AIRPORTS
AND
THE ENVIRONMENT

ORGANISATION FOR ECONOMIC CO-OPERATION AND DEVELOPMENT

CONTENTS

PREFACE

Since its formation in 1971, the Sector Group on the Urban Environment of the Organisation for Economic Co-operation and Development has been concerned with a variety of problems related to environmental conditions in cities as well as various aspects of urban growth.

More recently, the Group's concern with the conflicts between man and the equipment of modern life, has led it to direct its attention to the side effects of large scale developments. This report on factors which need to be considered in the siting of major airports is the first of a series of such impact studies.

Attitudes about how best to handle the growth of air traffic are continually changing and the possibility of decentralising some of the traffic handled by major international airports to regional airports is now being more actively explored. The effect of changing world economic circumstances on the volume and distribution of air traffic is uncertain; in addition, changes in aircraft technology could call for important changes in airport design. In view of these considerations and in view of concern over environmental problems, in particular noise, which are associated with the operation of major airports, the pressure to create huge new international airports, referred to in this report, is already decreasing in certain countries. Nevertheless, the influence of airports on urban growth and their effect on the environment, both central issues in this assessment, remain concerns of the governments of all OECD Member countries.

Since the report was prepared in 1972-73, some of the information contained in it may no longer be valid despite revision of the text at the time of printing. The contents of the report do not necessarily reflect the views of the OECD; nor does the Organisation vouch for the accuracy or validity of the data contained in it.

THE IMPACT OF AIRPORT DEVELOPMENT ON URBAN GROWTH AND THE ENVIRONMENT

The Conclusions of the OECD Sector Group
on the Urban Environment

INTRODUCTION

Construction of a major international airport, like any major land use development, can have a wide variety of effects. Some of these effects are undoubtedly desirable, such as benefits to air travellers, business interests and industrial activities of the region. At the same time there are some effects which can be undesirable and which help to account for the growing opposition to airport development. For example, the construction or major expansion of an airport may structure the development of the region in ways which are inconsistent with regional objectives. There will be higher noise levels in the communities surrounding the airport, increased traffic on the local road network, increased demand for local public services such as water and sewage disposal. Possible harm to wildlife, damage to fragile ecology, loss of agricultural land and open spaces are other reasons why new airports are increasingly unwelcome in rural areas as well as in urbanised regions.

The task of airport planning is further complicated by uncertainties concerning the future development of air transportation and the prospect of future development in aircraft technology. For example, much quieter equipment capable of using shorter runways and steeper angles on take-off and approach (QRTOL aircraft) could significantly modify the present requirements for airport location, and could open up hitherto unusable sites within metropolitan areas. But will such aircraft be developed, and if so, on what time scale? Many countries faced with an urgent need to expand airport capacity feel they cannot afford to wait until these questions are resolved.

Compounding the difficulties are uncertainties in areas over which the aviation sector has little control. For example, will the trend toward increasing decentralisation of employment and

7

residence continue, and if so, what implications will it have for airport size and location? What is the prospect for high-speed surface transport and what is its likely impact on short-haul air travel demand between metropolitan areas? Will the growing scarcity of fuel resources and the cost of environmental protection affect the economics of air transport sufficiently to dampen future growth of the air travel market? What might be user response to changes in marketing and the prevailing patterns of service?

The growth of aviation has been sustained, the number of passengers doubling every five years for the past twenty-five. Growth may continue in the immediate future, but in the longer term it seems unlikely that air transport demand and provision of transport facilities can continue to expand along the same exponential curve. Demand forecasts tend to be self-sustaining. So the important thing is to set independently determined goals for the future supply of airport facilities. Obviously, even a reduced rate of growth will demand serious efforts if rising levels of congestion, noise and other disamenities are to be avoided. In the following pages the Sector Group considers what options are open to Member governments to accommodate future changes in air transport and examines the key policy issues that must be addressed in the airport planning process. For purposes of this report these options have been grouped under five headings. In practice many combinations of these basic choices can be and are used within the various OECD countries. Governments are invited to look carefully and continuously at all these options; their decisions must, however, depend on a variety of national and local conditions.

The New Airport

In 1973 some twelve Member countries(1) were planning or building new, very large "third generation" international airports. Because large tracts of undeveloped land near big cities are increasingly difficult to find and assemble, and because the insertion of an airport into an already established densely settled area would be politically and environmentally unacceptable, most of these airports are being located in more or less remote areas, away from population centres. Only in a very few countries are convenient and environmentally compatible sites, like the undeveloped island of Saltholm, some 20 kilometres from Copenhagen, available for a large new airport.

---

1) Australia, Canada, Denmark, Germany, Greece, Italy, Japan, the Netherlands, Norway, Portugal, the United Kingdom, the United States.

A long distance between city and airport, however, creates an economic disadvantage and an inconvenience to the users of the airport. To compensate for this physical separation, arrangements are therefore made to provide the airport with superior motorway access and, increasingly, with a direct rail link to the city centre. This is the strategy which is being considered by a number of countries, among them the United Kingdom, Canada, Sweden, the Netherlands, the United States, Denmark, Japan and Norway. An advantage of this strategy is that a larger airport can be built capable of accommodating the anticipated needs of a metropolitan region for many decades while providing an opportunity to control land use in the surrounding area on a scale and to a degree not possible in a more urbanised region.

Although this policy minimises the impact of airport noise and problems of land acquisition, it can have a major impact on the local ecology and, in most cases, on the urban development patterns of the surrounding region. Inserting a new airport into a hitherto undeveloped area may seriously affect wildlife, disturb the sensitive ecological balance of wetlands and destroy the peaceful character of the countryside. In addition, major new airports become growth centres. The airport itself, a major employer, generates a demand for housing and supporting services. A number of related activities find it convenient to be near their markets and settle nearby, thus contributing to the development. The superior roadway system, built to serve the airport, will tend to attract additional development unrelated to the airport, which if uncontrolled could further increase the urbanisation of the surrounding areas. The positive and negative impacts of these urbanisation effects are discussed further below.

Expanding the Capacity of Existing Airports

Another option is to expand the capacity of an existing airport through additional investment in runways, terminals and supporting facilities.

In expanding existing airports, environmental concerns, community opposition and the scarcity of land emerge as the major constraints. Most existing airports are either surrounded by densely populated areas or located in greenbelts perpetually free of development. Thus, opportunities for the extension of runways, construction of new runways and addition of terminal facilities are often limited.

Airport expansion will often lead to higher noise levels in the vicinity of the airport. Increased runway and terminal capacity will attract additional traffic, subjecting local population

to higher levels of annoyance. For this reason airport expansion
plans have often met with spirited opposition on the part of the
neighbouring communities. Re-zoning of the areas most severely
exposed to noise, or the outright purchase of land is a possible
solution. However, since it is not always practical to consider
re-zoning large, densely populated areas surrounding existing
airports, secondary measures must be considered aimed at minimising
or reducing the level of annoyance, such as sound-proofing or
compensation.

Regional development impacts of airport expansion are generally
less pronounced than those of a new airport. More intensive use
of an existing site has not always resulted in a large jump in the
level of urbanisation or in the demands placed on public services
such as water or sewage disposal, although it has sometimes imposed
some strain on the local economy, for instance creating pressure
on the local labour and housing market. It has also sometimes
generated additional vehicular traffic, putting additional strain
on the existing road network. The scale of these local and
regional impacts may be much greater in the future because the
activities most responsible for the urbanisation impacts -
activities such as hotels, warehousing and conventions - are likely
to expand faster than in the past.

With the introduction of larger aircraft the primary strain
on capacity may first be felt by the terminal and access facilities
rather than by the runway system. Giving priority to establishing
more efficient transportation to and from airports, such as rail
links to the central city, may therefore prove to be the most
effective method of solving the immediate airport capacity problems.

Development of a Regional Airport System

While expansion of existing major airports and the construction
of new hub airports represent essentially a continuation of the
traditional airport planning philosophy, development of a regional
airport system requires some modification to the prevailing concept
of air service.

A regional airport system involves an effort both to disperse
air traffic to a number of points within a region and to introduce
a certain specialisation in the nature of services offered by
different airports. For example, the hub airport might primarily
serve scheduled international services and long-distance traffic
while private aviation, short-haul charters and cargo services
(i.e. those not requiring large aircraft and long runways) and
certain scheduled domestic flights are removed to smaller airports.
More importantly, the concept of a regional airport system

acknowledges the current trend toward metropolitan decentralisation
and the increasing dispersal of trip origins and destinations by
offering direct short-haul service to and from a number of points
within metropolitan areas. San Francisco/Los Angeles, Tokyo/Osaka
and Toronto/Montreal are three city pairs exploring ways of
expanding air services to a number of points between their metropolitan areas. In Scandinavia two new secondary airports -
Roskilde west of Copenhagen, and Sturup east of Malmo in Sweden -
already act as regional airports for the Sound Region around
Copenhagen. Careful attention should be paid to the type of
services that can be shifted to the regional airports. For example,
long-distance charters, heavy cargo and other air services that
use large planes should be kept at the hub airport so as not to
increase the noise footprints at the secondary airports.

The practicality of a regional airport system is dependent
upon the availability of sufficiently large undeveloped parcels
of land in metropolitan areas or of facilities (e.g. military
bases) that could be converted at reasonable cost to service short-
range aircraft including perhaps charters, and the willingness
of communities to accept small airports as neighbours. This
willingness, in turn, may largely depend on the development of
the quiet reduced take-off and landing aeroplane (QRTOL).(1) Even
if these conditions were met, the regional airport system would
still raise a number of questions. For example, could the air
traffic control handle the complex pattern of aircraft movements?
How much investment would be necessary to improve the road access
to the secondary airports and how much additional land would have
to be included in the buffer zones? Above all, is it desirable
to spread the negative effects of airport activity over a wide
area and thus expose additional communities to noise annoyance,
or is it preferable to concentrate environmentally disrupting
activities in as few locations as possible? The answer to these
questions will depend upon the objectives and constraints of a
particular comprehensive regional plan into which the airport
development must be integrated, in particular on the compatibility
of the airport site with the present and intended land use around
it.

Improving the Efficiency of Existing Facilities

Alternatively or in parallel to investment in a new airport
or in expanding an existing airport, steps can be taken to ease
the pressure on the existing airport facilities. Much of the

---

1) Such aircraft require runways of 4 - 5,000 feet instead of the
   8 - 12,000 feet runways needed by conventional aircraft.

congestion at major airports has a simple and basic cause: too
many aircraft compete for the use of limited facilities at peak
hours, mostly occurring in early morning and in late afternoon.
Such mode of operation will continue as long as airline operations
are not restricted or given incentives to shift to off-peak hours.

A rational policy of alleviating peak-hour congestion
and related capacity problems might include restrictions against
charter flights during peak hours, removal of general aviation to
secondary airports, encouragement of flight consolidation and
increased pooling between airlines, and a differential landing
fee policy, consisting of higher fees during peak hours and increased
minimum fees for general aviation. With the help of such methods
commercial operations could be distributed more evenly throughout
the day and private planes diverted away from busy airports. The
result could be a significant decrease in airport congestion,
providing longer term relief from saturation, and reducing premature
investment in additional ground facilities.

Standing Still

The final strategy is the converse of all those mentioned
above - a standstill policy which allows only for continued operation of the existing airport without any additional investment
in runways or new terminal facilities, and which lets congestion
and noise standards regulate the ultimate level of activity.
While this may be inappropriate in most countries as a national
policy, it may be acceptable as a strategy for an individual
airport either because further growth would drastically reduce
its working efficiency or because public opposition has foreclosed
virtually every other option. In 10 or 20 years time this option
may be given serious consideration by some governments.

Data on the effects of the null or do-nothing alternative
should be developed to a level of detail consistent with that for
other alternatives, and the null alternative can serve as a
reference point for identifying on a relative or comparative basis
the adverse and beneficial effects of any other alternative proposal.

Conclusions on Airport Planning Options

A review of country experience suggests that there is a
range of alternatives available to accommodate rising air transport
demand while providing for an acceptable urban environment. One
of the critical needs is to determine when the increased use of
existing runways, terminals and access systems will come into
conflict with the standards for acceptable environment, and what
costs will be involved in maintaining those standards.

Exactly which course of action to pursue is a decision involving delicate trade-offs between on the one hand the objectives of transport efficiency and convenience, and on the other hand considerations external to the aviation sector: regional development objectives, competing claims on the use of land, noise impact, effect on the local ecology, and public attitudes in the communities affected by the existing airport and its possible expansion or by the construction of a new airport.

The trade-offs and the uncertainties about future air transport demand, patterns of urban development, aircraft technology and user response to changes in patterns of service will be perceived differently in different countries, making it impossible to single out any one of the alternatives as the preferred or most "rational" strategy. For each large international airport the government will have to make an independent decision in the light of its best assessment of the competing considerations and weighing the conflicting interests of different groups after full consultations with the public.

MAIN ENVIRONMENTAL AND PLANNING ISSUES IN AIRPORT DEVELOPMENT POLICY

Whatever strategy a given region or nation may adopt, there are certain issues common to all nations, concerning which the Urban Sector Group believes it can offer some constructive suggestions. Three issues stand out as warranting particular attention: the problem of airport noise; the growing scarcity of land suitable for airports and problems surrounding its acquisition; and the need to consider airport planning in the wider context of comprehensive transport, regional and environmental planning.

The Problem of Airport Noise

Noise from aircraft is by far the most serious constraint facing airports today. It is the source of mounting complaints and litigation on the part of people living in the neighbourhood of airports; it is the main reason for organised protest against the expansion of existing airports; it is the cause of the growing trend to close major airports at night (with the attendant repercussions for air transport industry such as loss of freight revenue, forced idleness of equipment on the ground, problems of transcontinental flight scheduling, etc.); and it is a major factor in public opposition to the building of new airports. Ways to deal with aircraft and airport noise, therefore, should be accorded priority attention.

13

Recommendations to limit aircraft noise at the source have
been adopted by the International Civil Aviation Organisation (ICAO)
in 1971. This initiative has already resulted in some concrete
improvements. New types of aircraft emit 10 to 15 EPNdB (effective
perceived noise decibels) less than earlier jet equipment. As an
illustration of the impact these noise reduction improvements
have had, the 90 EPNdB noise footprint of a long-range jet aircraft
of the first generation (B-707) was 120 square kilometres; the
90 EPNdB footprint of the latest long-range jet complying with
ICAO recommendations (e.g. DC-10 or Tristar) has been reduced to
20 - 30 square kilometres. Efforts to produce even quieter
aircraft are being pursued in the United States, the United Kingdom
and France.

Present noise emission requirements apply to new type subsonic
aircraft and, in 1976, will apply to all production aircraft
whenever originally designed. There are, however, no proposals
to apply the ICAO rules to all existing aircraft in service.
Although the use of the new, large-capacity aircraft may reduce
the number of noisy overflights around airports, the older, noisy
equipment will continue in existence in sufficient numbers to
constitute a nuisance for many years to come. Only retrofitting
of the older aircraft would help to improve the noise situation
in the short and medium term.

Attention, therefore, should be focussed on the possibilities
of improving the airport noise environment at the local level -
where measures can have a more immediate effect. Three sets of
measures can serve this end: operational measures designed to
limit the production of noise by aircraft; measures aimed at
changing the land use in areas exposed to heavy noise; and measures
aimed at reducing the impact of noise at the point of reception.

Included in the first set are special take-off and landing
procedures, restrictions on the total number of noisy aircraft,
banning night traffic, partial diversion of traffic (especially
at night) to more isolated airports, and establishment and enforce-
ment of local airport noise regulations. Many such measures are
already in use. For example, some European airports have imposed
night curfews. Schiphol (the Netherlands) and the major German
airports permit night operations only to those aircraft that meet
the ICAO noise standards; while the London airports permit more
night flights to airlines whose aircrafts meet the ICAO requirements. Another approach - which so far is only in the discussion
stage - would impose an overall limit on the total noise emitted
by all aircraft of a given airline during a given period of time.
The virtue of this concept - known as "Fleet Noise Level" - is

that it would provide airlines with more flexibility. They could switch to quieter equipment or reduce the number of movements, whichever seemed more advantageous, so long as they remained within the overall noise emission ceiling. All these measures would tend to promote the commercial introduction of quiet aircraft.

A second approach consists in minimising the contact between human activities and airport noise through the co-ordination of airport planning with regional and local land use policy. This approach can be implemented most easily in the case of new airports situated in areas which are not yet intensively developed. However, even around existing airports within metropolitan areas possibilities arise to re-zone heavily noise-impacted areas over a period of time so as to minimise the exposure to airport noise of private dwellings, schools, hospitals and recreation areas. Re-zoning may involve heavy costs in purchase and clearance of residential houses; in some cases it may be possible to convert existing structures and areas, for instance into airport-related activities, industrial parks or sports stadiums.

Land can be acquired or restrictions on the construction of private housing can be imposed at the outset in such a manner as to establish a buffer zone between a new airport and the surrounding development. This has been done in the case of the new Montreal airport, where an area of 360 square kilometres was acquired although only 82 square kilometres were needed for the airport itself; and in the case of the new Paris airport at Roissy, where a prohibition has been imposed on the construction of private dwellings, schools and hospitals within the zone of the most intense noise. At existing airports, such as Zurich and Geneva, the problem of incompatible land uses near the airport has been dealt with by legislation. In addition, around these airports as well as around the Los Angeles and Roissy airports, large numbers of dwellings have been bought from their owners at considerable expense rather than risk a continuing threat of legal action. In the Scandinavian countries certain criteria have been laid down by the Ministries of the Environment as to existing and future land uses and their compatibility with different noise levels.

The third approach - which must be regarded as a secondary one compared to the first and second sets of measures - concentrates on providing protection against noise at its point of reception.

Sound-proofing of private dwellings, hotels, offices, etc. may prove to be the only way of dealing rapidly with noise disturbance around existing airports where land development has already seriously encroached upon the buffer zone. This technique has been used in connection with Heathrow (United Kingdom) and, more recently, Schiphol (the Netherlands) and the German Federal airports. In the case of Heathrow 4,000 dwellings have been sound-proofed since 1966 in the most exposed areas. However, sound-proofing remains an incomplete measure as it does nothing to improve the outdoor environment.

A practical programme of noise abatement requires a two-pronged approach, co-ordinating anticipated improvements in noise reduction at the source with protective measures carried out around the airport. In most situations there will be a need to modify to some extent the use of land where it does not comply with the proposed zoning plan. Priority could be given to those properties which could not expect significant relief from noise even under the most optimistic projections of future reductions in aircraft noise. Such a plan would provide a systematic basis for negotia-tion and action between the various interests involved. Zurich airport has been the first to experiment with such an approach as a basis for reconciling land use and noise impact in the long run, after 1980.

Where noise levels still remain unacceptably high in spite of all remedial efforts, a solution of last resort is to provide com-pensation to home owners for the property's loss in value due to noise. In return, the airport acquires a "noise easement" on the property. In the United States, where compensation has been used it has amounted to roughly 20 per cent of the value of the property. Although there is much virtue in the principle of compensation, it should be stressed that it is regarded as the final means of redress when other positive measures to minimise the adverse effects of noise have all been taken. Monetary compensation does not guarantee that the money will be spent on remedial measures and that the tenants living in the affected dwellings will there-fore be protected. For them, as well as for those who do not qualify for compensation, sound insulation and noise abatement zoning are the only effective solutions. The issue of compensation is already being addressed by the Sector Group in another context.

The Use of Economic Instruments

The possibility of using economic instruments to promote aircraft noise abatement also deserves attention. Airlines are already subject to landing charges, although today these charges are based on aircraft weight. Landing surcharges could also be assessed on noisy aircraft. Such charges could provide an important source of revenue which may be earmarked for financing airport noise abatement programmes, e.g. sound-proofing of exposed dwellings, hospitals and schools; land acquisition for buffer zones; and compensation grants. The use of such taxes as a source of revenue for airport noise abatement is still the subject of considerable debate.

It has also been argued that, set at a proper level and generally applied by the large airports, noise surcharges would act as a continuous incentive for airlines to minimise the noise impact of their activities. For instance, at operational level, charges would prompt the airlines to make the most rational use of their existing fleets of aircraft by diverting noisy equipment to long-haul runs and to airports where noise causes little disturbance (and where noise charges, therefore, would be set low), while concentrating the quiet aircraft on the heavily travelled, short-haul routes characterised by frequent landings and take-offs at noise-sensitive airports. At the same time, the noise tax could act as a continuous inducement for airlines to retrofit existing aircraft or to accelerate their retirement and their replacement with quieter models, and to purchase the quietest aircraft available on the market. All this, in turn, would provide an incentive to aircraft and engine manufacturers to devote maximum effort to the development of quieter engines and more effective retrofit devices and techniques.

Some problems remain to be resolved before a surtax on aircraft noise could be introduced. However, the use of charges to finance local noise protection programmes and to induce airlines to shift to quieter equipment already in production deserves serious attention. This issue is already being addressed by the Group in another context.

Airports and Comprehensive Planning

There is a need to integrate airport planning with the larger problems of land use, ground transportation, regional development and environmental protection. Only in this way can air transport objectives be reconciled with other pressing national and local needs. Issues concerning the planning process are dealt with toward the end of this paper.

Evidence examined by the Group indicates that the zone under the airport's influence is much larger than the area of the airport itself. It includes the surrounding noise buffer zones, associated service areas, large-scale residential development for airport employees and a network of access roads. Because of the size of the area involved, it is becoming difficult to find suitable sites for airports. It is increasingly important, therefore, to reserve

sufficient land in advance of development to cover both the needs
for the airport itself, its possible later expansion and the
buffer zones needed to minimise noise annoyance.

Urbanisation Effects of Airports

There is general agreement that the construction and expansion
of a large international airport and of its access links to the
metropolitan agglomeration can have a substantial impact on urban
development patterns in the surrounding sub-region. The airport
itself is a major employment centre in the region, attracting a
number of related services - airline companies, aircraft workshops,
warehouses, car-hire agencies, catering firms, hotels, convention
and exhibition centres, as well as public services and interna-
tionally oriented service firms. Similarly, employees of the
airport and of the airport-related activities will follow to a
considerable extent the short journey-to-work tradition and settle
in relative proximity to their work - inducing further development
of secondary and tertiary activities.

Whether this is to be regarded as a positive or a negative
effect will depend upon the general goals of national and regional
planning. Where the policy is to stimulate the growth of a
hitherto under-developed area, a new airport can serve as a powerful
tool of that policy. Where, on the other hand - as has been the
case in recent years in a growing number of countries - the goal
is to slow down the further expansion of an already highly urbanised
region or to preserve the area as a valuable agricultural, open
space or recreational resource, the construction of a new major
airport or a major expansion of an existing airport cannot but be
viewed as going counter to that goal.

Airport Planning in the Context of a Comprehensive Transport Policy

One aspect of aviation's success is its ability to drastically
shorten journeys over long distances; another is its ability to
serve in an economic way dispersed locations between which the
density of passenger traffic is not heavy enough to justify fast
and frequent rail service. On the other hand, over short distances,
in heavily travelled corridors traversing densely populated,
congested urban regions, improved rail service will be offering an
increasingly viable alternative to flying. This observation is
supported by evidence. Where fast, frequent and reliable rail
service has been introduced, as for example between London and
Manchester and between Tokyo and Osaka, people have switched from
air to rail travel in impressive numbers. Since the introduction
of high-speed trains on the London to Manchester run, the proportion

of travellers going by air has decreased by more than 40 per cent while rail travellers more than doubled. In Japan, the Tokaido line has had a similar effect on travel behaviour between Tokyo and Osaka: air traffic has dropped from 22 per cent to 8 per cent of the total in a period of eight years.

Improvements in rail transport thus offer another significant way in which relief could be sought from future airport saturation problems. But to bring about major modifications in the prevailing patterns of travel will require some re-adjustment in the ways of thinking. All too often the relationship between the different modes of transport is viewed as one of competition rather than of partnership. Each mode is regarded as sufficient unto itself whereas, in fact, they should be considered as complementing each other and functioning as parts of a total transportation system. In such an integrated transport system, rail, road and air transport do not vie for traffic but co-operate to give the traveller and the shipper the best possible service from origin to destination. Such intermodal co-operation can take many forms: joint reservation services, co-ordinated timetables, inter-connection of rail and air terminals as is proposed in the Netherlands and Switzerland. Underlying this philosophy is recognition of the fact that no one transport mode could possibly satisfy the many diverse needs of transport users or combine all of the attributes desired by the traveller. Each form of transport has certain unique features enabling it to serve particularly well certain transport needs. The goal of a national transport policy should be to exploit each mode for the purpose for which it is best suited: to assure, in other words, that the right kind of transportation is available in the right place for the right purpose.

This approach to transport planning could be widely applied. In a growing number of countries sufficient space for major airports is increasingly difficult to find. At the same time, improvements in high-speed ground transport are extending the acceptable distance for access travel to airports. These conditions suggest that there might be value in considering airport provision at an international or at least bilateral level. The Group believes that more attention should be devoted to examining the possibilities of developing shared airport facilities.

Environmental Issues and the Planning Process

The traditional technique for evaluating alternative plans for airports, as indeed for any major public facility, has been that of benefit/cost analysis. In this procedure, positive and negative effects of each alternative are evaluated in monetary

terms, the direct and indirect social benefits and costs are added
up separately and a benefit/cost ratio is computed. The alternative
whose ratio of benefits to costs comes out highest is ranked as
the preferred alternative. Although rather sophisticated methods
have been developed in recent years to assess the value of seemingly
unquantifiable matters, such as historical landmarks or the visual
beauty of a landscape, the benefit/cost approach still contains
serious shortcomings. To begin with, it employs monetary valuation
of items that are not subject to the influence of the market
mechanism. Secondly, it uses discount rates and amortisation
periods for public investments, whose lifetime, benefits, and
possible technical evolution are arbitrarily fixed; thirdly, it
aggregates all the impacts of the analysis and in so doing it
conceals the essential fact that the impacts will not fall evenly
on all the groups concerned: some people will benefit from the
proposed project while others will be affected adversely.

The Group feels that methods of evaluation need to be improved
so that the planning process may become more sensitive to social
and environmental issues and more responsive to community concerns
than is possible with the conventional benefit/cost analysis. In
particular, the evaluation should deal not only with costs and
benefits that can be quantified in monetary terms but also with a
full range of other impacts, such as health, safety, amenity,
equity, freedom of choice and attractiveness of the physical
environment. In such a planning process several principles are
of importance:

   i)   There must be a range of alternatives available. The
        range of alternatives must be sufficiently broad to
        represent real choices, including the option of not
        doing anything.
  ii)   There must be information on the effects of the alter-
        natives. This information must include both the bene-
        ficial and the adverse effects of the alternatives; it
        must include all effects that any particular segment of
        the public thinks are important, whether or not those
        effects are readily quantifiable; and it must identify
        explicitly which groups are benefited and which groups
        are hurt by any proposed alternative.
 iii)   There must be full opportunity for public involvement
        in the process so that every group which may be poten-
        tially affected by the proposed project has access to
        all relevant information and has the opportunity to
        influence the process.

iv) Where adverse impacts result for some groups in order
that benefits may be provided to other groups, consideration must be given to how those adversely affected can
be compensated.

v) Environmental damages and benefits must be evaluated
not in monetary terms but in terms of their falling
above or below certain conventionally fixed threshold
values expressed in non-economic units - e.g. noise
levels, pollution levels or acres of recreational land
consumed. The weighting of these factors is of necessity
a political act carried out in the context of the total
planning process. It is possible to list all money
value factors and environmental factors in a total
"evaluation scheme", but not to add up all factors into
one grand total.

vi) Sensitivity analyses should be used as supplementary
tools in the assessment of alternative policies,
location decisions and investment choices in order to
test the effects of varying the assumptions in the
benefit/cost analysis and in assessing the influence of
levels chosen for environmental and other threshold
values.

Chapter 1

AVIATION UP TO 1990

OECD Secretariat

INTRODUCTION

Profound changes have taken place in the objectives and philosophy of the air transport industry in the last twenty years as services catering largely for the business-man have been supplemented by others catering for a more diversified and fast-growing mass market. During this period OECD Member countries have accounted for 80 per cent of all passengers, supplied most of the technology and are becoming the first to face new problems - especially in the development of airports.

Twenty years is a long time in a rapidly developing field. Aircraft and airports have gone through a series of significant developments in this period as the number of passengers carried has grown by 12 per cent per year. However, today aircraft are increasingly reaching a technological plateau. The very rapid gains in aircraft productivity brought about by increases in speed and size in the 1950s and early 1960s should slow down over the next 10 to 15 years in the face of economic and operating limitations.

Airports grew significantly in size, cost and complexity of operation in the 1960s in response to rapid growth in passenger and freight jet aircraft movements. At the same time neighbourhoods adjacent to airports have become increasingly critical of noise and other environmental nuisances. The expansion of existing airports and the construction of new ones have meanwhile become either so costly or politically inexpedient that several major cities, such as New York and Munich, failed to create any new runways in the 1960s. Other regions faced with demands for additional runways are increasingly finding the solution of these problems to be beyond their abilities and resources. Central governments are therefore taking increasing responsibility for new aviation developments. Despite these institutional changes, governments in OECD Member countries are still experiencing difficulties in constructing the newer, larger airports.

LARGE NEW AIRPORTS

A few metropolitan regions have succeeded in developing large new airports at only moderate distances from population centres. In some cases decisions were taken before public opinion had become sensitive to environmental issues, in others suitable sites were available due to historical and geographical chance. However, there is a growing trend to locate airports on or next to water where this is a possibility, as in the United Kingdom and Denmark, or at considerable distances from metropolitan areas, as at Narita to the north of Tokyo, or as is proposed for Los Angeles at Palmdale. The future is likely to see further examples of this practice and although it should go some way towards reducing environmental damage, a new set of problems could arise at the regional and sub-regional levels. Urbanisation and airport access are likely to be the principal new problems, but looked at positively they could offer a new framework for regional development.

Future international airports are likely to be based on models now appearing at Dallas-Fort Worth and Charles de Gaulle. They will be flexible in function and modular in form. It also appears likely that they will be two or three times as large as the airports of today, consume five to ten times more water and power, and be major centres of communications. When fully developed they can be expected to handle between 50-100 million passengers a year. The huge size and cost of such airports means that no more than six are likely to be constructed throughout the world in the coming decade and that once built they will be able to handle all the air transport needs of the regions they serve.(1)

FORECASTS OF AIR TRAVEL DEMAND

As airport projects have increased in scale governments have found themselves playing an ever larger role in their financing and development. One result of this involvement has been an increase in attempts to forecast demand for air travel. The evolution of this demand may be correlated with a number of factors: the most significant being national economic growth, disposable incomes, education, levels of fare, service, frequency and comfort.

---

1) Major international airports proposed or under construction: Dallas-Fort Worth, Charles de Gaulle, Hamburg Karlten Kirchen, Saltholm Denmark, Kansas City International, Los Angeles Palmdale. A site for a similar 4-runway airport is being sought for in the Netherlands.

Yet forecasts remain imprecise for several reasons. Mass tourism, for instance, is an important and growing part of the demand for air travel but is highly price sensitive and prone to disruption by short-term economic fluctuations such as sharp rises in unemployment. Moreover, rises in fuel prices, wage increases and environmental taxes could make fare levels grow much faster than the cost of living and cause departures from the trends of the last 20 years.(1) **This** in turn could dampen demand in the rapidly growing tourist sector of the air travel market.

No more than 5 to 10 per cent of the population in OECD Member countries travels once a year or more. The potential market for air travel is thus huge and any factor that lowers trip costs in real terms could provoke a significant increase in demand. A number of airlines have attempted to exploit this possibility by expanding into non-aviation activities such as hotels. This enables them to offer a range of cheap package tours. Further developments in this direction seem likely to ensure that tourist travel becomes an increasingly dominant part of all travel.

The rate of air cargo growth is also uncertain. Most forecasts show ton-kilometres carried growing steadily through the 1970s and 1980s somewhat more rapidly than total passenger traffic. Revenues from cargo should remain at less than 20 per cent of the total, unless the use of containers becomes feasible on a larger scale. This development could make air cargo revenues more important than passenger revenues and attract newcomers into the business. The implications for airport development would be far reaching since more space would be needed for warehousing and related facilities within and without the airport's boundaries. Airline operations would also be significantly changed since the bulk of air cargo is expected to be carried in the holds of passenger aircraft rather than in all-cargo aircraft.(2)

Various factors may modify air transport demand but there is a consensus that passenger numbers will grow about three times, cargo tonnage about five times and aircraft movements about one and a half times in the next decade. Aircraft movements will clearly grow at the slowest rate as a result of wide-bodied aircraft providing greater seat capacity at cheaper rates than earlier jets.

---

1) In the past 20 years the continuous improvements in aircraft speed and size allowed significant increases in aircraft productivity per seat mile. This trend has permitted a continual reduction in air fares.

2) As yet only one aircraft model can carry the 8' x 8' x 10' intermodal (road, rail and sea) container, namely the Boeing 747F. Only one all-cargo aircraft is now operating on the North Atlantic, but a number are on order by all cargo-operators.

Tourist charters permit higher load factors and denser seating than scheduled services and on a number of high-density routes other forms of transport modes may prove increasingly competitive. As some 60 per cent of services in Europe are accounted for by trips of less than 500 to 600 kilometres new forms of high-speed ground transport could play an important part in the development of future short-haul air traffic demand. All or any of these factors should reduce aircraft movements while increasing the throughput of passengers. Such developments combined with the shifting of general aviation onto subsidiary airports and enforced scheduling of flights may enable the largest airports to accommodate 1980 air traffic demand at 1970 aircraft movement levels. Awareness of this possibility is recent and helps to explain increasing demands for a reappraisal of the present trend to ever larger and more costly airports. Beyond this there is the possibility that developments in technology such as reduced take-off aircraft and air traffic control coupled with quieter engines will permit the re-use of airports now considered obsolete.

Chapter 2

AIRCRAFT NOISE AND MAN

OECD Secretariat

OBJECTIVES

Studies of the effects of noise on man and his environment
have been undertaken in many countries in order to design measures
to control aircraft noise. Most of the measures are intended to
be used locally and may be divided into three types: the delineation
of noise zones with a view to controlling the use of land; the
altering of airport and aircraft procedures so as to minimise noise
in certain places at certain times; and the locating of new airports away from settlements so as to minimise the nuisance they
cause and to permit the use of the surrounding land to be controlled.

These studies are intended to establish criteria for assessing
monetary and non-monetary effects of aircraft noise; an appendix
to this report (Appendix A) describes them in detail and gives their
main conclusions.

CRITERIA

The extent to which aircraft noise interferes with health and
well-being has been revealed by social surveys. The method used
is to find out how often and to what extent such activities as
sleeping, resting, listening to the radio, watching television,
talking or reading are disturbed by aircraft noise. This enables
empirical standards of judgement about specific forms of annoyance
to be formulated.

The monetary effects of noise can be assessed by comparing the
cost of escaping from it with the cost of putting up with it.
Amongst possible indicators of such costs are falls in the value of
houses affected by noise; the cost of moving house in order to
get away from noisy areas; and the difference between the market
value of houses and the subjective value which owners attach to
them due to their surroundings, familiarity, proximity to friends

and so on. Attempts have also been made to assess the cost of noise annoyance itself by asking inhabitants what sum would compensate them for the inconvenience it causes them.

FINDINGS

Social surveys have shown that annoyance due to aircraft noise is mainly dependent on the number of activities disturbed and on the degree of this disturbance. On the basis of these surveys, noise indices have been worked out combining in a single formula such contributants to annoyance as average intensity, duration and frequency of occurrence.

Surveys of this kind have shown that the annoyance suffered by groups of people exposed to the same noise conditions were faithfully reflected by these noise indices with hardly a variation from country to country. This means that the number of persons likely to be annoyed at each noise level can be estimated and changes in the level of annoyance resulting from measures to control aircraft noise and movements predicted. Noise curves have already been traced for the surroundings of many airports on the basis of the findings of such surveys. The curves mark out areas in which land use and house building have to be controlled, compensation paid and so on.

Studies of the monetary effects of noise, on the other hand, have given results varying, not only from one airport to another, but from one place to another in the neighbourhood of the same airport. This is not surprising when it is remembered that there are housing shortages in most countries so that factors other than noise enter into house prices. Moreover the methods currently used to assess the cost of annoyance raise problems of interpretation:

a) Many people cannot say how much money would compensate them for the noise they put up with or else consider that no amount of money could compensate them for the damage they suffer.

b) But even when people do succeed in quoting values they can only assess what they are familiar with and it is far from certain that an estimate made near a typical urban airport today will reflect the value of annoyance at a rural location tomorrow.

Thus there is a risk of under or overestimating the monetary effects of noise, unless the methods of analysing them are improved.

27

CONCLUSIONS

There are well-established relationships between the daily frequency and average intensity of aircraft noise and annoyance and interference with certain activities, but the monetary effects of noise can only be assessed in certain cases and under certain conditions. The criteria used for measuring the damage caused by aircraft noise are inadequate. Those based on social surveys are ill-suited for cost/benefit analysis, while those based on real estate values often give unreliable results.

A better knowledge of the monetary relationships between noise and its effects is needed if cost/benefit calculations are to serve as a more rational basis for noise control policies. This calls for comparisons between the indirect cost of noise, for instance its effect on house prices, with its direct social costs measured in terms of expenditure on medical attention and pharmaceuticals, losses in labour productivity and educational attainment, and its effects on family life and neighbourliness.

Chapter 3

HOW TO REDUCE AIRCRAFT NOISE

OECD Secretariat

I. METHODS OF REDUCING AIRCRAFT NOISE

A. Modifying aircraft engines

The new types of aircraft introduced since 1972 - the DC10, the Lockheed Tristar, and a new version of the Boeing 747, emit 10 - 15 EPNdB(1) less than earlier jet aircraft. These new models are the first to comply with the United States regulations instituted in 1969 and the recommendations issued by the ICAO in 1971(2).

As an illustration of the progress already made, a Boeing 707 or a DC8 produces more than 90 EPNdB (one take-off plus one landing) over an area of 120 km^2, while a DC10 produces this noise over only 20 km^2. As regards new models now in production - the Airbus and the Mercure for example - their noise emission characteristics will be virtually the same as those of the DC10 or the Tristar.

These efforts to reduce noise from new aircraft are continuing, mainly in the United States, where the NASA and the FAA are financing the "Quiet Engine Program", whose purpose is to reduce noise during take-off and landing by 23 to 26 EPNdB compared with the noise of a Boeing 707 or DC8(3). Work on noise reduction is also going on in the United Kingdom, where Rolls Royce are trying to lower by a further 5 EPNdB the noise emitted by the engines fitted to the Tristar.

---

1) The noise of aircraft is measured in dBA, PNdB, or EPNdB. Values expressed in EPNdB or in PNdB exceed those expressed in dBA by by some 13 - 15 units. The three units of measurement, like the human ear, take account of middle and high rather than low frequencies. Moreover, the EPNdB embodies two other parameters: the duration of the noise and the presence of harmonics which are considered to be especially annoying.

2) The United States Regulation is the one usually known as FAR-36, which deals with the noise emission certification of new types of aircraft and which was published on 21st November, 1969. The ICAO recommendation was published under the title: "Aircraft noise - Annex 16 to the Convention on International Civil Aviation", ICAO, August 1971.

3) "Transportation Noise and Noise from Equipment Powered by Internal Combustion Engines", U.S. Environmental Protection Agency, Washington, 1971, p. 42.

In the short and medium term however, the new regulations concerning noise emission will not be sufficient to significantly reduce the annoyance suffered by persons living near airports, because:

i) regulations concerning noise emission relate only to new types of aircraft,

ii) existing aircraft have an average economic life of about 12 years (this is the amortization period used),

iii) to some extent, the steady increase in air traffic is negating the noise reductions achieved, which for the moment cover only a small fraction of all aircraft,

iv) the noisiest aircraft are the major contributors to annoyance.

For all those reasons, it would seem that the engines of existing aircraft should also be modified (by retrofitting).

Research so far carried out shows that retrofitting would especially reduce noise on landing (a reduction of 10 to 15 EPNdB), whereas noise during take-off would be much more difficult to abate (3 EPNdB less). The capital cost of such retrofitting would range from $200,000 to $1,000,000 per aircraft and the operating cost would increase by 4 to 9 per cent(1).

It is estimated(2) that in 1975 there are about 3,000 jet aircraft not covered by the new standards (excluding aircraft built in Eastern European countries), and the very substantial cost of retrofitting can well be imagined. In view of this cost and the fact that only widespread retrofitting would reduce the annoyance to people living near international airports, some international agreement would appear necessary, otherwise some airlines - those adopting retrofitting for their own aircraft - would be heavily penalised with respect to their competitors.

In any event, such an agreement would produce tangible results only gradually, because of the time needed for retrofitting.

Therefore a cost/effectiveness analysis should be carried out covering all existing aircraft to see whether the costs of general retrofitting could be compensated by substantially decreased annoyance both in terms of time and space. The costs, benefits and disbenefits of retrofitting could then be compared with those of other solutions which we shall now examine.

---

1) "Civil Aviation Research and Development Policy Study DOT-NASA, Washington, 1971: Supporting Papers", p. 5-9; "Transportation Noise and Noise from Equipment Powered by Internal Combustion Engines," op. cit., p. 40.

2) "Transport aérien et prix du silence" /Air Transport and the price of silence7, by C. Abraham, paper read at the seminar on "Les nuisances acoustiques" /Noise Pollution7, Paris, 1972, p. 13.

No assessment of retrofitting can however be meaningful unless all existing aircraft are covered; it is clear that if only one country is analysed retrofitting would prove far too costly and in any case would give partially ineffective results.

B. Flight procedures for noise abatement

1. During take-off

The area affected by take-off noise is much greater than that affected by noise during landing. This is the reason why restrictions on night flying are stricter for take-offs than for landings (see below, paragraph C.2).

One method is already in use at many airports for cutting down noise during take-off: this consists in taking off under full power and climbing at the steepest possible angle in order to gain height before flying over densely populated areas, and then in reducing power at an altitude of some 300 metres in order to keep the noise level as low as possible while overflying these areas. To this take-off pattern is often added a turn immediately after take-off whenever a flight path can be used above a sparsely populated area.

This method may however well increase the period during which the noise can be perceived on the ground.

Other possible methods include the preferential use of certain runways (when weather conditions permit and when a minimum number of people are flown over as a result), and above all the concentration of take-offs in a small number of strictly defined flight corridors. If take-offs are concentrated rather than spread out, fewer people are in fact inconvenienced. Yet while fewer people are inconvenienced, the degree of annoyance suffered by people under the flight path is greater, since the noise occurs more frequently.

The concentration of take-offs does nevertheless have an important advantage for land-use planners, since the noise can be limited to a well-defined area. Thus any soundproofing and planning schemes involve a smaller area than if the noise were spread around the airport. Clearly, however, the concentration of take-offs can be an effective solution only if the aircraft follows the flight paths exactly, and only if the flight paths are fixed once for all time by the authorities concerned.

2. Landing

There is at present no specific procedure laid down for reducing noise during the landing phase, which takes place at an angle of approach located somewhere between 2.5 and 3°.

Various modified procedures have however been tried out in recent years. The most promising seems to be the two-segment approach. The first would take place at an altitude of 1,000 metres (at present carried out at 450 metres); then, at some 9 km from the airport, a 6° descent would begin, levelling out at 3° when the aircraft is some 2 km from the start of the runway. Tests with Boeing 727s and 737s show that noise can thus be reduced by 15 PNdB 8 km away from the airport by 12 PNdB at 5 km and 10 PNdB at 3 km. At less than 3 km from the end of the runway, the improvement gained is promptly lost, falling to zero when the aircraft makes its final approach at an angle of 3°(1).

This procedure still involves safety problems and will probably require the use of refined automatic approach instruments. However its adoption would significantly reduce the areas affected by landing noise: a two-segment approach made by a large three-jet aircraft, for example, would produce noise greater than 90 PNdB over an area of only 350 hectares compared with 900 hectares when the current landing procedure is used(2).

C. Restrictions on airport use

Apart from technical methods of reducing noise at its source (engine modifications, adoption of new take-off and landing procedures), regulatory measures can be taken on a purely local scale, although these often have repercussions at national or international level.

These measures consist in establishing noise limits at certain airports, closing the airport at certain times (especially at night), sharing aircraft movements between several regional airports whenever possible and beneficial from a noise standpoint. There are other non-technical ways of restricting airport use in order to reduce noise: we shall examine these in Part II of this paper, since they are political instruments rather than direct ways of controlling noise.

1. Noise limits

Aircraft landing at or taking off from Kennedy Airport in New York must respect a limit of 112 PNdB, measured at dwellings closest to the airport.

---

1) "Noise Measurements During Two-segment Approaches at Los Angeles International Airport", Bolt, Beranek and Newman, Report 2208, Los Angeles, 1972, figures 5, 6, 7.

2) "Airports for the 80s" paper read at the 4th World Airports Conference, London, 3rd-5th April, 1973, p. 25.

The same applies to London - Heathrow Airport, although in this case the limit for night is much stricter than for daytime (102 and 110 PNdB respectively).

Establishing such limits clearly calls for constant monotoring of the noise emitted by each aircraft. Moreover, because of the night restrictions at London Airport, certain aircraft cannot take off during the night, while others must take off with a reduced fuel load: this raises obvious economic problems, but from another stand-point may be regarded as directly inciting airlines to use quieter aircraft complying with the limits imposed.

2. Banning of night traffic

There are now very many airports where night traffic is for-bidden: all those in Switzerland, many in Germany, Paris Orly, Copenhagen, and London Heathrow in summer (during winter the limit of 102 PNdB is maintained). It is also probable that an increasing number of airports will have to eliminate night traffic under pressure from people living nearby.

The time of shutdown varies from one airport to another: six to seven hours in some cases, only four hours in others.

Shutting down airports at night of course entails significant practical and economic disadvantages such as loss of income if air-freight companies prefer to use airports where there are no restric-tions on night flights; some aircraft are too long idle on the ground; there are problems of arranging take-off schedules for long-distance flights to allow for time differences (flights between Europe and the Middle East or the Far East, for example); and so on.

These total or partial bans on night movements will nevertheless be necessary for airports located in highly urbanised areas, where complaints and organised protests are apt to be strongest.

3. Sharing traffic between several airports

Air traffic may be so distributed as to subject the least number of people to noise whenever possible, as when a city is ser-ved by at least two airports.

In Stockholm for example, the airport closest to the city - Bromma - is barred to jet aircraft, which must use Arlanda airport 40 kilometres from the city.

Large new airports now under construction or planned will most often be located in sparsely populated areas. Since these new air-ports usually complement existing facilities located in some densely populated area, it will probably be possible to share traffic between airports, for example by transferring all night flights to the new sites.

D. Reducing noise at point of reception

Since regulations concerning aircraft noise are very recent and apply only to models put into service from 1972 on, and since no agreement has yet been reached regarding the reduction of noise from existing aircraft, and finally since quiet take-off and landing procedures are still in the experimental stage, current efforts to reduce noise at its source should not be expected to produce significant results for many years to come.

In the immediate future therefore, other measures must be considered: those designed to provide protection against noise at its point of reception. While the measures described above were the primary concern of aircraft manufacturers, airlines and airports, those we shall now discuss come more especially under town planning, land-use planning and construction authorities.

1. Zoning

Noise maps now exist for most airports in O.E.C.D. countries. These maps show a number of zones, each bounded by a noise contour(1).

As a general rule, two or three distinct zones are defined, within which land-use and house buildings are subject to certain restrictions. Only for future airports can these restrictions however become completely effective.

The fact is that since the last war, urbanisation around airports has proceeded apace and there has been great demand for building land, even in the noisiest areas, while at the same time air traffic was rapidly growing and jet aircraft, much noisier than propeller-driven types, were being introduced. Only partial remedies are possible around such airports, such as purchase of the most exposed dwellings, overflying charges to provide financial compensation, restrictions on further urban expansion, etc. Around future airports, preventive measures can however be envisaged.

Around the future French airport of Roissy, three zones have thus been defined: in the zone of intense noise (more than 115 CNR), no dwellings, schools and hospitals can be built; in the other two zones (107 and 102 CNR), certain restrictions concerning soundproofing, density of housing, etc. are in force.

---

1) These contours take account of the loudness and daily frequency of noise. They are expressed in terms of NNI, CNR, NEF or other indices. A detailed description of these indices and the reasons for their use are given in Annex A.

Generally speaking, whereever dwellings, schools and hospitals are not to be built, activities which are not incompatible with a high noise level may be established instead (industrial estates, warehouses, workshops, soundproofed and air-conditioned offices, etc.). There is a clear possibility that land-use and building regulations will often be opposed by landowners and be subjected to pressure from house seekers. How such regulations are received will depend on the consistency of land-use planning (since to forbid the construction of dwellings in certain areas means that other land should be released for construction) and on the compensation whicn landowners affected by the regulations are paid.

The effective implementation of such regulations will also call for close co-ordination among the various authorities concerned, including the airport authorities insofar as they are able to take action affecting the decisions concerning land-use and house building. We mentioned, for example, that take-offs might be limited to a small number of specified flight paths; in this case, the area of land covered by the regulations also might be relatively small. The same would apply if landing procedures were to be changed. The application of noise limits (as in London and New York for example) or a ban on night flights would likewise influence decisions to be taken regarding land-use and the construction of dwellings.

2. The soundproofing of dwellings

The soundproofing of dwellings (as well as of schools, hospitals and other buildings where noise abatement is necessary) is a partial solution rather than a cure in that people are compelled to keep their windows closed and the outside environment remains unchanged. However, in areas of intense noise, especially around existing airports, soundproofing is often the only way of rapidly reducing the inconvenience whenever rational land-use planning is no longer possible. The techniques of soundproofing are simple and well known: double glazing, better fitting outer doors, mechanical or electrical air-conditioning. In this connection, one particularly interesting achievement is worth mentioning: since 1966, 4,000 dwellings situated around Heathrow Airport - London in areas where noise exceeds 55 NNI, have been soundproofed. A government grant is paid to residents on request; however this grant has so far been limited to 75 per cent of the actual cost of soundproofing, with a ceiling of £200 per household.

Dwellings, schools and hospitals also have been or are being soundproofed in different countries, as a result of the adoption of new regulations (on this topic, see OECD working document U/CHG/73.61).

The cost of soundproofing varies according to the amount of noise reduction sought, the number of rooms to be treated, the size of windows, the type of dwelling (house or apartment), the country and so on.

A recent study concerning Los Angeles for example showed that an additional reduction in noise of 10 to 15 PNdB costs some $30 per square metre of floor area (i.e. $3,000 for a 100 m^2 house), including the installation of sealed double windows, acoustically treated doors and a special ventilation system[1].

The real problem is to decide whether the cost of soundproofing the dwellings which are most exposed to noise should be borne by their tenants and owners, or whether partial or total grants should instead be considered, in view of the fact that noise reduction at the source will produce results only very gradually.

As regards new buildings, when the demand for housing is high and the only solution is to allow dwellings to be built in a noisy area, the granting of building permits subject to some minimum amount of soundproofing, varying according to the site of the dwellings, may be considered (as around the airport now under construction at Roissy).

Construction regulations, grants and compensation can serve as alternative or complementary instruments in the soundproofing of dwellings most exposed to noise, as will now be seen.

II. POLITICAL INSTRUMENTS FOR CONTROLLING AIRCRAFT NOISE

The political instruments for effectively controlling aircraft noise are either of a legal or economic kind. They are different according to whether the action is carried out at international, national or local level.

A. Regulations

1. Noise emission standards

As mentioned in part one of this paper, there are now international noise emission standards for new models of subsonic aircraft. These standards have already been adopted by the United States, the United Kingdom and France. To be made fully effective, they should however be:

- extended to cover supersonic aircraft and aircraft designed before 1972 which are still being built,

---

1) "Aircraft Noise Impact. Planning Guidelines for Local Agencies", U.S. Department of Housing and Urban Development, Washington, D.C. 1972, p. 114.

- applied to existing aircraft so that these can be altered within a reasonable time,
- gradually made more strict.

Since most aircraft are used on international routes (especially in Europe), international noise standards need to be adopted, otherwise certain airlines would be penalised more or less than others.

Few countries however build airliners and any agreement therefore primarily depends on these. Yet countries without an aircraft manufacturing industry may adopt certain national or local regulations more strict than the international standards whenever the will to improve the environment of airports is such that any consequent financial or other sacrifices are found acceptable.

These national or local regulations may consist in establishing daytime and night noise limits for each airport (like those in New York and London). Setting limits of this kind will result in the noisiest aircraft being diverted to other airports.

The economic repercussions may however be considerable, above all for air cargo services (such economic effects are also likely to arise when other national or local measures are adopted, as will later be seen).

2. Regulations concerning airport utilisation, zoning and the soundproofing of buildings

Different psychological and physiological studies have shown that beyond certain limits noise becomes intolerable(1). The measures adopted in different countries are based upon the results of these studies, and consist in marking out different noise zones within which the construction of dwellings is controlled, in restricting use of the airport at night, and so on.

Regulations of this kind are both a means of direct action and political instruments designed to carry out the action. Since such means have already been described briefly in Part I of this paper, the subject will not be reverted to here.

3. Miscellaneous Regulations

Various regulations as yet not applied might be considered for implementing the different methods and techniques of noise control mentioned above. Adoption of these regulations by national, regional, local or airport authorities is however still apt to be hindered by unsolved technological problems such as two-segment landing procedures, limited numbers of closely defined take-off paths, etc.

In this connection, one proposal for special regulations appears feasible and is worth mentioning. So far it concerns only United

---

1) See Annex A.

States aircraft flying domestic routes, but its adoption would speed up the reduction in noise emitted by existing aircraft.

It would consist of limiting the total noise emitted by all aircraft of a given airline. This concept of overall limitation is known as "Fleet Noise Level"(1). It is based upon principles governing the sale or allocation of a pollution ceiling or right(2).

The total noise emitted by an airline's entire fleet would be fixed on the basis of data collected during a typical three-month period. This total noise would then be a maximum level which the airline should not subsequently exceed. If its traffic were to increase, the airline would then have to counterbalance the increase in total noise by reducing that of some of its aircraft.

Moreover, this limit would not be fixed once and for all but would be lowered by successive stages so that noisy aircraft could be gradually modified or replaced.

It must be stressed that this regulation is still in the tentative stage and would not apply to aircraft used on international routes. Yet it is reasonable to assume that in the medium or short term, international discussions might be held to look into the possibility of applying this overall system of regulation to all existing airlines.

B. Economic instruments

Economic instruments may complement or replace standards and regulations. We shall not embark upon a comprehensive analysis of the advantages and disadvantages of economic instruments compared with those of regulations, since this problem has already been covered by various studies undertaken within the O.E.C.D. Environment Directorate by the Central Analysis and Evaluation Unit(3). We shall simply list the main economic instruments already used or envisaged in the specific field of aircraft noise.

1. A noise surtax

At present, aircraft landing at an airport are subject to a landing charge, one usually proportional to their weight and capacity. Consideration might be given to supplementing this tax on "space occupied" with another proportional to the noise emitted during landing and take-off.

----

1) Press Communiqué No. 73-21 of the United States Federal Aviation Agency, dated 29th January, 1973.
2) See J. Dales: "Pollution, Property and Prices", University of Toronto Press, Toronto, Canada, 1968.
3) See "The Polluter Pays Principle and the Instruments for Allocating Environmental Costs", ENV/71.21, O.E.C.D., Paris.

A surtax of this kind would virtually be an incentive causing the noisiest aircraft to be modified or replaced. Certain local problems might also be resolved if the tax were adjusted for different landing and take-off times and the particular airport used. Income from this surtax could be paid either into an international fund designed to finance aircraft noise control research, or into a local fund financing such direct action as soundproofing, compulsory purchase, etc.

The relative competitive positions of the different airline companies using a given airport would not be affected, since a tax of this kind would clearly apply to all aircraft arriving at the airport.

On the other hand, airlines with aircraft solely of a noisy type would clearly be at a disadvantage.

Moreover, should some airports in a given region levy a charge while others did not, it is highly likely that at least cargo aircraft, and certain charter flights, would land only at airports where no charge was made.

Thus the principle of a noise surtax has advantages and drawbacks which require assessment. Also research is necessary to determine the optimum amount of the surtax so that it can be an effective inducement for reducing aircraft noise.

2. A passenger surtax

However a uniform charge paid by each passenger might be preferred to the noise surtax. This solution has already been adopted by the French Government for the airports of Orly and Roissy. Each passenger will pay an embarkation surtax of one franc for domestic flights, three francs for international flights.

Such embarkation surtax, however, has the disadvantage of not being linked to noise emissions, since a passenger in a quiet aircraft - a DC10 or Tristar for instance - will pay the same amount as a passenger in a noisy aircraft.

The levy is simply intended to finance a special fund for compulsory purchase or the soundproofing of dwellings, schools, hospitals and public buildings which are most exposed to noise.

While the surtax proportional to noise is an incentive for reducing the noise at the source, the passenger surtax simply provides local finance for compensating or protecting people living near airports. In France, this financial assistance for soundproofing will be limited to 66 per cent of the actual cost, although the proportion can be raised to 100 per cent for persons who are granted certain kinds of welfare benefits. As regards dwellings, this assistance cannot exceed Frs.6,000 per main room for blocks of flats and

Frs.10,500 for individual dwellings, the limit being three rooms, plus Frs.4,500 for a kitchen.

3. A company tax

Consideration could also be given to establishing a company tax to finance the purchase and destruction of the noisiest aircraft. This tax would be payable by all airlines on the principle adopted ten years ago by shipping lines to eliminate certain types of tanker (the Intertanko Plan)(1). The economic instruments of which we have spoken so far should be a permanent incentive for the reduction of noise in application of the general principle of pollution charges. In any event, they do at present provide sources of finance for action against aircraft noise.

The economic instruments we shall now discuss constitute means of direct action which require financing from a special fund (for example, the income from one of the taxes mentioned above) or from a State or regional budget.

4. Grants

In the first part of this paper, we pointed out that the occupants of dwellings most exposed to noise around London Heathrow Airport, received, since 1966, a special grant for soundproofing bedrooms, limited to 75 per cent of the total cost of the operation, or £200 per dwelling. Such a system of partial payment could be envisaged for other airports and especially for those sited in fairly dense urban areas where compulsory purchase or other measures dealing with the rational use of land would be too difficult to employ.

Moreover, as we saw in paragraph 2 above, the surtax adopted in France will in fact be used to finance such soundproofing grants.

5. Land purchase

It has been calculated that in the United States the total cost of buying up land exposed to noise regarded as annoying (1,300 square miles exposed to a noise index greater than 30 NEF) would reach $17,000 million which would fall to $1,600 million if the noise from each aircraft were reduced by 10 PNB(2). Expenditure of this order is hardly conceivable. On the other hand, it is sometimes possible when airports are being built - and if they are set up in agricultural areas - to consider purchasing much more land than would merely suffice for the airport and its infrastructure.

---

1) The idea of this tax was recently suggested by the Managing Director of the French airline, U.T.A. (Le Monde, 24/25 March, 1973).

2) "Civil Aviation Research and Development Policy Study - Joint DOT-NASA Report, op. cit., pp. 5-6.

In Canada, for example, a total area of 360 km^2 was bought to establish the new Montreal airport, although 82 km^2 only were needed for the airport and its installations(1). In this way control of the ground becomes complete: the construction of dwellings can be completely forbidden, but the establishment of activities compatible with noise may be authorised. Instead of being put out of action, the land can be rationally used.

Usually, however, and especially in Europe, it is impossible to find any vast tract of virgin land or even areas where the population density is very low. Therefore the only other possibility is to consider purchasing the land most exposed to noise or setting up a system of compensation and easement.

6. Noise easements

An easement linked to aircraft noise consists in paying the owner of a dwelling exposed to such noise the monetary value by which his dwelling is reduced. In theory, compensation paid under the easement reflects the dwelling's loss in value, and is paid to make up the loss caused by noise. A limited right is moreover acquired by the airport on the property under the easement, since compensation is paid in exchange for the noise endured.

Noise easements have been established around different airports, especially in the United States (Columbus, Ohio; Denver, Colorado; Des Moines, Iowa; Seattle, Washington; Jacksonville, Florida(2). In areas where the noise index exceeds 30 NEF, the cost of these charges is estimated to be 20 per cent of the value of properties exposed to the noise(3).

For airports and the authorities responsible for providing protection against noise, easements have the advantage of costing appreciably less than the purchase of land and dwellings exposed to noise. People living near airports thus receive financial compensation which can help them to soundproof their dwellings.

On the other hand, if the cost of such easements were to be borne by the airlines, they would be induced to adopt flight

---

1) "L'implantation du super-aéroport de Montréal et son impact sur le milieu naturel et social", by Pierre Dansereau, Forces, No. 118, Montreal, 1972.

2) The Economic Impact of Noise, op. cit., pp. 18, 19, 20.

3) "Aircraft Noise Impact - Planning Guidelines for Local Agencies", op. cit. pp. 119, 120. However, it should be noted that such estimates are always relatively uncertain (see in particular: Mrs. M.E. Paul "Can Aircraft Noise Be Measured in Money?" Oxford Economic Paper, Oxford, November, 1971.

procedures minimising the areas exposed to noise and to replace noisy
aircraft by quieter types.

o
o   o

It is probably a combination of the various regulatory and
economic instruments available - some of which call for international
agreement so that they will not hamper international trade and competition between airlines - which would produce the best result,
i.e. a rapid and substantial reduction of the noise affecting people
living near airports.

Chapter 4

Part 1

<u>THE MANAGEMENT OF AIRPORT PLANNING:</u>
<u>A UNITED KINGDOM VIEW</u>

F.A. Sharman

Partner, Sir William Halcrow & Partners, London

COST OF ACCESS

No more than ten per cent of the whole cost of air travel -
including the surface journeys of passengers - is influenced by
airport location.(1) And of this ten per cent an even smaller
proportion represents the different cost of travelling between any
pair of airports. It follows that even if a large increase in
airport-connected costs is added to air fares, the damping effect
on demand for travel would be unlikely to exceed more than a year
or two of growth.

This conclusion makes the task of the analyst easier than it
would otherwise be. It is difficult enough to balance "quality
of life" considerations against those of efficiency, but when the
issue is complicated by fear of crippling a major industry the
issue becomes inescapably passionate. If analytical methods are
to have any hope of contributing to decision-making, it is essential
to establish in good time their place and their limitations within
the political framework.

DEALING WITH ENVIRONMENTAL CONCERNS

Protest groups have become an important and sometimes decisive
influence in the choice of airport sites in many parts of the
world. The aviation "experts" have been guilty on occasions of
using tendentious or insensitive arguments in order to lull the

---

1) Sharman, F.A., "The Third London Airport as a Project Assessment
   Problem", Regional Studies Vol. 5, pages 135 - 143, 1971.
   Commission on the Third London Airport (1969), Stage III Research
   and Investigation (Papers and Proceedings, Vol. VII, HMSO).

fears of potential protesters. Equally, the protest groups have
an in-built tendency to exaggerate. Both would serve the
community better if they could express their cases in recognisably
objective terms.

In Britain any proposal to establish a new airport or to
change an existing one has to be subjected to a searching process
of examination before the Government takes a decision. This
examination, called a public inquiry, is devised to allow the
most unsophisticated and economically powerless individuals to be
given a hearing along with organised groups, local authorities
and airlines. The famous Roskill Commission of inquiry into the
Third London Airport arose out of dissatisfaction with the
expansion of Stansted Airport that was expressed at such a
public inquiry and itself gave rise to four more public inquiries
held near the sites of other possible locations.(1)

At many of these inquiries, local authorities and pressure
groups retain experts to give evidence for them as well as
commissioning leading lawyers to examine and cross-examine all the
experts giving technical evidence. Such inquiries have been
concerned with domestic issues but the world has been searched
for examples and methods of assessment to deploy before them and
strenuous efforts have been made to balance the advantages and
drawbacks of airport development. Some of the difficulties
encountered during these balancing exercises are discussed in the
following paragraphs.

Planning factors

Even the economists of the Roskill Committee Research Team
were baffled by the problem of expressing town planning considerations in financial terms. This points to the necessity to discuss
whether airport activity enhances or detracts from local, regional
or national planning objectives in general terms. However,
planners are seldom unanimous about such aims and many of them
regard such questions as matters of policy to be decided at a
political level. Nevertheless, in many cases it is possible to
establish a consensus amongst experienced planners which should
be given due consideration. For instance, if a proposal was made
to locate a new airport in the midst of beautiful countryside, few
people in the locality would be prepared to oppose it. The local
authorities might welcome the material prosperity and importance
promised by the airport. It would then be left to the regional

---

1) Commission on the Third London Airport, Stage II, Local
   Hearings, Vol. III (Foulness), Vol. IV (Nuthampstead),
   Vol. V Cublington (Wing), Vol. VI Thurleigh (Bedford).

planners and perhaps the national conservation organisations to
argue that the project would deprive many people of the enjoyment
of unspoiled countryside.

Equally, only national and regional planners can be expected
to be objective about the intensification of employment brought
about by an airport and the consequent thinning-out of it elsewhere.
In all this, it is appropriate to support an argument for a
particular solution with population, employment and productivity
figures but in the end, the case must be based on a description
of objectives and judgements about their importance.

NOISE

There are many methods of measuring the effects of aircraft
noise on those who live and work near airports. In Britain and
at all recent British public inquiries into airport developments,
the Noise and Number Index (NNI) has been relied on as the best
available method, and it has been frequently asserted that other
methods used in Scandinavia and America give similar results when
used to describe the same situation. The NNI method arose from
a report by the Wilson Committee(1) in 1963 and was based on a
social survey in the vicinity of Heathrow Airport which correlated
the degree of annoyance expressed by residents with the actual
number and loudness of aircraft noises heard. A defect of this
work was its failure to distinguish between night and day effects
and a follow-up survey in 1967(2) failed to make good the defect.

However, as a result of evidence given at a public inquiry
in 1972(3) it was judged that the correlation between the
readiness of people to complain about airport noise and noise
levels expressed in perceived noise decibels experienced as a
maximum during the passage of different types of aircraft using
the airport fairly frequently was superior to the NNI method. The
lesson of this and other public inquiries where people suffering
airport noise confront those who organise its cause, is that
indignation can be reduced and the considerateness of operators
increased when both parties are asked to agree on methods of
measurement and systems of record.

---

1) Committee on the Problem of Noise, Final Report, July 1963,
   Cmnd. 2056, HMSO.

2) The Second Survey (1967) of Aircraft Noise Annoyance around
   London (Heathrow) Airport, 1971, HMSO.

3) Developments at Luton Airport: Inquiry 4th January - 9th February,
   1972: Reports of Inspector and Assessor dated 3rd May, 1972.

45

Forecasts

One obstacle to describing the nuisances of airports is
uncertainty about the quantity and quality of future air traffic.
Should present sufferers be asked to put up with an increasing
burden for two, three or four years, rather than ask for the
imposition of a new burden on hitherto unaffected people? Can
we rely on continued success in reducing engine noise and so make
do with an airport pattern that would otherwise seem intolerable?
The only way of validating such possible futures is by describing
them clearly and publishing them widely.

FORECASTS OF AIR TRAFFIC

Since the Second World War aviation has grown irrepressibly
with passenger movements generally increasing at 10 per cent per
annum compound.(1) To translate this increase into the requirements
of an individual airport, local and national factors, trends in
aircraft seating capacity and airline maintenance facilities
need to be taken into account. Nevertheless, forecasts can turn
out to be wide of the mark though growth in aviation is such that
these errors are usually mended by time.

CHANGES IN TECHNOLOGY

The introduction of jet engines and recent increases in
seating capacity illustrate the effect that changes in aircraft
design can have on airport requirements. This makes it reasonable
that investment in airports suitable for a 1973 mix of aircraft
should be challenged when the life of such installations is
expected to last well into the next century. Clearly, if new
aircraft requiring less landing space and causing less noise were
to become economic, many machines now in use and under design
would be displaced and current ideas about airport systems would
have to be rethought. In the nature of things, however, one
cannot rely upon this happening. As long as fuel is an important
part of in-flight costs, heavy flying machines will be more
economical if their engines are used to help them glide up and
down rather than to rise steeply and descend against thrust. The
discovery of a dramatically cheaper source of energy would change

_____

1) Business Monitor CA2: Monthly Statistics on Air Passengers
   in Britain, 1972, HMSO.

this but it would revolutionise transport generally and no one can rely upon that heppening within the life span of existing airports.

Other constraints on change are the inherent dangers of marshalling large numbers of aeroplanes in a small volume of air space and a diversity of destinations that will tend to limit the size of aeroplanes no matter how great the growth of traffic.

AIRFIELD CAPACITY

Improvements to navigation aids, automatic landing and sequence control have enabled the intensity of use of runways to be steadily increased. Further improvements may be expected but it is hard to imagine that they will raise the standard busy rate of any runway far above today's rates.

THE SEARCH FOR GENERAL SOLUTIONS

It is tempting to the mathematical analyst to make assumptions about the distribution of population, about the relationship of the cost of surface and air travel and about the propensity of people to fly and then attempt to deduce how many airports would be needed and where and of what kind. It even seems reasonable to hope that this would give some guide through the dilemmas now facing airport planners.

Yet as far as I know, no such exercise has been seriously attempted because of inadequacies of data and the difficulties of assessing economic benefits. The idea of a rationally spaced hierarchy of airports is, however, in the minds of many planners and Figure 1, which is taken from a recently published document on regional planning in France, illustrates how the matter is being approached in that country. It is hoped that further advances may result from a national airport study shortly to be undertaken on behalf of the British Civil Aviation Authority.(1)

MAJOR LOCATION STUDIES

Searches for a fourth New York and a third London airport both led to major studies aimed at locating new airports in existing urban and aviation complexes. In the case of New York, the search

1) Civil Aviation Authority, "Airport Planning: An approach on a National Basis," HMSO.

Figure 1

A THEORETICAL AIRPORT HIERARCHY FOR FRANCE
UNE HIERARCHIE THEORIQUE DES AEROPORTS EN FRANCE

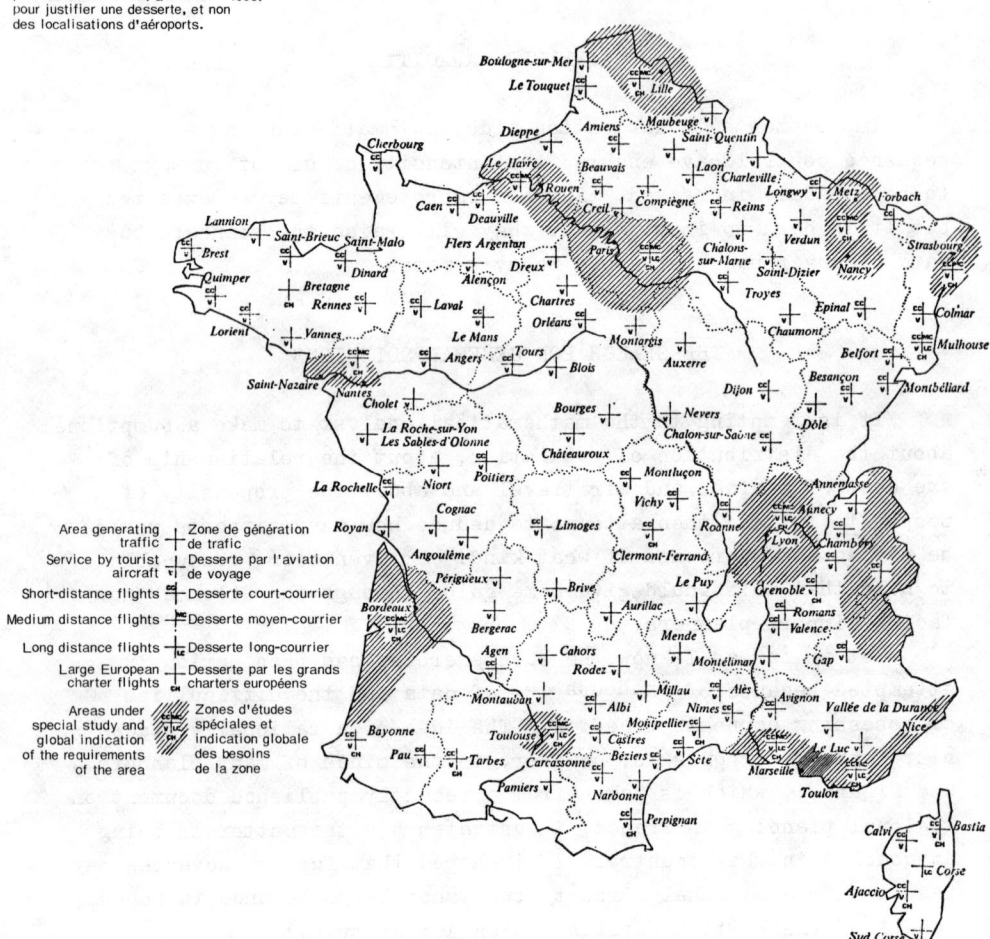

Nota bene

The symbols used below indicate potential requirements
for airport services for 1985 and are not the
location of airports.

Les symboles ci-dessous indiquent les besoins
potentiels suffisants, à l'horizon 1985,
pour justifier une desserte, et non
des localisations d'aéroports.

Area generating traffic	Zone de génération de trafic
Service by tourist aircraft	Desserte par l'aviation de voyage
Short-distance flights	Desserte court-courrier
Medium distance flights	Desserte moyen-courrier
Long distance flights	Desserte long-courrier
Large European charter flights	Desserte par les grands charters européens
Areas under special study and global indication of the requirements of the area	Zones d'études spéciales et indication globale des besoins de la zone

has so far not produced a result. In the second case, the United
Kingdom Government decided to choose what was widely believed to
be the most expensive, but least nuisance-prone site (this project
was subsequently abandoned following a change in government).
Nobody would now repeat the long and demonstrably wasteful process
by which decisions in these two cases were made, refused or evaded.
The lesson would seem to be that polarisation of opinion should
be avoided by the widest possible consultation.

OTHER LOCATION STUDIES

Innumerable airport feasibility studies have been carried out where less is at stake than at London and New York. In many of them the terms of reference lay down or imply constraints on location which result from power politics rather than from any logical optimisation. Such studies cannot, therefore, be relied upon as guides to airport location planning.

NATIONAL POLICIES

Airports can be regarded as growth points for employment, commercial activity and everything connected with passenger and freight transport, and as such, governments can use them as instruments for redistributing prosperity between one region and another. In pursuing such an aim, however, no government would wish to reduce the national wealth more than a limited amount in the course of seeking to distribute it more evenly.

The Roskill Commission's attempt to measure the national loss and the regional variations resulting from different locations has not met with universal credence. This illustrates the difficulty of arriving at reliable conclusions, even when large research resources are available and when the will to obtain an objective answer has triumphed over political considerations.

REGIONAL POLICIES

Regional planners and politicians will find it easier than their national counterparts to envisage the effect of a proposed airport, to decide whether or not to accept the development, and to identify amendments to it. Road and rail links will, in many cases, transform existing surface transport patterns and the position of the airport's noise shadow will effect patterns of residential development. In addition, industry and warehousing associated with the airport will have regional implications.

SOCIAL AND ENVIRONMENTAL EFFECTS

Attacks are sometimes launched on cheap air travel on the grounds that it loosens community bonds and gives rise to disoriented groups without the locational centres essential for the development of social values.(1) An attempt has also been made to correlate the social characteristics of individuals with the distances they travel. While it would be wrong to dismiss this line of thought as irrelevant, it may be wise to set it beside estimates of the relief from tedium offered to industrial workers by holiday travel.

Most of the other social effects of airport development are produced by other changes in place of work and residence and other forms of transport. Such changes are inevitably regarded by some as dangerous and by others as opportunities for modernising backward regions and redistributing wealth.

It is widely assumed that land, air and water are always damaged by the establishment or expansion of an airport. Again, it is desirable to take a balanced view of this. If the airport is established in neglected or rundown country, improvement as well as disturbance may result. Furthermore, the large numbers of spectators drawn to airports reveals that many people regard them as places of great interest.

PRODUCING AIRPORT PLANS

Ideally, every nation should have a national airports plan and policy and should co-ordinate its intentions with its neighbours. In practice, decisions about the siting of airports have hitherto largely been in response to pressures from users and operators, and counter pressures from local and national amenity groups. In no case has a nation defined and pursued an airports policy designed to optimise the national interest and obliged other interests to conform to this regime.

The British practice of seeking to expose and justify an airport proposal at a local public inquiry, though it has had good results in some cases, has become increasingly inadequate to prevent a polarisation of forces for and against each proposal. The more elaborate procedure followed for the Third London Airport, though it appeared appropriate at the time, proved in practice to be an extravagant failure of decision forming.

Yet it is clear from the instances reviewed in this paper that the preparation of a national or regional airports policy calls for expertise ranging from sociology to engineering. Trusted bodies of facts and well-authenticated forecasts that all can rely upon when expressing their own legitimate aspirations are no less important. Then there is the question of the impartiality of the research team.

---

1) J.G.U. Adams, "London's Third Airport", The Geographical Journal, Vol. 137, Part 4, December 1971.

Government departments and aviation interests may be tempted to give terms of reference that reflect their own particular responsibilities and interests, but it is in the end to nobody's advantage if a technical team is shown to have been biased by its instructions. Whether the technical experts come from the civil service, local authorities, private consultancy, statutory bodies or from commercial firms, they should therefore be responsible to a committee on which all relevant interests are represented and should receive instructions only from that source. As a further safeguard, the technical report, however qualified by members of the directing committee, should be published and made widely available.

Part 2

THE MANAGEMENT OF AIRPORT PLANNING:
A CANADIAN VIEW

P. Beinhaker and J.M. Choukroun

Ministry of Transport, Canadian Air
Transportation Administration

AIRPORT PLANNING AND MANAGEMENT IN CANADA

In Canada, the Federal Ministry of Transport is responsible for building and operating all international and most other airports. However, airports are not concerned solely with transport. They affect the entire social, political and economic fabric of the regions in which they are located. This gives all levels and departments of government an interest in them and makes it necessary for airport planning to be a collaborative effort.

The planning of the new Montreal International Airport followed this pattern but had some special characteristics. Effort was made to ensure that this airport would not become quickly obsolete as had occurred elsewhere. Emerging and future technology was carefully studied. Environmental issues were taken more seriously than hitherto - indeed, one reason for embarking on a new airport was the predicted disruption of communities around the existing one. Regional development was to be considered so that socio-economic benefit could be maximised. And the government was anxious to use the venture to promote new Canadian technology.

The planning of the new Montreal International Airport was therefore carried out against the background of new aspirations and within an intricate inter-organisational context.

THE NEW MONTREAL INTERNATIONAL AIRPORT

Background

In 1966 the Canadian Ministry of Transport commissioned a study of the airport capacity needed in the Montreal region up to 1985. The study indicated that while Dorval could be expanded, the cost, mostly the purchase of land, would be very high. It also showed that growth in air traffic would conflict with the expansion of adjacent suburbs and lead to widespread noise nuisances as well as costly restrictions on flying. It was therefore decided to make a study of the benefits and costs of developing a new airport. It was subsequently decided that a new airport and Dorval would provide Montreal with a more cost-effective airport system than Dorval alone. In July 1968 a decision was made to build a new airport at one or other of several sites. This choice was discussed with the other levels of government and in March 1969 a decision was made to build the airport at Ste. Scholastique, some 30 miles north-west of downtown Montreal. Ste. Scholastique met transport requirements and appeared to offer regional benefits.

Following the decision, a New Montreal International Airport Project Office was created. The project team obtained approval for a master plan. Funds were allocated and 1975 set as the date for the airport to begin operations. Meanwhile, the Provincial Government set up a regional planning agency for the airport and a development commission for the Greater Montreal Region. These agencies were to focus on the regional development aspects of the airport and subsequently worked with the federal authority.

Planning the airport

Planning an airport is a complex business because it entails two different but inter-acting contexts. On the one hand there is the need for a facility that enables travellers to board and leave aircraft, shippers to load and unload cargo and aircraft to take off and land. Providing for these needs calls for airport facilities planning. On the other hand, an airport has a number of other, wider functions.

  a) It is part of an area airport system that in Montreal's case is likely to have three future elements - an international, a domestic and a downtown, short take-off-and-landing airport.
  b) An airport system is part of a national air transport system involving relationships with other area systems and, in this case, Toronto's. Growing pressure from the airlines

and the public to make Toronto and not Montreal a terminal
for international flights indicates the economic nature of
such relationships.

c) An airport is part of a world-wide network.

d) An airport has an impact on the development of its region
that is felt in several ways:

   1. employees of the airport will move to the area, creating
a demand for housing and community services;

   2. airport-related industry and commerce will locate in the
area;

   3. industry and commerce shipping by air or making great
use of passenger services will locate in the area;

   4. the population with direct links to the airport will have
to be served by commercial and other activities which
will have a multiplying effect on the local economy;

   5. land, expropriated because of the noise inconvenience,
can be developed to increase the economic potential of
of the airport;

   6. ground transportation links built for air travellers will
also serve residents of the airport district thereby increasing its accessibility. The outcome is likely to be
increased urbanisation.

e) The airport has a direct impact on the environment. It
generates noise and air pollution as well as altering the
landscape.

These are indirect functions of the airport and call for environment planning (Diagram 1).

Facility planning and environment planning are closely linked
at the stage when the issue is whether a new airport is needed and,
if so, what kind and where. They become more distinct after the
site has been selected and construction begins. The early phase
may conveniently be called "strategic planning".

Once this phase of the work is completed, the process branches
out into "facility planning", the object of which is to come up with
an operational airport, and "environment planning", whose objective
is to plan for the non-air transport functions of the airport.
Facility planning can, in turn, be divided into airport master planning and airport operations and development planning.

Airport environment planning is more difficult to define. In
the case of Montreal, it can be defined in terms of various geographical scales. They are pictured in Map 1. The area delineated
in black in the first scale is 70,000 acres and is the land bought
compulsorily to control its development. The airport itself covers
another 18,000 acres.

Diagram 1 - Schéma 1

OVERALL PLANNING CONTEXT
CONTEXTE GLOBAL DE LA PLANIFICATION

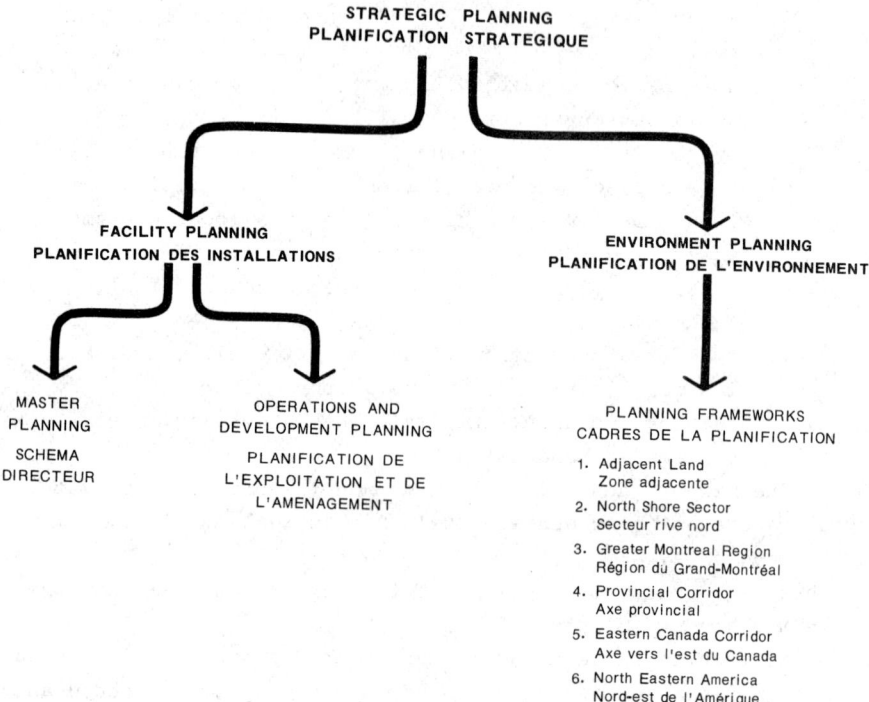

STRATEGIC PLANNING
PLANIFICATION STRATEGIQUE

FACILITY PLANNING
PLANIFICATION DES INSTALLATIONS

ENVIRONMENT PLANNING
PLANIFICATION DE L'ENVIRONNEMENT

MASTER
PLANNING

SCHEMA
DIRECTEUR

OPERATIONS AND
DEVELOPMENT PLANNING

PLANIFICATION DE
L'EXPLOITATION ET DE
L'AMENAGEMENT

PLANNING FRAMEWORKS
CADRES DE LA PLANIFICATION

1. Adjacent Land
   Zone adjacente

2. North Shore Sector
   Secteur rive nord

3. Greater Montreal Region
   Région du Grand-Montréal

4. Provincial Corridor
   Axe provincial

5. Eastern Canada Corridor
   Axe vers l'est du Canada

6. North Eastern America
   Nord-est de l'Amérique

Strategic planning

Strategic planning of the Montreal Area Airport System started
as soon as the Canadian Air Transportation Administration, the air
transport arm of the Ministry of Transport, made the decision to
build a new airport instead of expanding Dorval. The objective was
to find a site and four sets of criteria were used to assist the
choice. Air space safety requirements had to be fully met. The preferences of air travellers and cargo shippers had to be considered.
The airlines had to be consulted. And the effect of the airport on
man and nature had to be assessed.

Air safety requirements were over-riding and led to the elimination of several sites. Ease of access was used as a barometer for
passenger preferences. Since access depends on the availability of
roads and rail links to the various sites, provincial road plans and
transit proposals were considered.

Map 1 - Carte 1

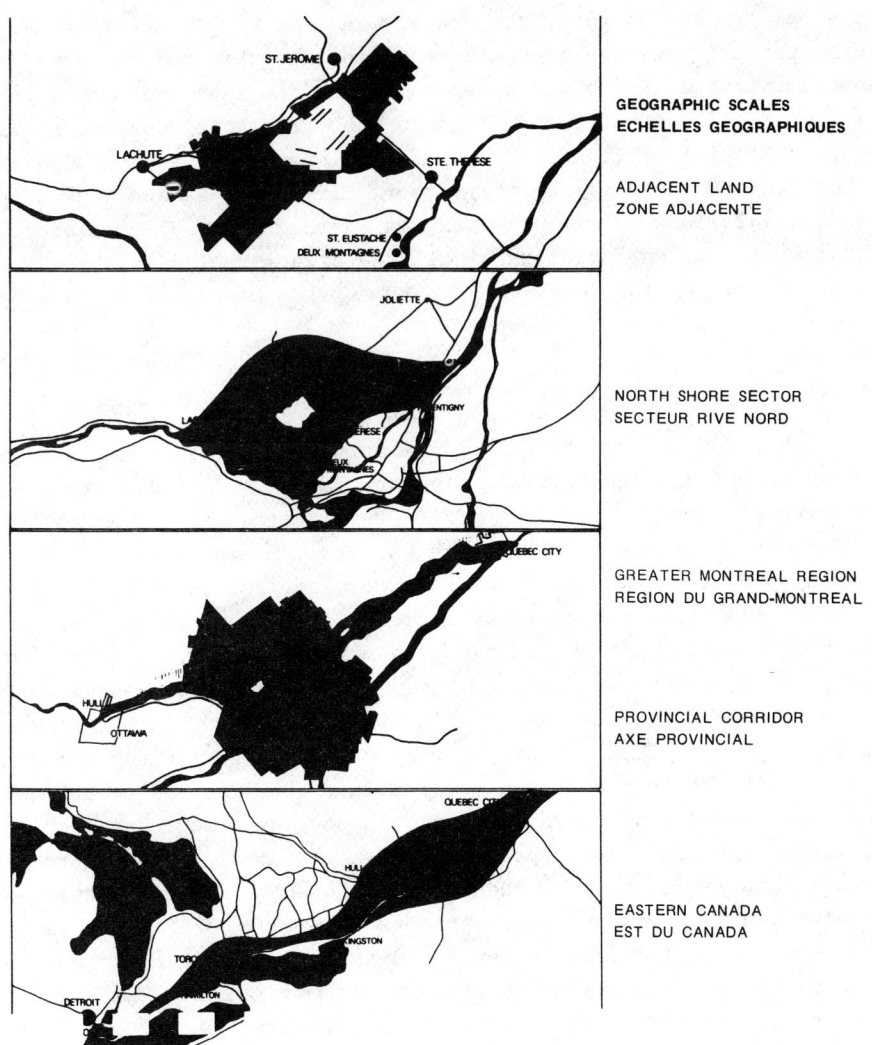

Shippers of air cargo prefer sites at some distance from cities
since this eliminates flight restrictions and provides inexpensive
land for warehouses.

The concerns of the airlines took two forms. The first turned
on the policy of the Canadian Air Transport Administration to finance
the running of major airports from fees charged to users. This made
the users wary of the cost of building and running the airport.
Other cost issues were raised by the prospect of the new airport and
Dorval being run as an air system since this promised to split the

operations of some airlines and add to their costs. It also led to a need for a good surface link between the two airports.

Since Dorval's environmental shortcomings were one reason for developing a new airport, the new site had to be planned to minimise nuisances and maximise economic benefits. To this end the Canadian Government took the bold step of acquiring the land that would be exposed to flight noise. At Toronto, the Provincial Government will achieve control through land-use regulations. At the same time the Government intended to use the airport investment as a stimulus for regional growth which meant siting it where growth was both needed and possible. Consideration of all these factors led to the selection of Ste. Scholastique.

AIRPORT FACILITY PLANNING

The second phase of work on the airport involved a master plan and an operations and development plan. These were the responsibility of the airport Project Office but increasingly of Ministry of Transport personnel in order to ensure a smooth integration of airport planning into the normal activity of the Ministry.

An original feature of the Project Office was the operations planning division set up in it at the very beginning. Its role was to build an airport to the requirements of the future operators. The personnel in operations planning were also the future managers of the airport. Their first job was to supply the planning/design people with the information about levels of service and performance and operational requirements. Once the physical plans had been decided they switched to operational management of the new airport.

The terminal layout chosen by the Project Office is linear and modular and involves bus-like vehicles to carry passengers to and from the aircraft. This concept permits flexibility in the operation of the airport and is convenient for passengers. The layout and the transfer vehicles are shown in Diagrams 2 and 3.

AIRPORT ENVIRONMENT PLANNING

People and services

The region around the airport, which is called the North Shore, has a present population of 315,000 and is expected to double it by 1985 and to triple it by AD 2000 without the added stimulus of an airport. The Greater Montreal Region is forecast to grow to some four million by 1985 and to 5.5 million by AD 2000 or double its present population.

Diagram 2 - Schéma 2

AIRPORT PLAN - PLAN DE L'AEROPORT

Spine Road Airport express
Express de l'aéroport
— TR2
● Passenger terminal
Aérogare voyageurs

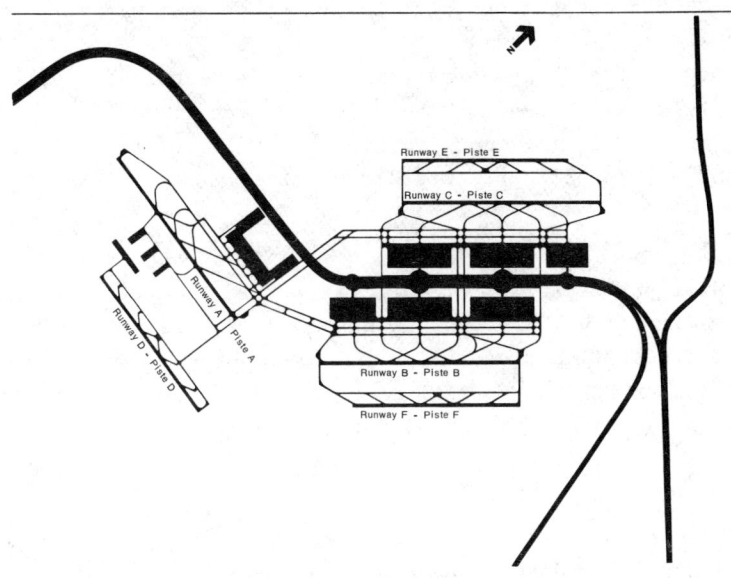

Diagram 3 - Schéma 3

TERMINAL TRANSIT VEHICLES

VEHICULE DE TRANSFERT DE L'AEROGARE

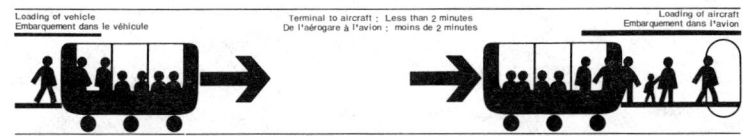

Illustration of vehicle loading at terminal building
Embarquement des passagers au bâtiment de l'aérogare

The airport's impact is not so much a matter of size but of technology and of the support required by its surrounding communities. This support must be of aviation quality. For instance, access must be good as schedules have to be met. The setting of high standards in such services as transport, power, sewers and water is bound to rub off on the surroundings of the airport too.

These surrounding communities and the technically oriented workers who will move into them will in turn attract light manufacturing and scientific industry capable of delivering high standards of transport, utilities and other services.

Land

Development of the 18,000 acres within and immediately surrounding the airport will be done within land-use controls reflecting the effects of flight operation. This land constitutes a major land bank that can be used to influence the development of the whole North Shore. An aviation business-industrial complex could be encouraged.

North Shore

The North Shore has ample space for housing, industry and agriculture and is located between the mountain resorts of the Laurentians and the great city of Montreal. The expected economic development of the region will greatly exceed changes induced by the airport. An airport cannot create development in a region without growth tendencies. But where such tendencies exist, an airport can act as a stimulator and influence the size and nature of growth. The North Shore is not today equipped to meet the demands of normal growth but plans exist for roads and new communities can be supported.

Greater Montreal

This is the primary market for the airport and accessibility from it for air passengers and air freight is vital. The airport should be part of communication and exchange systems covering airlines, hotels, hire cars, the media, banking, insurance and other institutions. Various transport schemes are possible for the region and a tri-level governmental group has been established to examine them and to invite the participation of private transport companies.

The Quebec and Eastern Canada corridors

Ste. Scholastique is located on the Quebec corridor which is part of the Eastern Canada corridor. Both corridors are developing and both need to have their linkages strengthened. The airport can contribute to the development of the two corridors partly through the aviation services offered and partly through being a part of an urbanised, well-developed North Shore. Interactions between airport and corridors will thus extend beyond air transport.

At the North American level, the airport is part of a network of airports, itself part of a network of urban centres. Judicious development of Ste. Scholastique could make it a major centre for inter-continental air cargo and an inter-governmental study is under-way to investigate this possibility.

The completion of the airport will not guarantee that all these developments happen. They will do so only if federal, provincial and local governments and a large number of private organisations get involved.

CONCLUSION

The planning of the Montreal Airport has proved an invaluable experience for at least three reasons:

a) it has given Canada an outstanding experience in planning airports for the long-range future;

b) it has given Quebec the opportunity to focus planning and regional development activities. It is interesting to note that in light of this experience the provincial government of Ontario advanced its regional planning so as to provide a more specific context for co-ordination at an earlier stage in the case of the new Toronto airport;

c) it has helped generate a new dimension of physical, social, economic and organisational planning in Quebec. An important by-product of the airport will be this new competence which can now be applied to other Quebec issues.

The combinations of these three consequences make the Montreal airport experience a worthwhile exercise in Canadian terms. Both the planning approaches and technical solutions adopted as well as the inter-agency co-ordination should prove useful in indicating guidelines to the planning of complex large-scale physical infra-structure.

Chapter 5

A PROGRAMME OF STUDIES FOR LOCATING AN AIRPORT

Reidar Persson,
Stockholm County Council Regional Planning Bureau

BACKGROUND

Greater Stockholm is the dominating urban agglomeration in Sweden and is part of a larger area, the Mälar-Hjälmar Valley, which contains a number of towns whose economies are mainly based on industry. The population of greater Stockholm is expected to reach two million, and that of the larger area about three million, by the end of the century.

This paper describes a number of studies proposed to be carried out in order to find sites for future airports in the Mälar-Hjälmar Valley.

FUTURE AIR TRAFFIC

A forecast of air traffic in the Stockholm region made by Professor Bo Björkman in 1969 indicates that passenger movements will nearly double every tenth year between now and the end of the century (this view was formed before the fuel price increases of 1973/4). (Table 1).

THE CONTEXT FOR AIRPORT PLANNING

In all planning it is desirable to observe a total system in operation and not to concentrate on its individual components. In planning an airport it is therefore necessary to consider an air traffic system of which the landing strip is merely a part. This system embraces airways and flight patterns, runways and terminals, air traffic control, a variety of types of ground equipment as well as passenger and cargo flows. What is more, an air traffic system must be considered as part of a wider system covering all forms of movement and as a factor in a regional land-use system.

The development of an air traffic system is largely determined by national and international forces and by non-geographical factors. Nevertheless regional and local land-use planning is affected by the location of airports. Collaboration between aviation authorities and regional and local planning authorities is therefore essential when a new airport is under consideration.

Table 1

FORECAST OF AIR PASSENGERS ARRIVING AND DEPARTING IN THE STOCKHOLM REGION

	1965	1970	1980	1990	2000
Passengers per year ('000)					
Domestic	675	1,100	2,000	3,400	5,300
Scandinavian	335	570	1,150	1,900	2,900
Scheduled International	430	750	1,550	2,600	4,000
Charter	300	650	1,750	3,400	5,700
Total	1,740	3,070	6,450	11,300	17,900
Passengers for a 24 hour period ('000)					
Domestic	3.0	4.7	8.2	14.2	22.0
Scandinavian	1.4	2.3	4.6	7.8	12.0
Scheduled International	1.9	3.3	6.5	10.8	16.5
Charter	2.4	4.9	11.8	22.5	36.5
Total	8.0	14.0	28.0	50.0	80.0
Passengers for a one hour period					
Domestic	560	880	1,400	2,400	3,600
Scandinavian	180	300	530	900	1,400
Scheduled International	200	340	670	1,100	1,700
Charter	160	400	900	1,700	2,800

Collaboration is particularly necessary on the following issues:

a) The reservation of land

Airports and their associated noise zones make sizeable demands on land and compete with housing and recreation needs. The definition of noise zones is therefore of prime importance.

b) Surface transport

Airports require good links with the towns and cities they serve but as high-capacity public transport services designed exclusively for air passengers and cargo are seldom economic, airports will generally need to be located on regional public-transport networks.

c) Long-term physical planning

Large airports probably have long term effect on shaping the regions they serve. They are likely, for instance, to influence the siting of businesses. This in turn makes it desirable for airports to be at places that are advantageous for industry and workers.

REGIONAL DEVELOPMENT

Familiarity with likely short and long term changes in the existing regional structure is essential in airport planning. Such changes will include pending residential developments, city centre expansions, major shifts in employment and proposed main road and rail links. The impact of airports on the regional structure should also be further analysed.

Studies required:

Investigate current national and regional land use policies.

AVIATION DEVELOPMENTS

New types of aircraft and improved air traffic control techniques play an important role in the development of air traffic systems. The introduction of jumbo jets, for instance, led to demands for longer and stronger runways and larger terminals. The prospect of short-take-off-and-landing (STOL) aircraft able to operate from runways of 600 to 1200 meters, of quiet STOL machines and of supersonic transports with long runway requirements and high noise levels may, in turn, bring about further changes.

The different kinds of aircraft used for different aviation activities raise other issues since a suitable location for an airport may vary depending on the kinds of aircraft to be operated from it. Thus if it is desirable to site an airport close to an urban area, then a first priority must be to ensure that it is used only by quieter aircraft.

The handling of aircraft is prone to change too. Current developments in air traffic control promise to disperse landing aircraft and their noise over fan-shaped areas instead of mar-shalling them along corridors. Runway layouts, taxiways, and

terminal buildings are meanwhile all being improved to permit
the handling of larger numbers of flights and larger aircraft as
well.

Studies required:
    a) Assess which types of aircraft are likely to be used in
       the various branches of aviation in the short and long
       term and identify those aircraft characteristics that
       affect the siting and layout of airports. (Figure 1).
    b) Assess the short and long term prospects for developments
       in air traffic control and describe how these will affect
       the location and design of airports.
    c) Evaluate developments in the design of small as well as
       large airports.

NOISE

The establishment of relationships between aircraft noise and
human reactions to it is essential to airport planning and is the
subject of a number of studies. A 1956 report on flight noise has
hitherto been used for this purpose in Sweden but this is under
review by a government committee and new standards are expected to
be proposed in 1975.
. The levels of noise to be expected around an airport can only
be defined when the noise vibration and climb performance of
individual aircraft and their patterns of use are known. The
method of making these computations is complex and has given rise
to difficulties. These are described in "Flight noise at Arlanda
airport 1985: Theme Report II."

Studies required:
    Identify the implications of current noise standards. Define
the procedure for making precise estimates of the noise levels
for a given airport.

DIFFERENT KINDS OF AVIATION

Aviation can be divided into categories based on function.
These categories may be further subdivided according to the types
of aircraft used and the resulting flight noise, runway lengths
and technical facilities involved. They can be subdivided even
further according to their needs to be close to densely populated
areas and other modes of transport. The variations amongst
scheduled services are especially large. (See Figure 1).

Figure 1

DIFFERENT KINDS OF AVIATION

Function	Type of aircraft	
Scheduled flights Charter flights All-cargo services Air-taxi flights	Civil transport aircraft, in general	More than 5,700 kg. take-off weight
Agriculture and forestry services Other non-transport operations (aerial photography, advertising, geophysical survey, powerline-, ambulance-, and emergency operations, traffic observation, forest fire patrol)	Aerial work planes or civil commercial	Civil aircraft in general less than 5,700 kg. take-off weight
Business flying Private flying Flying clubs School aeroplane activities	Private planes, non-commercial civil aircraft in general	

When examing an air traffic system encompassing a group of airports with partially specialised roles it is advisable to study the different categories of aviation individually before attempting to group them together. Political preferences for the organisation of the air traffic system may also be indicated.

Studies required:

    a) Forecast the number of aircraft movements for each of the different categories of aviation shown in Figure 1.

    b) Identify for each category of aviation its most desirable location in relation to densely populated areas and other forms of transport including other categories of aviation.

    c) Contrast the views of the public and of the aviation community on the development of the air traffic system.

    d) Indicate how the various categories of aviation might be combined at specific airports.

AIR TRAFFIC NETWORKS

Airways and airports together comprise air traffic networks and as new airports are commissioned and flying increases so the

network changes. It is therefore necessary to describe the
development of the system and to identify departures from the
present structure. The national character of air transport means
that this analysis will have to take into consideration other
regions and cover developments there too.

Studies required:

    a) Analyse national airway and airport developments in so
        far as these affect traffic within the region under
        study.

    b) Map the main structure of the air traffic network showing
        the size, function and technical standards of main air-
        ports and military aviation needs. Alternative structures
        should be shown where they are feasible.

    c) Show the development and alteration of the air traffic
        system in a series of step-by-step sketches.

OTHER LAND USES

Once the prospective air traffic system has begun to take
shape it is necessary to see how it fits other existing and proposed land uses. This calls for a land-use inventory showing
present uses and planned ones where binding decisions have been
taken. The inventory should cover houses, places of work and
other noise-sensitive sites. The latter may include recreation
resources and farms containing noise sensitive livestock. Land
subject to military restrictions against flying should also be
listed. Once all this land use data has been collated it may be
overlayed on a map illustrating the main elements of the existing
air traffic system.

Studies required:

Prepare an inventory of existing and planned land uses and show
them on a map.

DEVELOPMENT POTENTIAL AT EXISTING AND NEW AIRPORTS

Study should initially be confined to the development potential
of existing airports taking into account flight noise, civil
engineering implications and air traffic control requirements. In
a second phase a list of all conceivable sites for new airports
should be drawn up. The criteria for selection may be distance
from urban areas and from prohibited military zones and air traffic

control considerations. All these sites should then be analysed
for their noise disturbance characteristics and civil engineering
costs.

Studies required:

    a) Draw up an inventory of existing airports and analyse
        their potential for growth in terms of land requirements,
        noise, civil engineering costs and air traffic control.

    b) Map out areas where new airports could possibly be
        located.

    c) Examine all conceivable locations for new airports.
        Take flight noise and site preparation costs into account.
        Mark the potential sites and runway directions on a map.

CHOOSING A SITE AND RESERVING LAND

By this time the more promising sites should be apparent and
they should be subjected to further analysis. The volume and
composition of traffic at various stages of development should be
specified and surface access for passengers and goods looked into.
The airspace should be examined, meteorological conditions identified
and an estimate made of traffic distributed on airways. This will
in turn provide a basis for calculating flight noise and for
delineating noise footprints for all possible runway and airway
layouts. The implications of urban development should be examined
too.

At this stage a brief survey of civil engineering considerations should be made. Runways, taxiways and terminal buildings
should be sketched and their costs roughly assessed. The land
requirements for the preferred airport sites may now be formally
designated and further study made of noise nuisance to enable
zones likely to be at risk from flight noise to be determined.
Such zones will not be identical with the computed noise limits
for any given stage of development but possess a margin to cover
variations in flight patterns.

The delineation of risk zones will, of course, involve trade
offs with other land uses but once negotiations between competing
interests have been completed all development should be made to
conform to the noise zoning.

Studies required:

    a) Select a series of potential airport sites for investi-
        gation.

b) Specify the types of traffic and traffic volumes to be expected at various stages of development.
c) Analyse the travel time and costs of surface transport links for both cargo and passengers.
d) Construct airway patterns and distribute traffic on them.
e) Compute a theoretical limit for noise nuisance.
f) Identify sites and their associated civil engineering costs for runways, taxiways and terminals.
g) Negotiate the limits of a noise risk zone agreeable to the aviation authorities, communities and local authorities concerned.

Chapter 6

A THEORETICAL DISCUSSION
OF THE EFFECTS OF AN AIRPORT ON ITS REGION

R.P. van der Kind,
Planning Group, Second Airport,
Netherlands Department of Civil Aviation

INTRODUCTION

In the last few years aviation has found itself in an ambivalent
position. Passenger travel has expanded spectacularly but so has
opposition to aircraft noise, to road congestion around airports and
other side effects of aviation. The once widely held view that
aviation is good for a country from every point of view is not now
so readily taken for granted. However, there is expected to be a
shortage of airport capacity in the Netherlands in the next ten to
fifteen years. The resulting situation is one that merits careful
attention, especially in a country which is densely populated and
where receipts from transport play an important part in the balance
of payments.

Awareness of the prospective shortage has led to proposals to
expand existing airports such as Schipol and to build a new one.
Ten years ago investigations would have been concerned mainly with
the direct effects of such proposals, their cost and profitability
and the importanceof the airport to the Netherlands economy. Nowadays
it is felt necessary to look at the impact of these effects on the
community as well.

The Department of Civil Aviation has therefore set up a planning
group to study the economic effects, noise, impact on recreation
facilities and infrastructure costs of five possible airport sites.
This paper will only deal with one aspect of these studies - the influence of an airport on the development of its region. All other
national and international aspects of aviation will be disregarded.
The discussion will be in general terms, because the details of the
sites are not yet known at the time of writing.

THE SITE

Let us assume to start with that the region in which the airport is to be established is thinly settled and agricultural in character. Its inhabitants have low incomes and little more than basic schooling. There is little shortage of labour. The infrastructure is not very developed. The conurbation to be served by the airport is about 60 kilometers away. In short, it is more or less an ideal region for a national airport.

ECONOMIC EFFECTS OF BUILDING AN AIRPORT

Building activity is intense for eight to ten years while the airport and its road and rail links are being built but generally speaking, the revenue from this activity will not remain in the region. The extent of the work means that both contractors and labour will be drawn in from nearby cities because local firms and craftsmen will be insufficient to meet the demands placed upon them. Most of the wages earned in this phase of the development will therefore be spent outside the region in which the airport is located. The economic effects of the development will be on the national, not the regional, economy.

RUNNING AN AIRPORT

Airport services are labour intensive and form an important source of employment. Studies at Roissy (France) and Maplin (United Kingdom) mention figures of 90,000 and 100,000 workers. Such workers will not only look for housing near the airport, causing a surge of town building, but they will spend their incomes there too. The outcome is likely to be a considerable and lasting increase in regional income. This increase will in turn set off a multiplier effect, the extent of which will depend on the success of the airport and the purposes for which it is used.[1]

A similar multiplier effect will ripple through the labour market with primary employment giving rise to jobs in secondary, mainly service, industries.

1) See Waldo and Edwards, "The Economic Impact of Los Angeles
   International Airport on its Market Area" Los Angeles 1971.
   Malin and Poza, CEIR Study "Economic Relationship of Air Trans-
   portation to the New Jersey, New York Metropolitan Area",
   August 1960.
   "Economic and Social Impacts of Kansas City Airport", Kansas City,
   Metropolitan Planning Commission, 1970.

<u>Spending by passengers</u>

Air passengers and their friends can also be expected to contribute to the economy of the airport region. Many will earn their
income outside the region and, in a way that is analogous to foreign
tourists, their spending will be a contribution to the region's exports and in turn help to increase incomes within the region.

SECONDARY EFFECTS

The vicinity of an airport is an exceptionally attractive place
for various types of businesses, including trading companies and
banks which are in frequent contact with other countries, manufacturers of high-value products that are dispatched by air, distribution centres of more than regional importance, hotels (usually of the
more expensive kind), shopping centres (tax-free or otherwise) and
head offices of airline companies. In other words, secondary activities will develop around an airport making it more than an inter-
change between air transport and ground transport.

These secondary activities will, of course, require workers who
will need to be housed in the region and whose salaries will be spent
and cause multiplier effect in it.

Furthermore the trading companies, banks and manufacturers
attracted by the airport will generally sell most of their production
outside the region thus further improving the regional balance of
payments.

<u>Advantages for the original inhabitants</u>

Other secondary effects will flow from the opening up of the
region to provide access to the airport. For instance, the products
of the original inhabitants may be transported more cheaply and more
distant markets will become accessible.

THE EXTENT OF AN AIRPORT'S INFLUENCE

An impression may have been given that the influence of a future
airport on a region can be determined with precision. Nothing could
be farther from the truth. The direction of the expected effects
may be known but their extent will be dependent on the following
variables:
  a) The characteristics of the airport
  b) The characteristics of the airport region
  c) The size of the airport region

d) The quality of any road and rail links

e) Policies for industrial and urban development and environmental protection.

Such factors cannot be dealt with exhaustively in this paper,
but an attempt will be made to indicate their regional effects. The
order in which they are mentioned, beginning with the airport itself
and ending with central government policy, is arbitrary. If arranged
by importance the order could be different.

The characteristics of the airport

An airport's effects on its region will depend first and fore-
most on the extent and nature of aviation activities. For instance
employment will be closely related to the number of aircraft or
passenger movements. Large intercontinental airports may generate
90,000 to 100,000 jobs. Smaller airports will create correspondingly
fewer. A relationship therefore needs to be found between the number
of workers and the airport activities but existing information is too
sketchy for this to have been done so far.

The economic effects of airports specialising in charter,
scheduled or general aviation will all be different. For instance,
charter flights can be handled with smaller staffs than scheduled
ones and the same applies to domestic compared with international
flights.(1)

The prospects for freight traffic are also important. If productivity in this branch of aviation continues to improve as slowly
as in the past fifteen years then it is likely to account for an increasing proportion of airport employment.

The characteristics of the airport region

One hypothetical region has already been described. Let us
consider another that is less thinly populated and where labour is
tight. This will probably mean that service industries are already
well established and that the secondary effects of an airport on
employment would be less pronounced. However the arrival of a new
employer would make supplies of labour even tighter leading to
higher wages and prices which would in turn effect the region's competitive position.

Employees can also be expected to leave existing industries to
work in aviation services causing changes in the regional economy
which would partly offset the airport's positive effects. This
would be avoided only if the labour demands of the airport could be

---

1) Gatwick, a charter flight airport, handled 613 passengers per
   employee in 1970 compared with 323 per employee at Heathrow, a
   scheduled flight airport.

met by the unemployed in the region. In that event there would be a rise in regional income but such a situation is unlikely to arise frequently in Europe because of the tendency to site airports near large conurbations.

The employment created by an airport should therefore not be regarded entirely as a stimulus. It will have a negative influence too. The measures that may be taken to relieve labour shortages fall outside the scope of this paper. Nevertheless the problem is not a theoretical one in the Netherlands, where one of the five sites being considered for a second airport is in the sphere of influence of Rotterdam, a highly industrialised region where labour is in relatively short supply, and another is in the Markerwaard, a region with no inhabitants or economic structure at all because it has yet to be impoldered, and which is surrounded by regions where there is structural unemployment.

The size of the airport region

How should an airport region be defined - as a finite geographical area or as a sphere of influence that dwindles with distance? If the former is chosen, there is a risk that the effects will be considered only insofar as they occur in the region. If the latter is chosen, the matter becomes extremely complicated since infrastructure, industrial structure and the composition of the population all need to be taken into account.

The region as a geographical entity

Let us assume that an airport's region is defined as an area within a radius of 50 kilometers and that it is agricultural and sparsely populated. The establishment of an airport could mean, for example, work for 50,000 people, resulting in an increase of about 175,000 in the population. Urban development would be on a corresponding scale. Not too far away from the region thus defined, however, are a number of industrial towns with a total population of one million people, about one third of whom constitute the working population.

If the region is regarded in isolation and the average wage of an airport employee is taken to about 20,000 guilders, the direct stimulus to the regional income can be put at 50,000 x 20,000 = 1,000 million guilders or U.S.$370 million. If a multiplier of two or three is taken, (1) this means an ultimate annual increase of 2,000 million to 3,000 million guilders or U.S.$740 million to $1,100 million. Total employment from an airport can be calculated in a similar way. If the number of workers directly employed is

1) Los Angeles International Airport.
The Economic Impact of LAX on its market area. Secondary Economic Impact, p.63, Waldo & Edwards, Inc., 1971.

50,000 and multiplied by 2.5, it can be shown that employment for
125,000 persons will be generated. This is no mean figure for a
region needing development and is frequently used as an argument to ·
justify a decision to establish an airport.(1)

The outcome could, however, be quite different. For instance,
large numbers of airport employees are likely to come from nearby
towns leading to a fall in manufacturing industry and a rise in services. The employment multiplier of 2.5 must therefore be applied
to smaller numbers of people since it relates only to the creation
of new jobs not to shifts from one to another. If the airport region were to include such towns, far fewer new jobs would be created
than in the area within 50 kilometers of the airport. It is also
doubtful whether employees drawn from industry would move to live
near the airport thus reducing the demand for houses. If however
they were to move - to a new town for example - there would be an
increase in the number of houses available in the towns they had
left. This would be a positive effect in a time of housing shortage,
but if there were no shortage, it would cause house prices to fall,
giving a lower return on real property and would have to be counted
as a negative effect of the airport.

All this should help to show how the effects of developing an
airport will differ depending on the extent of the geographical region chosen for study. It also brings out how the size of an airport
region cannot be considered without reference to an actual site.
Thus in an empty area such as the Markerwaard, the effects of an
airport will be more far reaching than in an over-crowded area like
Rotterdam.

The region as a sphere of influence

If it is decided to treat an airport region as a sphere of influence, it will be necessary to decide which influences should be
included in the analysis. Account will also need to be taken of the
modifying effect on an airport's sphere of influence, of its function,
accessibility and other factors. The danger of this approach is
that it is precisely the information required - the influence on the
region - that is being used to define the region. This means that
the definition of the term "region" plays a very important part in
the determination of the airport's influence on that region.

---

1) See the Los Angeles International Airport document, and
   R.E. Goughter and R.C. Douglas in Economic Impact of the Dallas
   F.W. Regional Airport on the North Central-Texas region.

The quality of any road and rail links

Road and rail links decide an airport's market area. The better the links the wider the area over which effects are felt. This is true of the patterns of urban development generated by an airport too. The better the access, the further off airport-associated development is likely to be. Much of it may even lie outside the airport region and good links may be provided by governments expressly with this objective.

Policies for industrial and urban development and environmental protection

Government has at its disposal a wide range of instruments with which to influence the impact of an airport on its region. It may inhibit or shape urban development by zoning.(1) It can decide the function of an airport: this may be essential if a second airport is being created. It can determine the transport links to be provided and the kind and rate of housebuilding. Finally it can use systems of permits to control the establishment of secondary activities.

CONCLUSION

This paper has been largely theoretical. It indicates some of the difficulties that can be expected if an attempt is made to forecast the effects of a major airport on its supporting region.

Some experience of such difficulties has already been obtained in the Netherlands and has led to decisions not to study regional effects in general terms but to prepare specific models for each of the five possible airport sites. It was found possible to describe the nature of the anticipated effects in general terms, but impossible to determine their extent without more detailed employment forecasts than had been available hitherto, information about government policy and facts about local housing and labour markets.

Furthermore airports are part of very complex and wide-ranging systems. Government policy can affect them but it is in turn affected by national, international and other considerations. In other words, many extra-regional factors impinge on airports.

---

1) Depending on the standards applied, zoning could mean that areas of land up to 240 km^2 are not available for house-building.

Chapter 7

Part 1

FINDING SITES FOR MAJOR AIRPORTS:
THE EXPERIENCE OF OSLO

Åage Danielsen

Head of Economic P₁anning Studies,
Nordland Regional College, Bodø

BACKGROUND

On 4th October, 1968, the Norwegian Government appointed a committee to look into the airport needs of the Oslo region. The committee concluded that a new airport was essential and after examining 17 possible sites recommended closer investigation of seven of them. A new committee was appointed on 17th July, 1970 to evaluate the regional and environmental effects of the sites and to recommend one of them for development. Three of the seven sites were rejected but Gardermoen, Hobøl, Ås and Nesodden were selected for closer examination (Map 1).

OBJECTIVES OF THE PAPER

This paper uses the output from a Lowry model to trace the long-term effects of population distribution, transport and traffic policy of the three most promising sites for a new Oslo airport - Gardermoen, Hobøl and Ås. External diseconomies such as noise, disadvantages to agriculture and forestry and urban growth policy for the Oslo region are discussed. The main focus is, however, on changes in population distribution and in the structure of the work force, for it can be argued that most other regional impacts are derived directly or indirectly from these variables.

The study region comprises Oslo, the present airport at Fornebu and the three proposed sites. This region is, by definition, that area within which growth and structural change would accompany development at any of the sites. The region comprises 57 communes and had a population of 1,140,000 in 1969 (Map 2).

If the existing site at Forenbu were expanded, there would be little redistribution of the work force. However if any of the other sites were chosen for development the impact would be considerable.

Map 1 - Carte 1

ALTERNATIVE AIRPORT SITES

DIFFERENTS SITES D'AEROPORTS POSSIBLES

Alternatives considered in this paper marked with a circle.

Les sites étudiés dans ce rapport ont été cerclés.

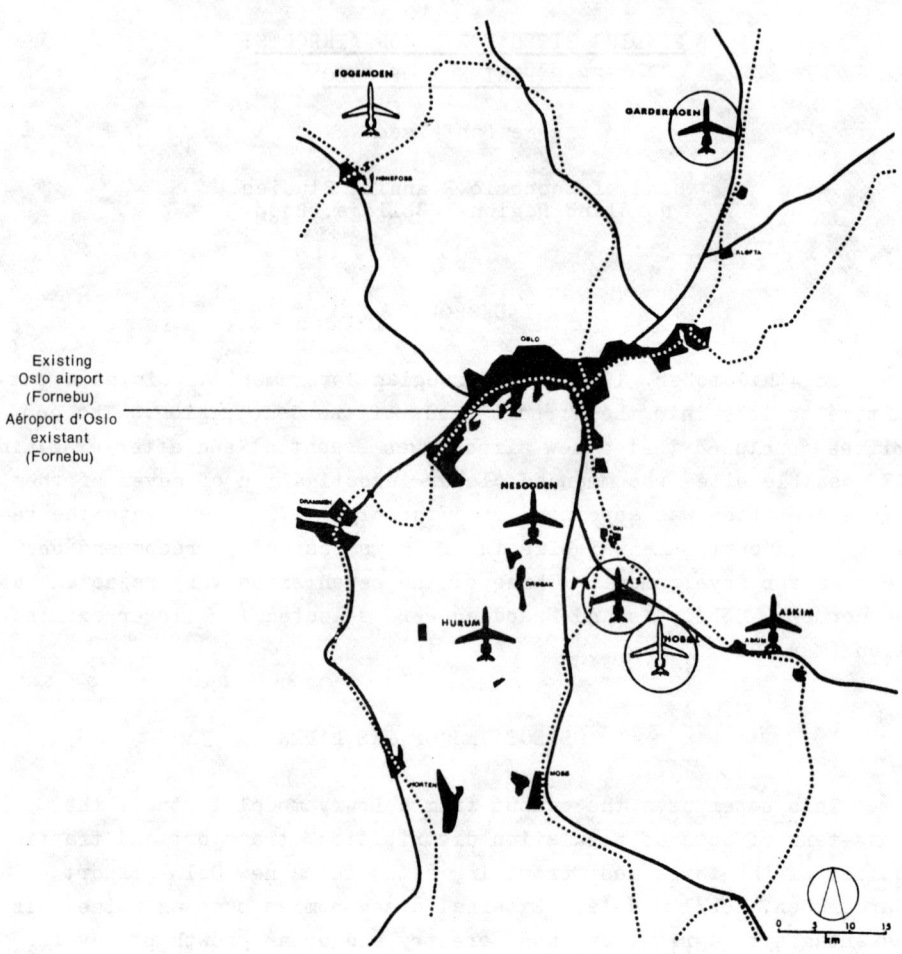

Existing
Oslo airport
(Fornebu)
Aéroport d'Oslo
existant
(Fornebu)

SUMMARY OF REGIONAL IMPACTS

An airport gathers around it those services essential to its
operation, here defined as <u>fundamental services</u>. In addition to this,
industrial and service activities not directly associated with aviation may seek to locate or expand in the vicinity of airports. These
are referred to as <u>secondary activities</u>. Employees in these activities
and their families will in turn cause an increase in population within
commuting distance of an airport. This will result in increased demand for public and private community services and additional expansion in tertiary employment. Increases in traffic between residential
areas, places of employment and service areas will accompany all these
developments and necessitate expansion of the existing transport network. These impacts along with disturbances to the natural environment may be said to be the main effects of a new airport on its
surroundings.

SIZE LIMITATION AND UNCERTAINTY REGARDING WORKPLACES

The study that is about to be discussed was based on forecasts
of population and employment in the Oslo region and on an assumption
that all air traffic is to be transferred from Fornebu to a new site
by 1980.

Fundamental service employment

The growth of air traffic to the region will depend on increased
national income, air transport prices, the competitive standing of
the air lines, upon travel time and the relative prices of other
forms of travel. Uncertainty clouds the future of all three factors
and made it necessary to work with several estimates of passenger
traffic (Table 1). These estimates provide the basis for calculations of all employment directly associated with the operation of
the airport - including flying personnel, technical and service
staff in charge of aircraft, freight and passengers. Alternative
assumptions are made about the future ratios of employment to traffic,
and consequential changes in productivity in the handling of freight
and passengers.

Secondary employment

The selection of a site will lead to readjustments in the location of certain industries and services. Firms shipping by air or
highly dependent on passenger services for their business may find
their existing locations disadvantageous. Some may consider it preferable to expand or relocate in the vicinity of the new airport.

Table 1

ALTERNATIVE ESTIMATES IN AIR PASSENGER
TRAFFIC INTO OSLO REGION IN 1990. ALTERNATIVES FOR
FUNDAMENTAL SERVICE AND SECONDARY EMPLOYMENT

	Passenger Traffic(1)	
	1970	1990
Alternative 1 Alternative 2	} 2,077,000	11,900,000 8,500,000
	Fundamental Service Employment(2)	
	1970	1990
Alternative 1 Alternative 2 Alternative 3	3,800	20,200 12,300 8,000
	Secondary Employment(3)	
	1970	1990
Alternative 1 Alternative 2 Alternative 3	} ?	7,200 5,000 3,700

1) Alternatives 1 and 2 for passenger traffic forecasts 1990 are
   given from the Committee of October 1968. The figure for 1970
   is statistics.

2) Alternatives 1 and 2 for Fundamental Service employment are computed from (1) by use of an estimate for future employment/traffic
   volume ratio. Alternative 3 is based on an indication of present
   ratio found later in the study period. The figure for 1970 is
   statistics.

3) Three alternatives are directly estimated. No registrations for
   1970 are done.

In the following analysis the effects on the structure of the region
of changes in both fundamental and secondary employment are considered.

Tertiary employment

As residential areas are built around a new airport, there will
be increased employment opportunities in local services. Estimates
of this increase were based on two surveys done in 1960 and 1969 of
existing employment in local services in the 57 communes that make
up the study region. This led to the definition of two categories
of local employment - local services and basic activities. The former
include retail trade, most types of private and personal services
and local government (Table 2). The ratio between local service
employment and population was found to be relatively constant
throughout the period surveyed, though the level of this kind of
employment was, as might be expected, significantly lower outside

than within Oslo. Uncertainties about how this situation might evolve led to the adoption of the 1969 ratio of 14 local service jobs per 100 inhabitants as a fixed factor.

Activity levels

Past levels of employment per 100 inhabitants in the region are given in Table 3 but the Central Bureau of Statistics expects these to decline in the future as a result of changes in the age structure of the population. The economically active population in the study region is therefore unlikely to be significantly greater in 1990 than in 1969.

Total population growth and degree of accuracy

The effect on population growth of a proposed airport may be estimated by using a model based on economic theory in which fundamental airport service employment and secondary activity are taken as basic. Calculations of this sort for the three sites are given in Table 4. They are based on low and high forecasts of 10 to 15 workplaces per 100 inhabitants, and on low and high levels of 39 and 43 economically active persons per 100 inhabitants. These exercises suggest that the population associated with airport development will lie between 35,500 and 114,200.

Where will these people live and what proportion of them will be newcomers to the airport district? An attempt to answer this question was made on an assumption that an airport district extends about 30 km from its focus. The conclusion was that a large part of the airport staff would live in such a district but that the total would be modified by the following factors:(Table 4)

a) a proportion of new jobs within the district will be taken by currently employed airport personnel or others in secondary activities who do not move house;

b) a proportion of new jobs will be taken by workers commuting into the district;

c) a proportion of the service requirements for the local population will be met by establishments outside the district;

d) an allocation of labour between establishments in the airport district from which the airport derives benefit.

These factors are expected to lead to reductions in the new population of the airport district given in Table 4 of between 20 and 50 per cent depending on the actual levels of fundamental and secondary employment, and on the airport site selected.

Table 2				Table 3		
LOCAL EMPLOYMENT PER 100 INHABITANTS IN 1960 AND 1969 IN THE STUDY REGION				ACTIVITY EMPLOYED PER 100 INHABITANTS IN 1960 AND 1969 IN THE STUDY REGION		

	1960	1969			1960	1969
Oslo	21.4	21.4		Oslo	46.4	47.9
Rest of Region	9.2	9.5		Rest of Region	39.8	40.7
Total	14.8	14.6		Total	42.9	43.7

Table 4

POPULATION ESTIMATES WITH ALTERNATIVE EMPLOYMENT
LEVELS IN PRIMARY AND SECONDARY EMPLOYMENT

Alternative for Fundamental Service and Secondary Employment(1)	Employed Popn. per 100 inhabitants(2)	Employment in Service Sector(3)	
		10 workplaces per 100 inh. ("low")	15 workplaces per 100 inh. ("high")
1	"Low" : 39	94,500	114,200
	"High": 43	83,000	97,800
2	"Low" : 39	59,700	72,100
	"High": 43	52,400	61,800
3	"Low" : 39	40,000	48,700
	"High": 43	35,500	41,800

1) See Table 1.

2) High and low estimates based on Table 3.

3) High and low estimates based on Table 2.

ANALYSIS OF THE REGIONAL DISTRIBUTION OF POPULATION GROWTH

A version of the Lowry model employed by the Roskill Commission
on the Third London Airport was used to calculate the probable distribution of population at the three airport sites.(1)   It was
calibrated according to employment, commuting and travel time data
for 1969 using travel time estimates for 1990 taken from the
Norwegian Road Plan.

---

1) E.L. Cripps and D.H.S. Foot: "The Empirical Development of an
   Elementary Residential Location Model for Use in Sub-Regional
   Planning", Environment and Planning 1969, Vol. 1, pp. 81-90.
   M. Batty: "Some Problems of Calibrating the Lowry Model",
   Environment and Planning 1970, Vol. 2, pp. 95-114.
   E.L. Cripps and D.H.S. Foot: "The Urbanisation Effects of a
   Third London Airport", Environment and Planning 1970, Vol. 2
   pp. 153-192.

Assumptions about the growth of employment and population for the region up to 1990 that were fed into the model are shown in Tables 5 and 6. By then the region is expected to contain 38.9 per cent of the country's employment compared with 34.7 per cent in 1969. Maps 2 and 3 show employment changes 1960-90 by commune assuming the trends of 1960-69 continue.

Population patterns in 1990 for the three sites were compared by demonstrating first of all that if the existing airport were expanded to handle all air traffic, all fundamental service employment would be located in Baerum Commune. Construction of an airport at any of the other sites would, on the other hand, result in some growth being attracted to Gardermoen, Hobøl and Ås respectively. Secondary employment would then shadow the pattern set by basic employment and basic employment in the Oslo region would be reduced too. However it was assumed that only a half of the secondary employment would find a location in the airport commune and that the other half would settle in the communes between the airport and Oslo.

In fact the model indicated that population growth in the communes near the sites would be considerably higher than they could be expected to absorb due to lack of suitable land for house building. Some population would therefore settle in communes further away from the airport sites. Table 7 shows populations for each commune, taking these limits on growth into account.

The proposed sites

The effects of the various proposals is set out graphically in a series of maps. The first (Map 4) shows what would happen between 1970-1990 if the existing airport were to absorb all future growth. Map 5 shows changes in the residential structure should the airport be built at Gardermoen. Note that the maximum population of Oslo and therefore congestion is not reduced. On the other hand, there is reduced growth in the communes West of Oslo. Map 6 shows the effect of an airport at Hobøl. Hobøl's growth in the immediate vicinity of the airport is constrained to not more than 5,400 inhabitants in 1990, hence the population growth is spread over many communes. The construction of a proposed motorway linking Hobøl and Tune/Sarpsborg must also be considered. This road could be used to generate new residential areas in Tune, thereby reducing pressure on the farm land in Ås and Vestby. The motorway would also reduce travel time between Hobøl and the existing residential areas by about 30 per cent. An estimate of the effects, which change the original calculations for Hobøl, are shown in Map 7. Map 8 shows the changes in the residential structure if the airport is built at Ås.

Table 5

POPULATION AND WORKPLACES IN THE
STUDY REGION AND NORWAY 1950-1990

Thousands

	1950	1960	1969	1990
Workplaces	419.7	456.1	508.0	651.8
Net commuting (est.)	0	6.0	9.0	0
Employed Population	419.7	450.1	499.0	651.8
Workplaces in % of total (Norway)	30.1	33.1	34.7	38.9
Population	904.3	1,022.9	1,140.7	1,503.0
Population % of Norway	27.6	28.5	29.5	32.4
Norway:				
Population	3,278.5	3,591.0	3,867.4	4,638.0
Workplaces	1,393.7	1,377.5	1,465.0	1,677.0

Table 6

PER CENT ANNUAL INCREASE IN WORKPLACES
AND POPULATION 1950-1990.
STUDY REGION AND NORWAY

	1950-60	1960-69	1950-69	1969-70
Workplaces				
Study Region	0.8	1.2	1.0	1.2
Norway	-0.2	0.7	0.3	0.7
Population				
Study Region	1.3	1.2	1.2	1.3
Norway	0.9	0.8	0.8	0.9

Split-operation

The forecasts just described are based on an assumption that
Fornebu airport will be shut down but the consequences of continued
operations at Fornebu, though with 60 per cent of total traffic
operating from another site, have also been calculated. If this
occurred, 7,900 fundamental service jobs would be located at Fornebu
in 1990 and 13,100 at the new airport. In addition 3,200 secondary
jobs from the Oslo Region would shift to the new airport district
giving a total of 16,300 jobs compared with 25,200 if Fornebu were
shut down. This is shown in Maps 9, 10 and 11. Split-operation
produces about the same population effects in the airport districts
as full relocation, but with somewhat lower effects on fundamental
and secondary employment and a reduced commuting level between the
airport and peripheral communes.

Map 2 - Carte 2

CHANGE IN BASIC EMPLOYMENT 1960-1969

VARIATIONS PAR RAPPORT A L'EMPLOI INITIAL, DE 1960 A 1969

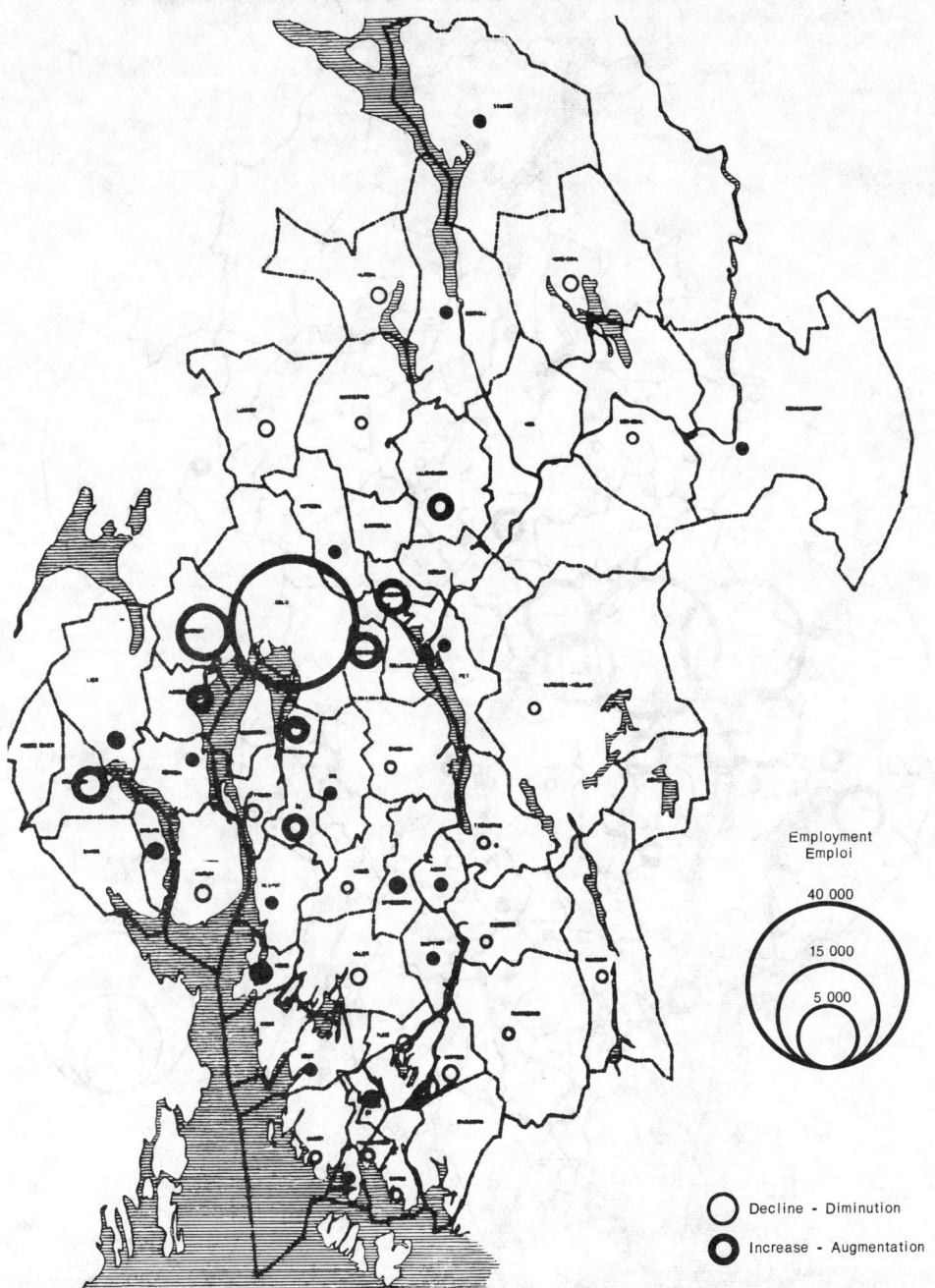

Employment
Emploi

40 000

15 000

5 000

○ Decline - Diminution

◉ Increase - Augmentation

Map 3 - Carte 3

ESTIMATED CHANGE IN BASIC EMPLOYMENT 1970-1990,
mainly based on Trends on Map 2. Basic proposal.

VARIATIONS ESTIMEES PAR RAPPORT A L'EMPLOI INITIAL, DE 1970 A 1990,
basées principalement sur l'évolution indiquée par la carte 2. Proposition initiale.

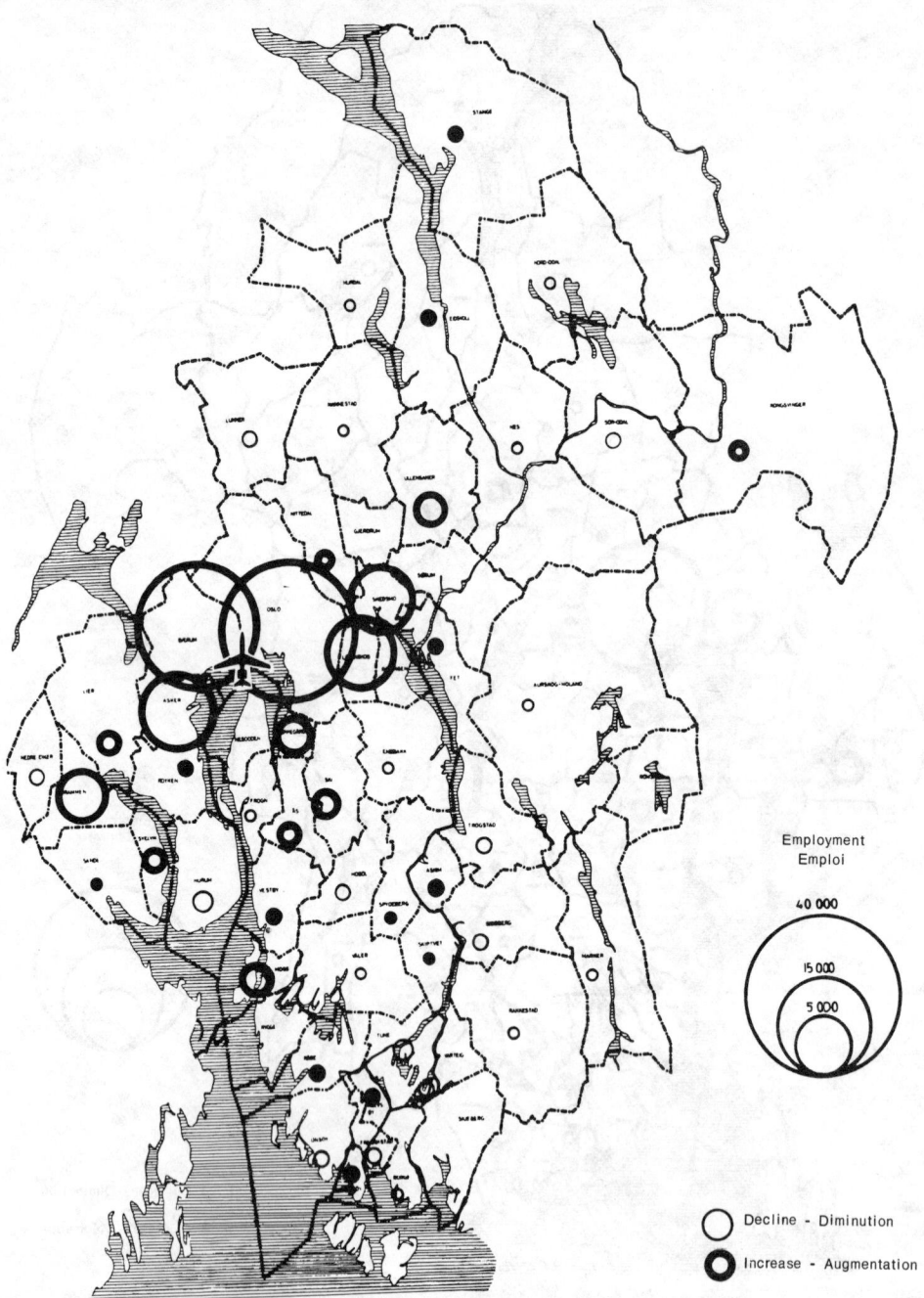

Employment
Emploi

40 000

15 000

5 000

○ Decline - Diminution

◉ Increase - Augmentation

Table 7

COMMUNES WITH IMPOSED CONSTRAINTS
ON POPULATION GROWTH

Communes	Population		Annual Increase 1970-90 %	Constraint effective with development at:			
	1970	1990		Basic proposal	Alt. G.moen	Alt. Ås	Alt. Hobøl
Oslo	487,000	520,000	0.3	x	x	x	x
Baerum	74,700	140,000	3.0	x			
Asker	29,850	75,200	4.5	x			
Skedsmo	30,500	62,900	3.5	x	x		
Ski	14,000	31,900	4.0			x	x
Ås	8,950	20,400	4.0			x	x
Frogn	7,350	18,500	4.5			x	
Oppegård	12,400	31,200	4.5			x	
Vestby	5,700	17,500	5.5			x	x
Sørum	8,100	18,600	4.0		x		
Gjerdrum	2,400	5,500	4.0		x		
Ullensaker	14,900	37,400	4.5		x		
Eidsvoll	13,500	22,700	2.5		x		
Nannestad	6,400	14,600	4.0		x		
Drammen	49,300	67,300	1.5	x	x	x	x
Moss	24,600	45,700	3.0				x
Spydeberg	3,300	7,500	4.0				x
Skiptvet	2,400	5,600	4.1				x
Våler	2,200	5,000	4.0				x
Hobøl	2,900	5,400	3.0				x

A COMPARISON BETWEEN THE ALTERNATIVES

The figures for the population growth effects derived from the Lowry model permit the three alternatives to be compared. Some of these results are grouped in Table 8. The total population increase 1970-90 shows little variation between the alternatives, except that Hobøl shows strongest growth. Hobøl also has the largest population in the initial state. Growth is associated partly with the airport, and partly with expected growth in existing activities. The individual airport district's population changes in relation to the basic proposal can, to a certain degree, be said to show the airport's net population effect on the district. The Table shows that in comparison with the basic alternative, Hobøl's district population increases by 47,000, whilst Ås and Gardermoen each increase approximately by 35,000. Note the effects of relocation of the airport on the Central District, which is made up of Oslo and eleven adjoining suburban

Map 4 - Carte 4

ESTIMATED CHANGE IN POPULATION 1970 - 1990.
Basic Proposal - future Fornebu Airport handling all Traffic.

VARIATIONS DE POPULATION ESTIMEES ENTRE 1970 ET 1990.
Proposition initiale. Ensemble du trafic aérien passant par le futur aéroport de Fornebu.

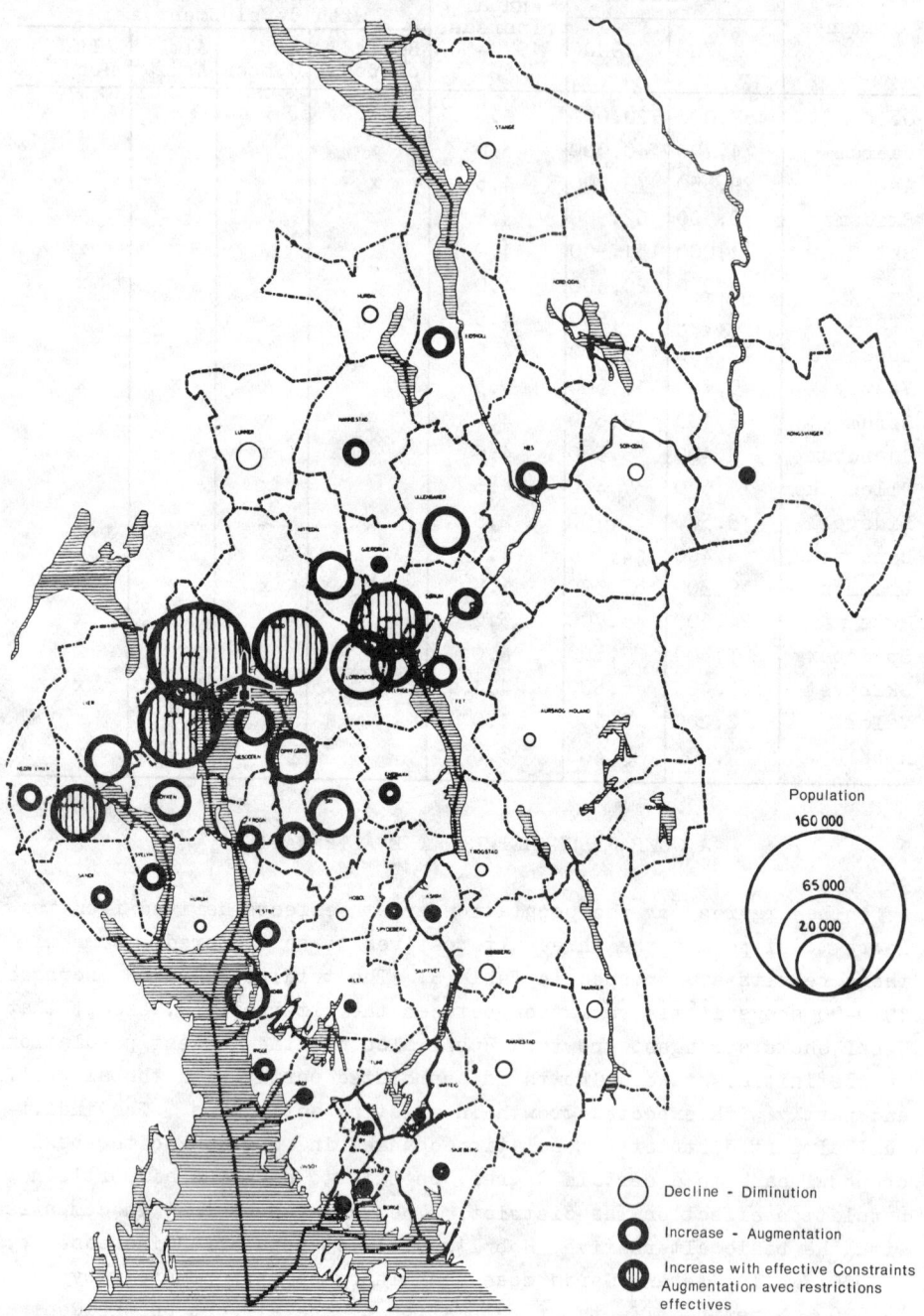

Population

160 000

65 000

20 000

Decline - Diminution

Increase - Augmentation

Increase with effective Constraints
Augmentation avec restrictions
effectives

Map 5 - Carte 5

GARDERMOEN

POPULATION CHANGE 1990 IN RELATION TO BASIC PROPOSAL

VARIATIONS DE POPULATION EN 1990 PAR RAPPORT A LA PROPOSITION INITIALE

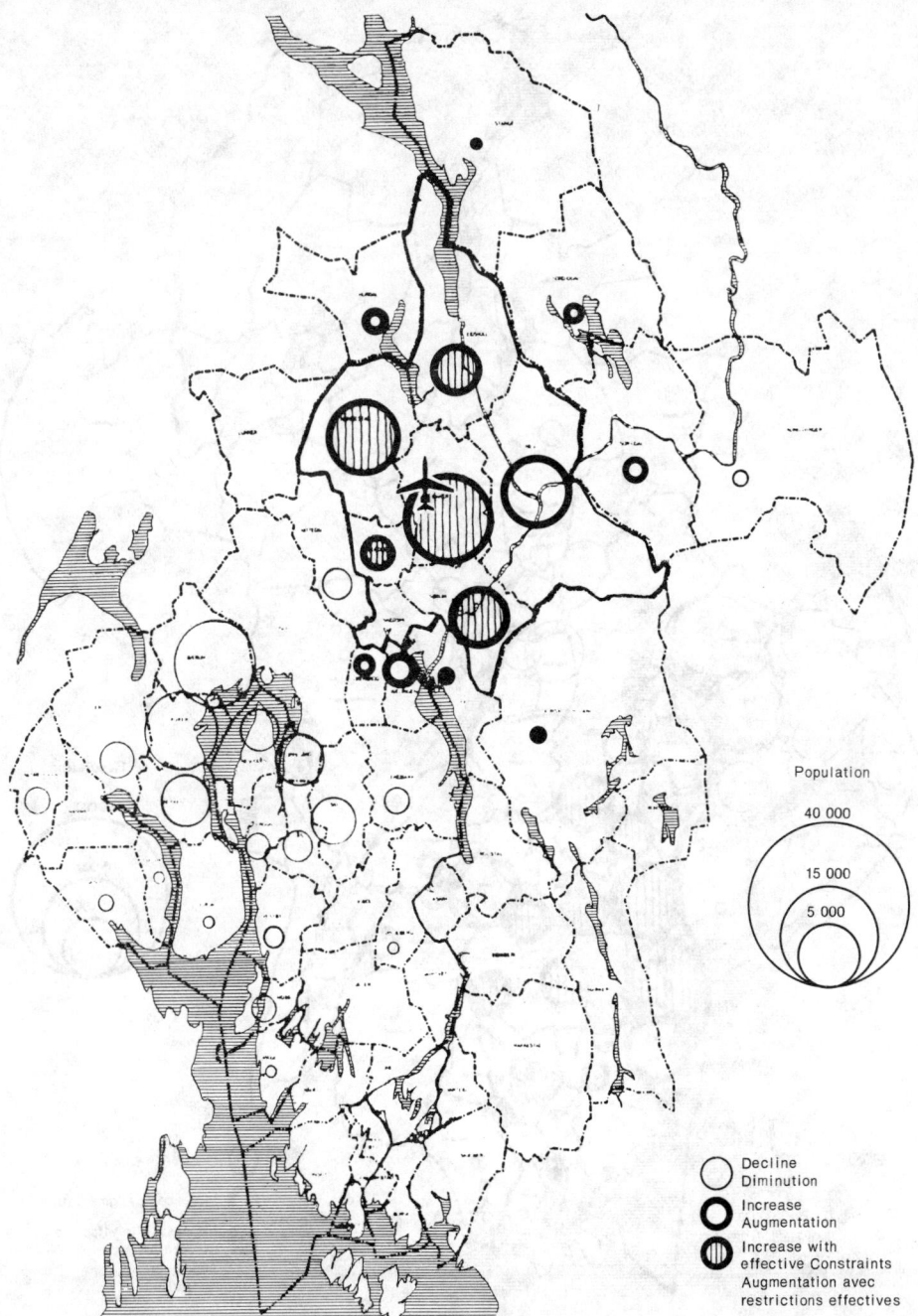

Population

40 000

15 000

5 000

○ Decline
Diminution

◯ Increase
Augmentation

◉ Increase with
effective Constraints
Augmentation avec
restrictions effectives

Map 6 - Carte 6

HOBØL

POPULATION CHANGE 1990 IN RELATION TO BASIC PROPOSAL
VARIATIONS DE POPULATION EN 1990 PAR RAPPORT A LA PROPOSITION INITIALE

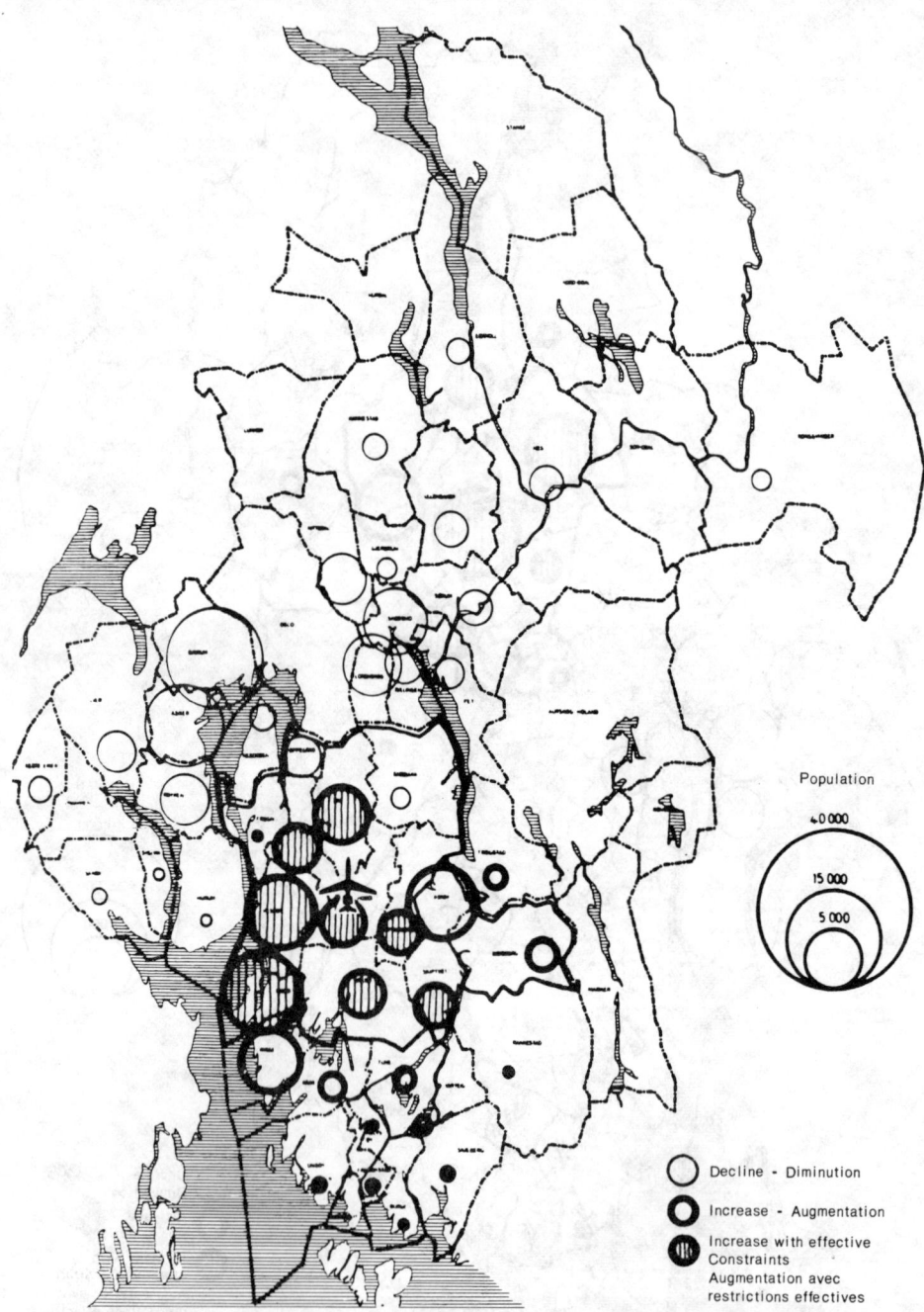

Population

40 000

15 000

5 000

○ Decline - Diminution

◎ Increase - Augmentation

◉ Increase with effective
Constraints
Augmentation avec
restrictions effectives

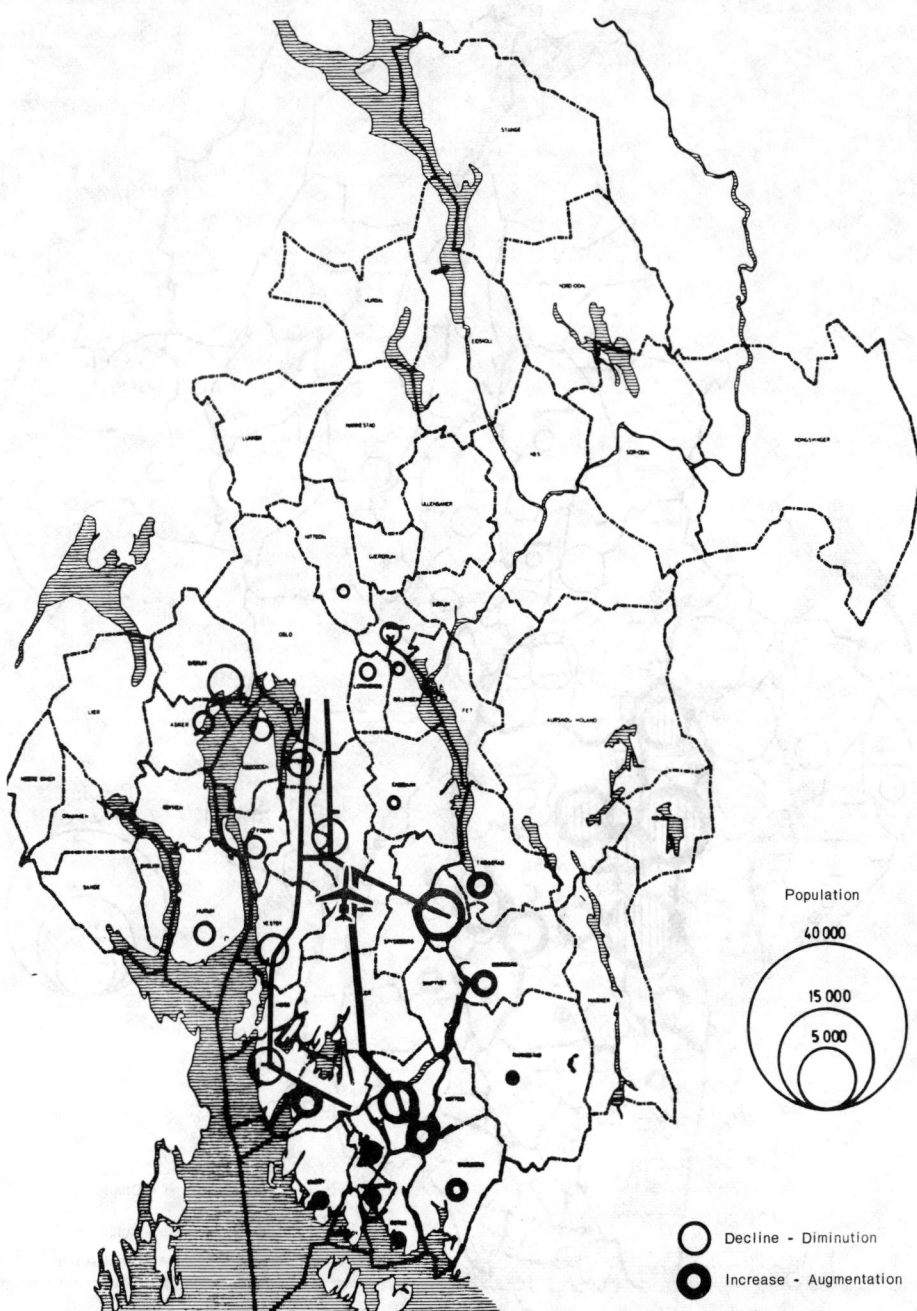

Map 7 - Carte 7

HOBØL WITH NEW MOTORWAY TO TUNE/SARPSBORG
Population Changes 1990 in relation to Map 6

HOBØL AVEC NOUVELLE AUTOROUTE VERS TUNE-SARPSBORG
Variations de population en 1990 par rapport à la carte 6

Population

40 000

15 000

5 000

Decline - Diminution

Increase - Augmentation

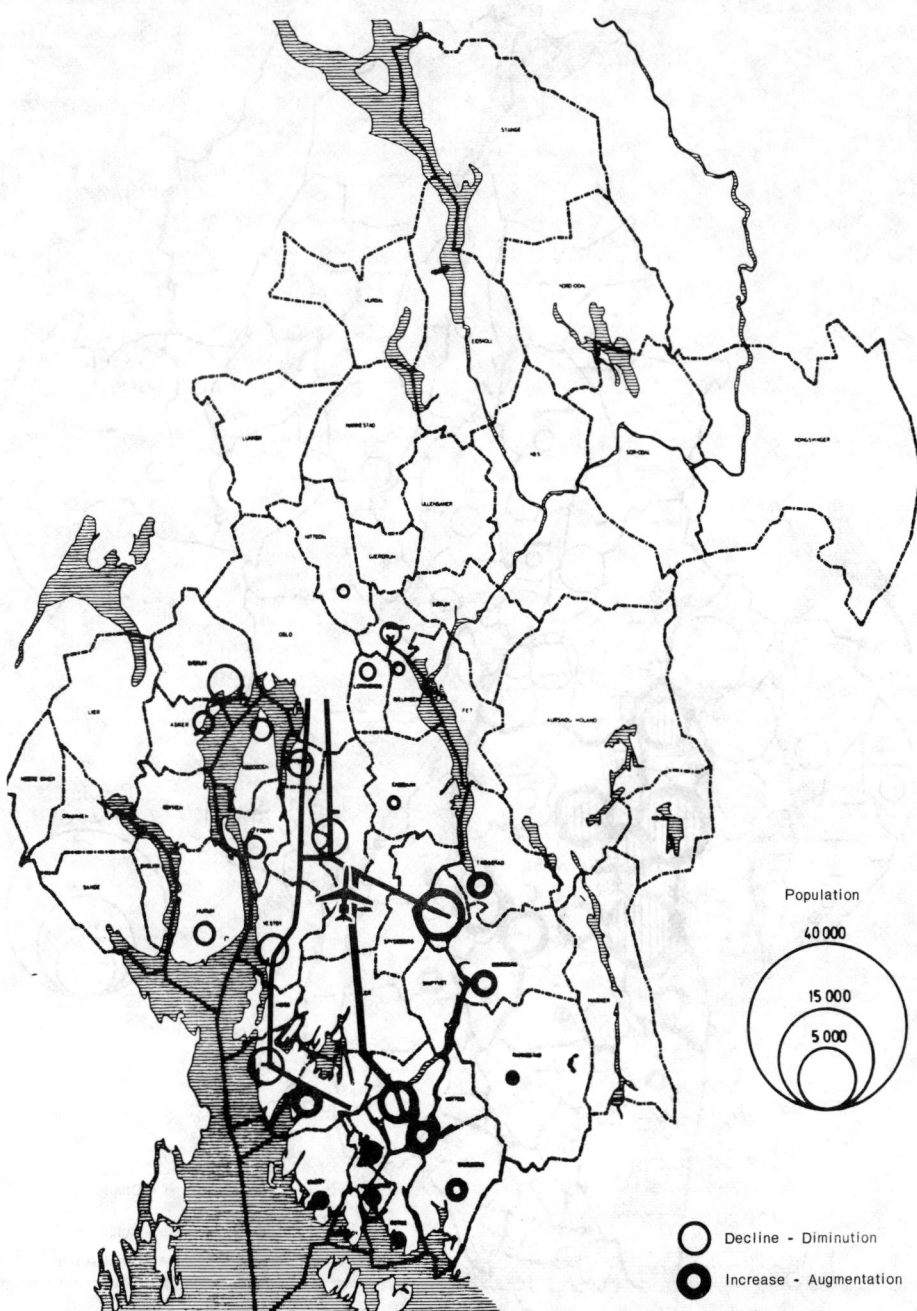

Map 8 - Carte 8

ÅS

POPULATION CHANGE 1990 IN RELATION TO BASIC PROPOSAL
VARIATION DE POPULATION EN 1990 PAR RAPPORT A LA PROPOSITION INITIALE

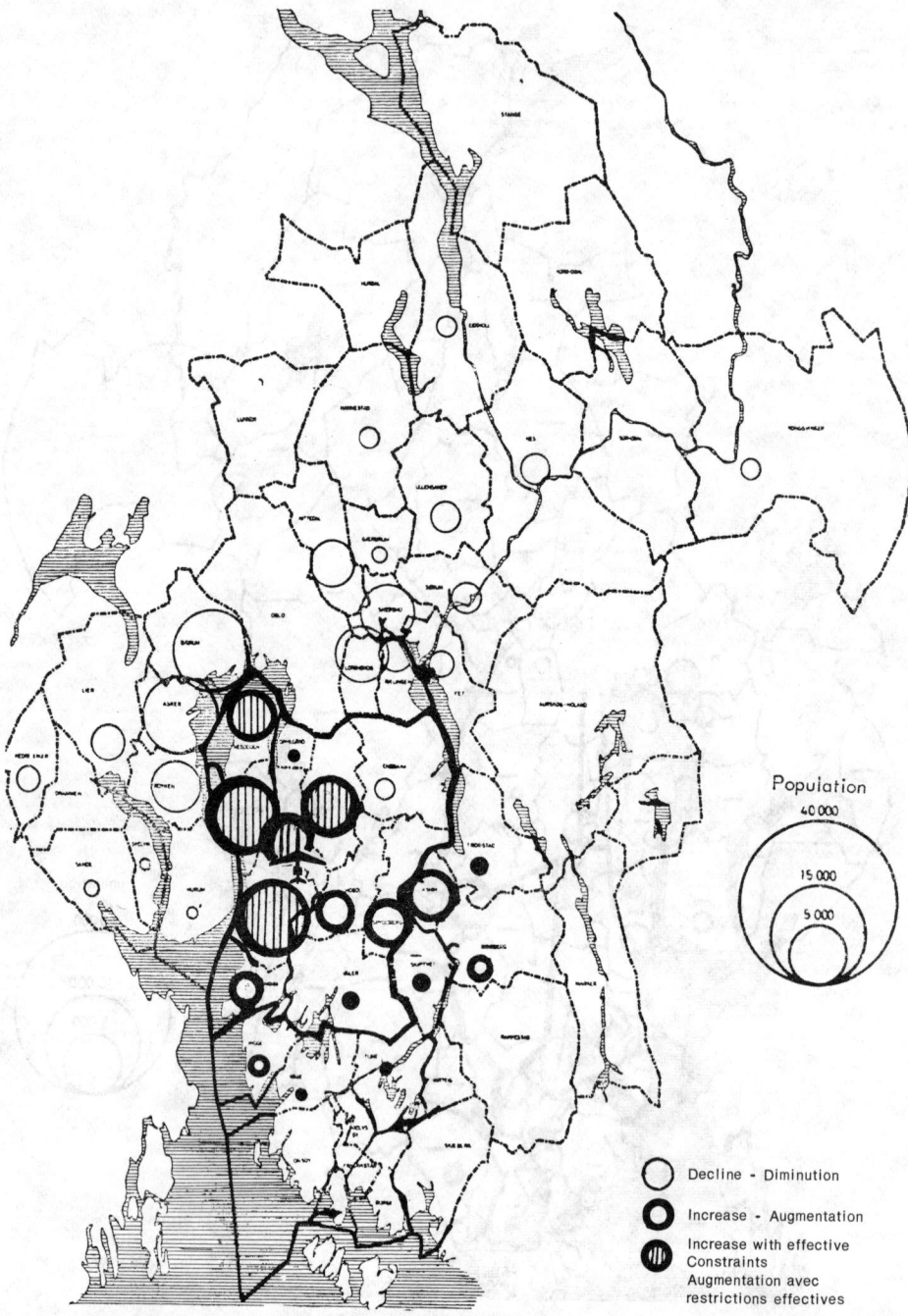

Population

40 000

15 000

5 000

Decline - Diminution

Increase - Augmentation

Increase with effective
Constraints
Augmentation avec
restrictions effectives

Map 9 - Carte 9

SPLIT OPERATION HOBØL/FORNEBU
Population Change 1990 in relation to Same Alternative without Split Operation
(Difference between Split Operation and Map 6)

EXPLOITATION PARTAGEE ENTRE HOBØL ET FORNEBU
Variation de population en 1990 par rapport à la même variante sans exploitation partagée
(Différence entre l'exploitation partagée et la carte 6)

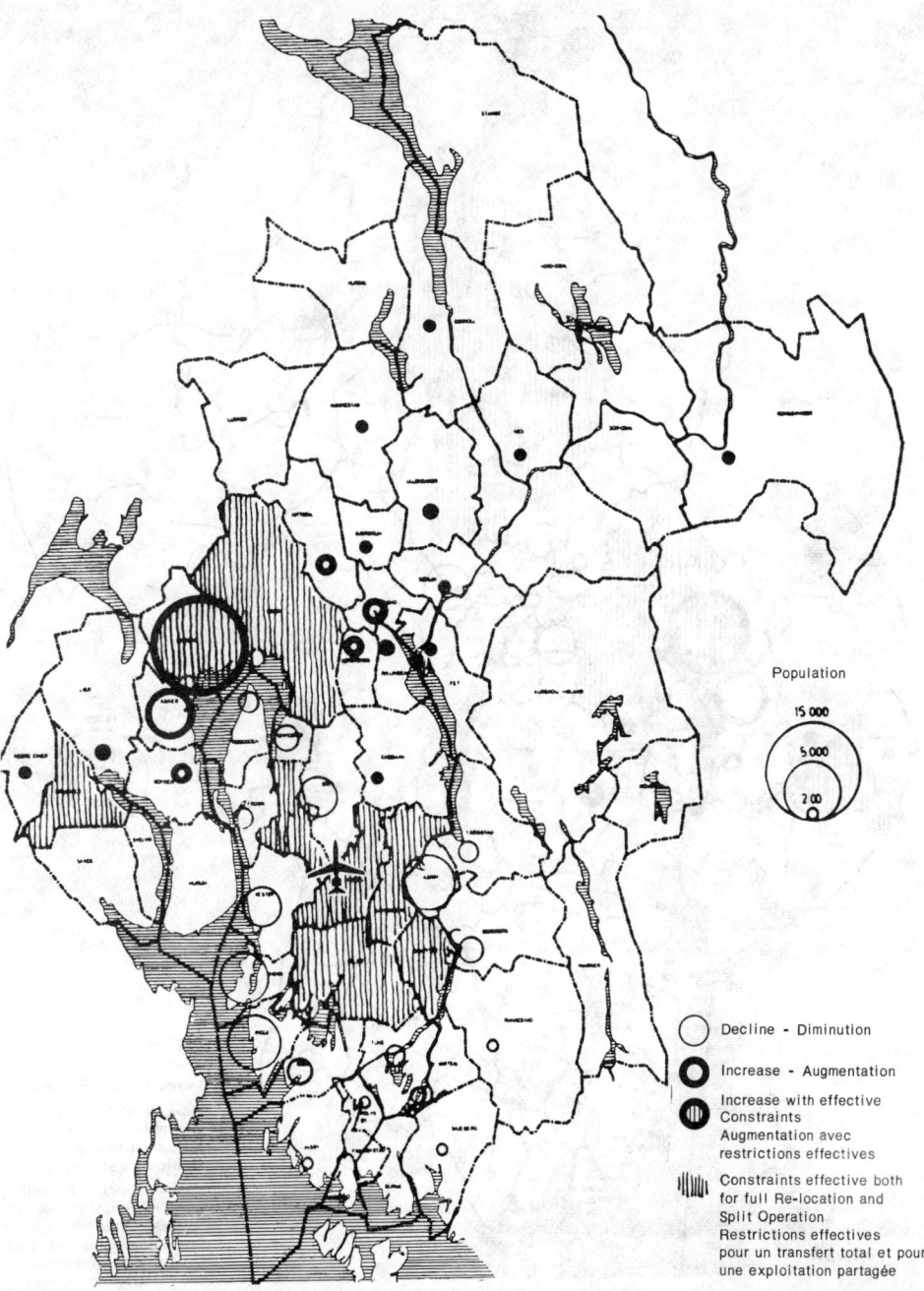

Population

15 000

5 000

2 00

○ Decline - Diminution

◉ Increase - Augmentation

Increase with effective
Constraints
Augmentation avec
restrictions effectives

Constraints effective both
for full Re-location and
Split Operation
Restrictions effectives
pour un transfert total et pour
une exploitation partagée

Map 10 - Carte 10

SPLIT OPERATION GARDERMOEN/FORNEBU
Population change 1990 in relation to same alternative without Split Operation
(Difference between Split Operation and Map 5)

EXPLOITATION PARTAGEE ENTRE GARDERMOEN ET FORNEBU
Variation de population en 1990 par rapport à la même variante sans exploitation partagée
(Différence entre l'exploitation partagée et la carte 5)

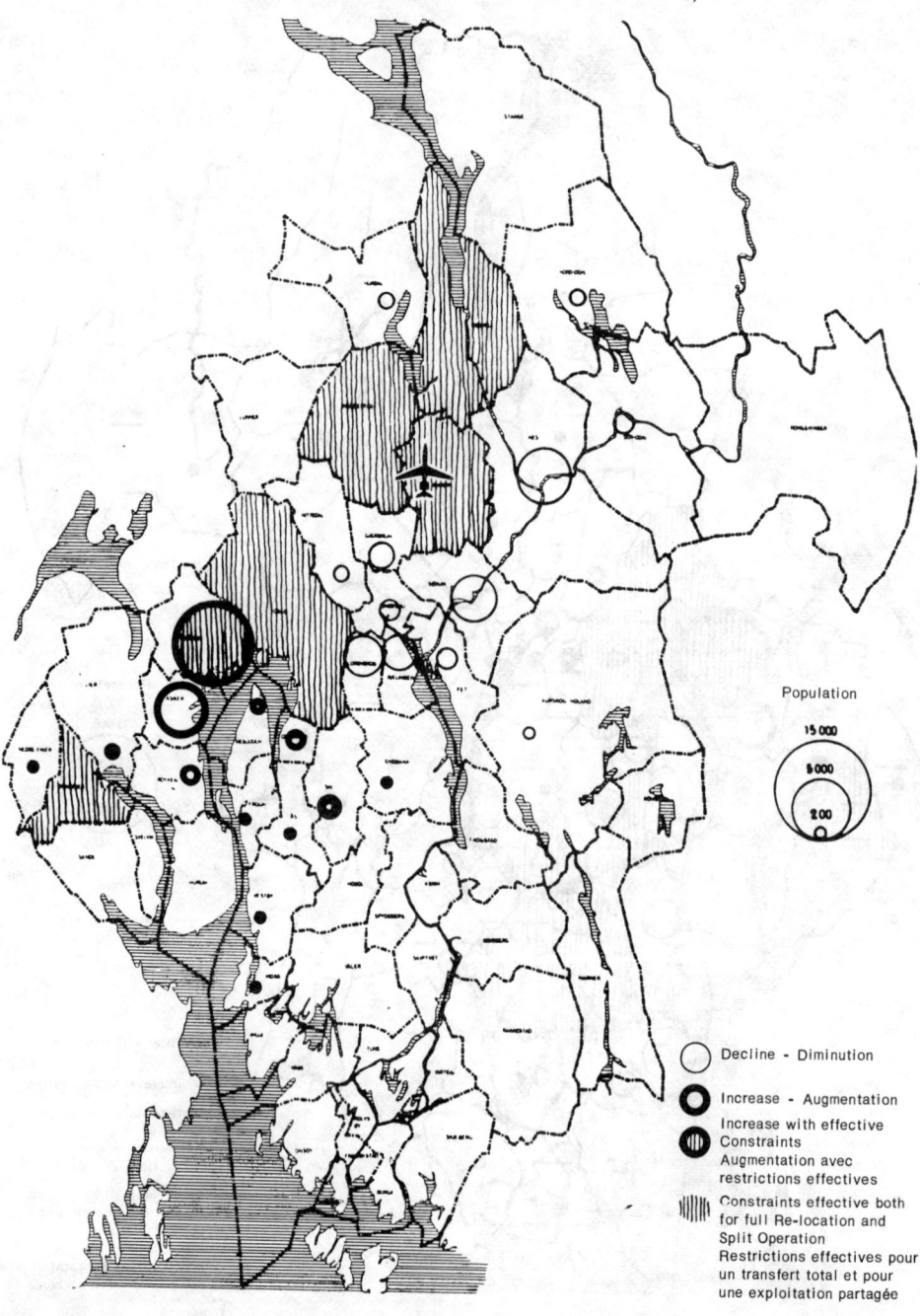

Population

15 000

5 000

200

Decline - Diminution

Increase - Augmentation

Increase with effective
Constraints
Augmentation avec
restrictions effectives

Constraints effective both
for full Re-location and
Split Operation
Restrictions effectives pour
un transfert total et pour
une exploitation partagée

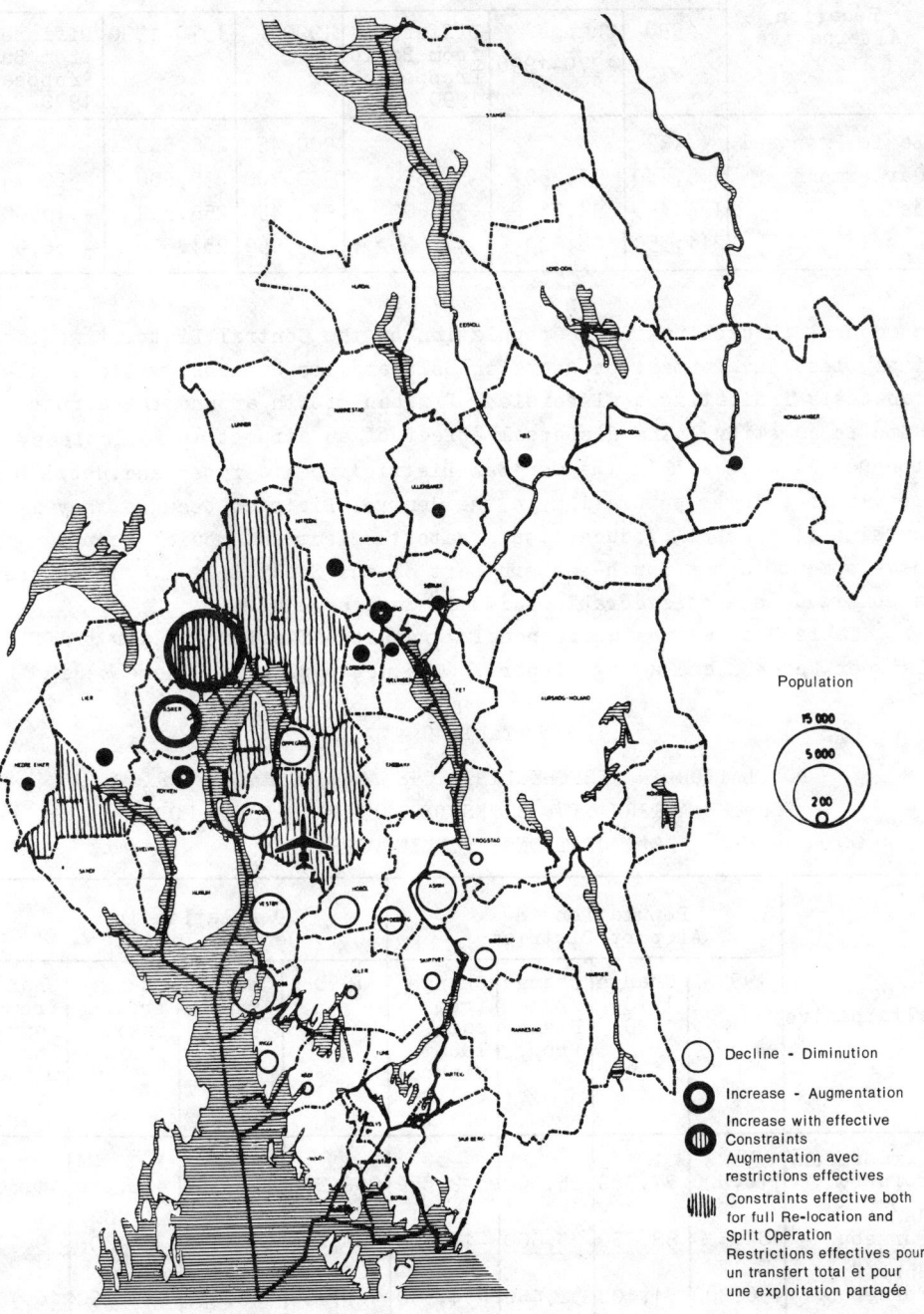

Map 11 - Carte 11

SPLIT OPERATION ÅS/FORNEBU
Population Change 1990 in relation to same Alternative without Split Operation
(Difference between Split Operation and Map 8)

EXPLOITATION PARTAGEE ENTRE ÅS ET FORNEBU
Variation de population en 1990 par rapport à la même variante sans exploitation partagée
(Différence entre l'exploitation partagée et la carte 8)

Population

15 000

5 000

2 00

○ Decline - Diminution

◎ Increase - Augmentation

◍ Increase with effective Constraints
Augmentation avec restrictions effectives

Constraints effective both for full Re-location and Split Operation
Restrictions effectives pour un transfert total et pour une exploitation partagée

93

Table 8

POPULATION IN AIRPORT DISTRICTS AND CENTRAL DISTRICT
DERIVED FROM LOWRY MODEL CALCULATIONS

Location Alternative	Population in Airport District			Population in Central District		
	1990	Change 1970-1990	Difference from Basic Proposal 1990	1990	1970-1990	Difference from Basic Proposal 1990
Basic Proposal				980,450	268,550	
Gardermoen	185,650	97,250	34,650	950,700	238,800	- 29,750
Ås	194,450	99,350	34,600	970,450	258,500	- 10,000
Hobøl	211,350	103,800	47,000	943,550	231,600	- 36,900

communes. A decline in the population of the Central District would
imply less development pressure on Oslo and its suburbs, while simultaneously indicating a dispersion of urban growth around the airport
site in question. The dispersal effect of an airport at Ås is least
because it lies within the Central District. Gardermoen and Hobøl both
result in a lower population in the Central District because they lie
outside it. Hobøl produces the greatest effect and would prompt
development in the South-Eastern part of the Study Region. Gardermoen
also produces a considerable shift in development.

Table 9 shows the corresponding results of splitting air traffic
between Fornebu and a new airport. The net population increase in

Table 9

POPULATION IN AIRPORT DISTRICTS AND CENTRAL DISTRICT
FOR THE ALTERNATIVE SITES DERIVED FROM LOWRY MODEL
CALCULATIONS: SPLIT-OPERATION

Location alternative	Population in Airport District				Population in Central District			
	1990	Change 1970-1990	Change from Basic Prop.	Change from same locat. without split-oper.	1990	Change 1970-1990	Change from Basic. Prop.	Change from same locat. without split-oper.
Gardermoen/ Fornebu	176,300	87,900	25,300	-9,350	962,200	250,300	-18,250	11,500
Ås/ Fornebu	183,300	88,150	23,500	-11,100	980,150	268,150	-300	9,700
Hobøl/ Fornebu	196,800	81,400	32,450	-14,550	960,250	248,350	-20,200	16,700

the new airport district would be between 25,000-32,000. With Hobøl
having the greatest relieving effect on the Central District. Split-
operation would result in there being less fundamental and secondary
employment at the new airport compared with full relocation and would
reduce commuting between the airport and peripheral communes. In
the communes close to the airport there would, in any case, be considerable population growth.

CHOOSING THE BEST SITE

Uncertainty about the future population of the Region and about
the effect of the three proposals on its distribution make it difficult to choose a best buy. There are also shortcomings in the Lowry
model. It presents a static view of the situation in 1990. It does
not, for instance, take account of developments in the housing and
labour markets. And even if the forecasts derived from the use of
the model did take place, they might not occur until after 1990 due
to inertia amongst workers or a slower than anticipated rate of
relocation.

Nevertheless, the evaluation provides a basis for comparing the
three sites. The Maps make clear the considerable differences between the effects of the various proposals on Oslo and, in the case
of Ås and Hobøl, the outlying communes as well. Which location is
preferable depends on which set of structural changes is considered
to be most desirable.

REGIONAL PLANNING CONSIDERATIONS

The best location for Oslo's new airport is one that contributes
most to the achievement of regional development objectives. The
choice therefore must be related to Oslo's growth.

The rate of residential growth in Central Oslo is decreasing.
It has been increasing to the East, West and South of Oslo, and to
a lesser extent to the North. Workplaces have however remained concentrated in Oslo resulting in a steady increase in commuting over
longer distances. Suburban service centres have not been developed
to a sufficient degree to counteract pressure in the centre. A tendency for rich and poor to polarise has also become noticeable. Incomes are significantly higher to the West of Oslo than to the South
and East. Those with high incomes have been moving mainly to the
West and little to the South and East.

The Regional Plan for Oslo is based on the existing infrastructure and favours concentrated urban growth in three ribbons: to the
East, West and South (Map 12). The Regional Planning Committee for

S.E. Norway (Østlandet) considers it desirable to decentralise population and workplaces to restrict growth in central Oslo and to promote it at Hamar-Gjøvik-Lillehammer to the North of Oslo and in Fredrikstad-Sarpsborg to the South (Map 13).

APPRAISAL OF THE ALTERNATIVES

From the point of view of regional growth objectives a site to the North or to the South of Oslo, in other words at Gardermoen or Ås/Hobøl, is to be preferred; but further confirmation is needed in order to decide which would result in the most desirable urban structure. Both alternatives have, or will have in the near future, good public and private transport connections with Oslo. In both cases, however, the only link with the Western districts is through Oslo. A Southern site could have a connection by means of a bridge over the Oslo-fjord but if this is not built, the difference in the effect of a North or South site on long-term economic structure would appear to be only marginal. But as there is a possibility that a fjord bridge will be built, the Southern choice must be favoured.

This is not the only factor favouring a Southern site. Urban development costs are higher in the North than in the South where the labour force is more concentrated and diverse. There is a more clearly defined hierarchy on centres in the South. And the Southern area contains a variety of fjords, forests and lakes used for recreation. The establishment of the new airport at either point would tend to increase social polarisation since contact between the urban extremities is slight. However, the scope for contact in the South could be improved if a bridge to the West were constructed. Restrictions on urban development in the interest of agriculture and maintaining water purity would probably be more effective in the South than in the North.

Assessment of the two main possibilities using these criteria points to the superiority of a site to the South of Oslo, a choice that coincides with the thrust of the regional development plan. An airport at either Ås or Hobøl would support the plan. One at Gardermoen would neutralise it. A Southern site would also encourage growth in Fredrikstad/Sarpsborg and give support to the proposals of the Regional Planning Committee for S.E. Norway (Map 13). The distance between Gardermoen and the Committee's Northern growth point is too far to expect significant region-wide growth effects. Either Ås or Hobøl is therefore superior to Gardermoen on regional planning grounds too.

The objectives set out in the regional plan are not sufficiently precise to enable a choice to be made between Ås and Hobøl. The distance between the two sites is short. Other factors need to be taken into account in making a selection.

Map 12 - Carte 12

DEVELOPMENT PLAN FOR OSLO
The Arrows shows expanding Directions

PLAN D'AMENAGEMENT POUR OSLO
Les flèches indiquent les directions de l'extension

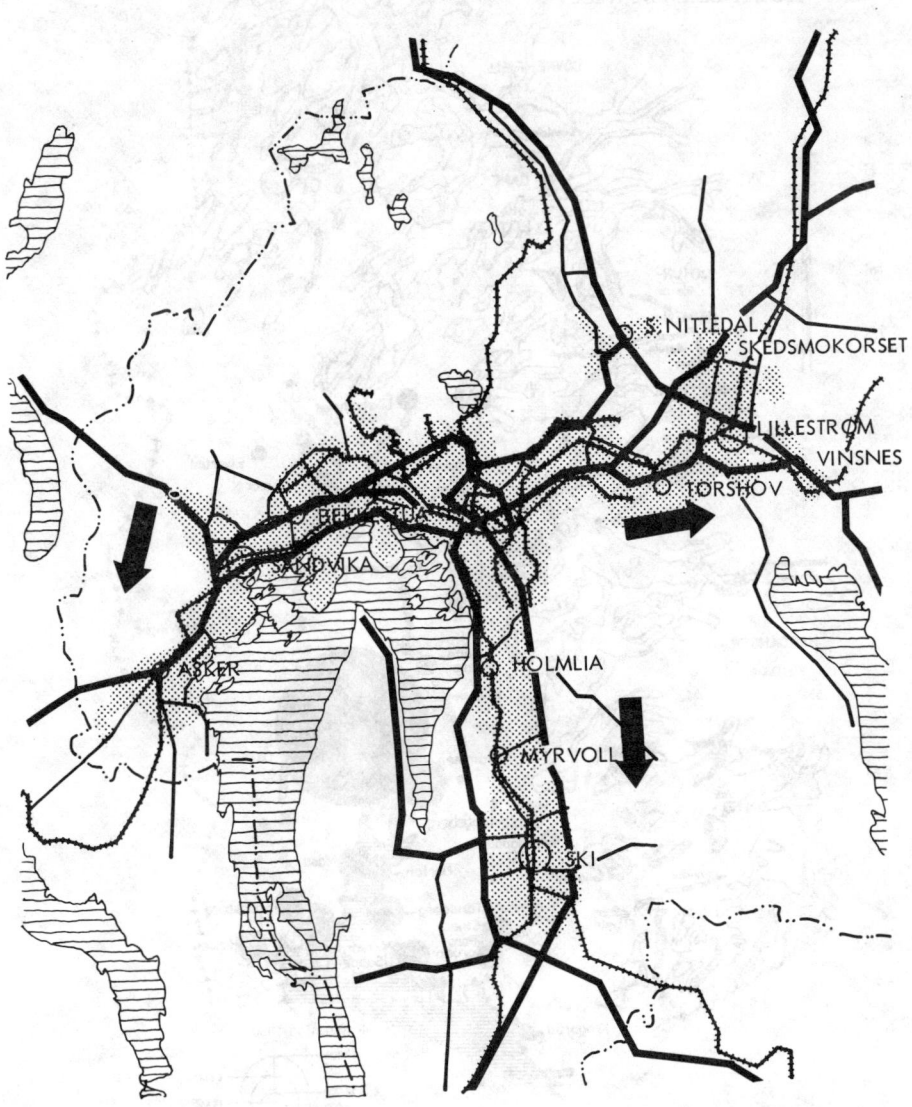

Map 13 - Carte 13

URBAN CONCENTRATION IN S.E.NORWAY 1960

CONCENTRATION URBAINE AU SUD-EST DE LA NORVEGE EN 1960

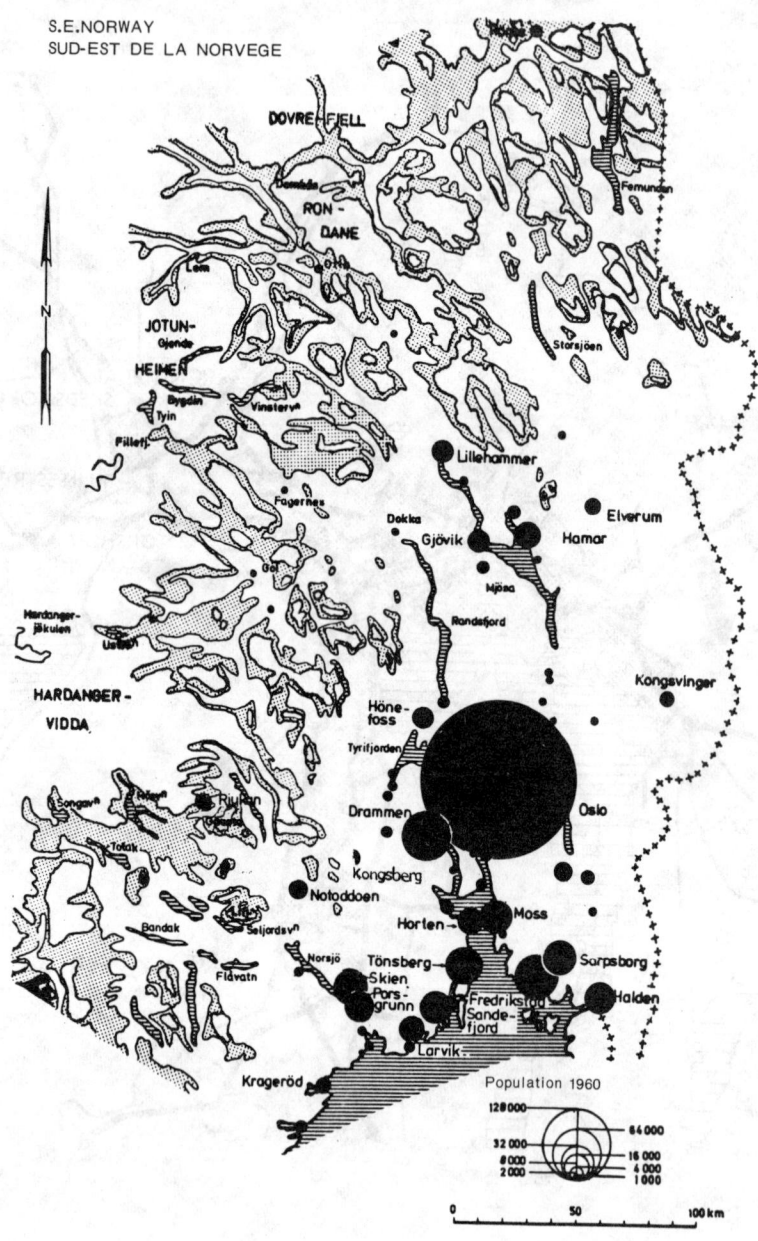

S.E.NORWAY
SUD-EST DE LA NORVEGE

Population 1960

CONCLUSIONS

This analysis has focussed on population and employment, their geographical distribution within the Study Region, and on the regional context. Statistical sources have been as widely used as possible but the results need to be qualified. For one thing the total population generated by airport development and its regional distribution cannot be forecast with certainty. Furthermore a decision was made to base the analysis on the maximum likely extent of fundamental and secondary employment, and their effects on tertiary employment and population. This was done so that the consequences of airport development would not be under-estimated but leaves open the possibility that they may have been exaggeratd.

It should also be borne in mind that whichever site is selected, the greater the increase in local population, the greater the cost of development, because it would require that much more investment to support the newcomers. It may also be expected that whichever site is selected, objections will be raised against noise and the prospect of rapid urban growth.

If such opposition raises acute political difficulties, an approach based on the experience of Fornebu, where growth was relatively slow, could be adopted. Development could be held to keep the growth of fundamental service employment in line with the low estimates which would result in lower population growth in the communes around the chosen airport site.

Part 2

FINDING SITES FOR MAJOR AIRPORTS: THE EXPERIENCE OF COPENHAGEN

Kai Lemberg

Director of General Planning,
City of Copenhagen

EXISTING AIRPORTS IN THE COPENHAGEN REGION

Civil aviation at Copenhagen is served by an international airport at Kastrup about 10 km South of the city centre and by a newly established secondary airport near Roskilde, about 25 km to the West of it. Kastrup is one of the biggest European airports while Roskilde is small and intended primarily for general aviation and, eventually, as a supplementary base for domestic and charter flights (Map 1). Traffic at Kastrup since 1960 and forecasts to the end of the century are given below.

Map 1 - Carte 1

EXISTING AIRPORTS IN THE COPENHAGEN REGION

AEROPORTS EXISTANTS DANS LA REGION DE COPENHAGUE

X Runway configuration - Disposition des pistes

Existing primary roads
Routes principales existantes

Planned primary roads
Routes principales en projet

Existing rail lines - Voies ferrées existantes

Map 2 - Carte 2

ALTERNATIVE AIRPORT SITES DISCUSSED FOR THE COPENHAGEN REGION

VARIANTES DE SITES D'AEROPORTS ENVISAGEES DANS LA REGION DE COPENHAGUE

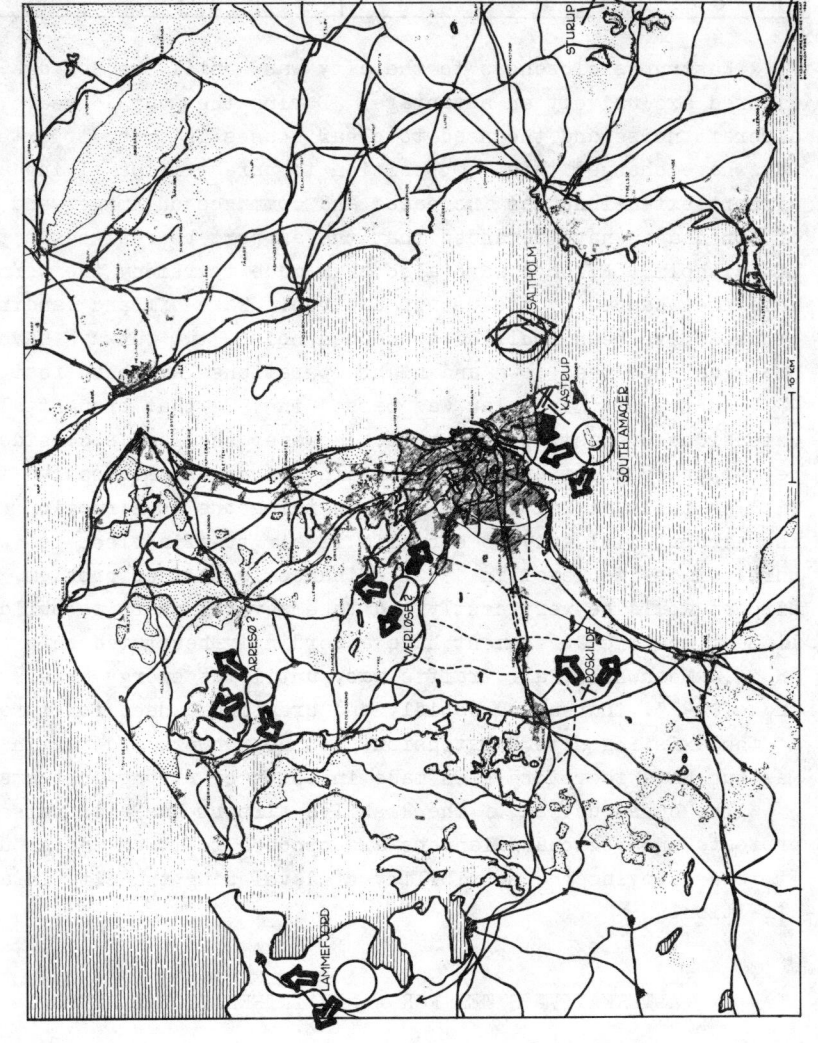

	Kastrup			Saltholm	
	1960	1970	1973	1985	2000
Annual passengers (in millions)	1.9	6.4	8.4	ca. 20	ca. 25
Annual flights (in thousands)	75	139	178	ca. 350	ca. 400

Kastrup's closeness to the city was, until the jet age, considered exclusively an advantage. During the last 15 years, however,
aircraft noise and the need to clear houses in order to extend runways have changed this. Opposition to unrestricted flying and to
airport extensions has increased and communes on Amager and the City
of Copenhagen have demanded that the airport be resited on the island
of Saltholm. Efforts have also been made to remedy the worst
nuisances caused by the use of Kastrup. Take-off and landing procedures have been modified to reduce noise, two runways have been
practically closed down and night operations have been restricted.

On top of this a law was passed in 1971 that brought all further
extensions of Kastrup to a halt. However the law is considered to
be temporary and there is no certainty that an alternative to Kastrup
will be built at Saltholm. For one thing the construction of the
new airport will only be economic if air traffic rises to two to
three times its level in 1972. Finance is another problem. The new
airport would be very costly and take several years to build. Parliament and the Government have accordingly hesitated before starting
on it. Meanwhile, air traffic was, until the energy crisis at the
end of 1973, increasing rapidly and creating a need for more capacity
at the existing site. Extensions to the runways and terminals at
Kastrup have therefore been made in spite of strong protests.

The construction of the Roskilde airport has also raised local
protests and regional planners are opposed to it on the grounds that
it is destroying the possibility of developing the city in a Westerly
direction.

ALTERNATIVE SITES FOR A NEW INTERNATIONAL AIRPORT

Discussion about sites for a new airport have gone on for the
last 10 years. Although some ecologically-minded individuals are
for stopping the development of air transport completely, most politicians, planners, industrial and commercial interests and the larger
part of the press agree that a way must be found to accommodate some
increase in air traffic. The following possibilities have accordingly
been put forward:
  a) the permanent extension and more intensive use of Kastrup;
  b) the construction of a new airport on South Amager and on land
     reclaimed from the sea and its use in conjunction with Kastrup;

c) the continued, but restricted use of Kastrup airport by large jets and the establishment of secondary airports elsewhere;

d) the construction of a new airport at Saltholm and the closing down of Kastrup;

e) the construction of a new airport at Sealand, about 70 km West of Copenhagen, and the continued but less-intensive use of Kastrup; and

f) a stand-still policy involving the continued operation of Kastrup, but without extensions and without new secondary airports.

A Government committee was appointed to consider the matter in 1962 and presented its final report in 1968. Sites at Saltholm and South Amager were shortlisted. However, when it became clear that Kastrup would not be given up if South Amager was proceeded with, it was decided to concentrate on the Saltholm solution. The Danish Parliament that authorised the start of planning of a Saltholm airport and negotiations with Sweden made it clear that the project would have to be financed solely by Denmark.

However, in 1972 the Swedish Government offered to connect Malmo and Copenhagen to Saltholm by bridge and tunnel provided the Swedes could collect tolls from users of it for an extended period. This has been agreed by the Swedish but not yet by the Danish Parliament.

In January 1973 the Danish Minister of Transport presented Parliament with a bill authorising a start to be made on an international airport on Saltholm in 1974. Two months later, the start was delayed by one year and in 1974 the Government proposed a further delay until 1976.

During this process some politicans, especially representatives from Jutland and other provinces, have fought against the Saltholm project. They are against it for financial reasons, because it conflicts with geographical decentralisation of investment or because they oppose the growth of air traffic on ecological grounds.

Since the completion of Roskilde Airport in 1973 it has also been suggested that the Copenhagen airport system should be completed by adding another secondary airport in North Sealand but this idea is heavily opposed by the regional planning agency for environmental reasons. The new Malmo airport at Sturup will probably serve as an Eastern secondary airport to Saltholm.

NOISE

Noise is the most important of all environmental factors. Future levels have been calculated at a number of airports by Danish and Swedish committees and experts but their investigations do not permit simple comparisons to be made because they have been based on different runway layouts, flying procedures, flight frequencies, types of aircraft, traffic compositions and flying schedules. The noise contours shown in the maps attached to this paper are not therefore comparable, though they do demonstrate the main differences between the sites investigated.

Map 3 was prepared by Professor Fritz Ingerslev of the Acoustic Laboratory of the Technical University of Copenhagen in 1971. The contours show the very unsatisfactory conditions that would arise around Kastrup in 1980 assuming a daily total of 850 take-offs and landings. Map 4 shows what conditions might be in 1980 if there were 1200 daily jet operations at Saltholm. The detailed assumptions underlying the contours cover:

a) runway layouts,
b) distribution of operations among runways taking climatic conditions into account,
c) approach and take-off paths,
d) number of jet operations,
e) breakdown of aircraft fleet into light, heavy and jumbo jets (supersonic aircraft will not be allowed to operate in Denmark), and
f) distribution of operations between the hours of 07.00 - 22.00 and 22.00 - 00.07 respectively.

Calculations based upon these assumptions were made according to the principles developed by the United States Federal Aviation Administration (FAA DS-67-10, 1967), which involve measurements of perceived noise decibels (PNdB) under take-off and approach power but not under taxi-ing conditions. The noise curves calculated in this way are translated into noise reaction contours using data on attitudes gathered by social surveying. The research showed that complaints about noise would be repeated and violent within the boundaries of zone 1 and that organised group action should be expected. Noise under zone 2 conditions could be expected to cause some - maybe strong - individual complaints and might lead to group action. No serious complaints would be likely in places with zone 3 conditions or less though noise might still cause inconveniences.

Noise zone 1 corresponds to a level exceeding 90 dB(A) and zone 2 to a level between 85 and 90 dB(A).(1) It is evident that given such conditions life around Kastrup will be intolerable under unrestricted 1980 traffic but that only very small areas of land would be affected by operations from Saltholm even with a larger number of flights. Saltholm will however create a noise nuisance for people enjoying sea recreation. The Western parts of Køge Bay,

---

1) The dB(A) values correspond approximately to PNdB values - 13.

Map 3 - Carte 3

NOISE CONTOURS ZONE 1 AND 2 FOR KASTRUP 1980 (INGERSLEV, 1969)

COURBES D'EGAL BRUIT - ZONES 1 ET 2 POUR KASTRUP EN 1980 (INGERSLEV, 1969)

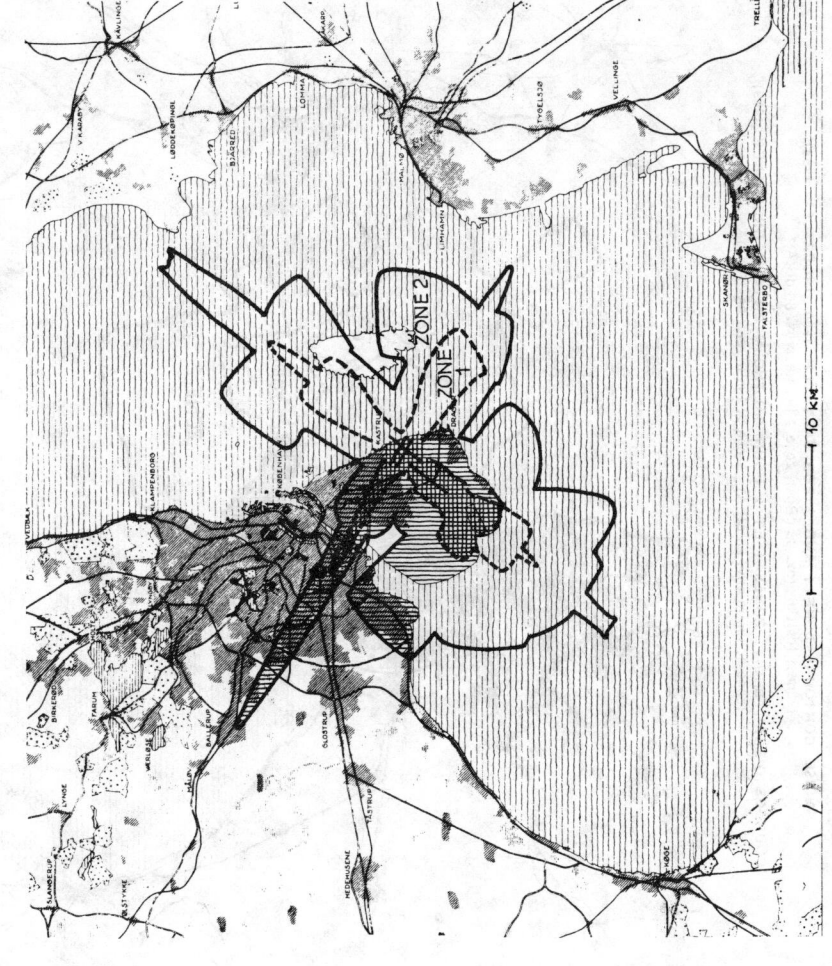

Map 4 - Carte 4

NOISE CONTOURS ZONE 1 AND 2 FOR SALTHOLM 1980 (INGERSLEV 1969)
(Zone 1 limit approx. 90 dB(A), zone 2 limit approx. 85 dB(A))

COURBES D'EGAL BRUIT, ZONES 1 ET 2 POUR SALTHOLM EN 1980 (INGERSLEV 1969)
(Zone 1, limite env. 90 dB(A) ; zone 2, limite env. 85 dB(A))

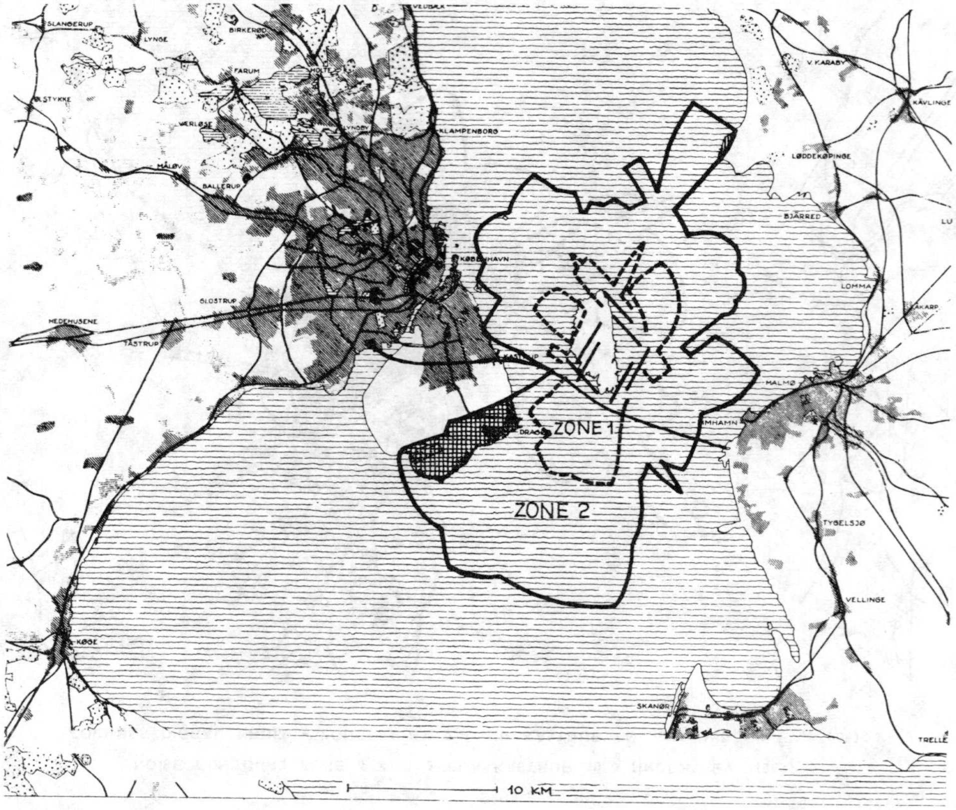

ZONE 1

ZONE 2

10 KM

the sound North of Copenhagen and the Swedish coast, which are the
most important waters for boating will therefore need protecting.

Rough estimates suggest the continued use of Kastrup would result in about 32,000 people living in noise zone 1 and a further
225,000 in noise zone 2 in 1980. But should the airport be moved to
Saltholm by 1980, (which is impossible) and should the level of air
traffic be 50 per cent greater than at Kastrup, no one would be living
in zone 1 and only about 10,000 inhabitants in the Southern part of
Amager would be in zone 2. However, a number of inhabitants in the
Southern part of Malmo would be living just outside the zone 2 contour
and a few thousands in Bärseback would find themselves straddling it.

The following description of noise levels may help to identify
the nuisances involved.(1)

dB(A)	Corresponding noise
130 - 150	a jet aircraft starting up 10 to 50 m away
110 - 130	a riveting machine
90 - 110	a noisy factory
80 - 90	a street with heavy traffic
70 - 80	a noisy office
60 - 70	someone talking from one metre away

The majority of the working group recommended that for zones A
105 PNdB should be the maximum noise level, that new housing should
not be permitted and that existing housing should be disused. For
zones B they recommended that 90 PNdB should be the maximum, that
new housing should not normally be permitted although existing housing
might be retained. And they estimated that about 15 per cent of the
population would feel heavily annoyed by the noise in B zones. A
minority recommended that the maxima be raised to 115 and 100 PNdB
for zones A and B respectively. Professor Ingerslev in another
dissenting report gave his support to the lower criteria, but proposed that exemptions be given exclusively to the international airport because of its importance to Copenhagen.

Later in 1972 new calculations were done for Saltholm by an
official Danish-Swedish working group on the basis of a different
runway layout. "Critical noise contours" were drawn around areas
within which 20 per cent or more of the population would feel
"seriously annoyed" on the assumption that DC-8, 9 and 10 type aircraft would be used in 1985 and aircraft less noisy than DC-10s
in AD 2000 (heavily and lightly loaded aircraft were classified
separately).

Map 5 shows a comparison between contours resulting from the
Danish and Swedish methods.(2) This indicates that the Swedish

1) Report of the working group on aircraft noise, Pollution
   Secretariat, Ministry of Pollution Control, p. B17, 1972
2) Taken from Danish Environment Directorate report "København
   Lufthavn Roskilde. Miljøtilpasning" 1973.

Map 5 - Carte 5

COMPARISON OF DANISH AND SWEDISH NOISE CONTOURS FOR SALTHOLM 1985 (1973)

COMPARAISON DES COURBES D'EGAL BRUIT OBTENUES PAR LES DANOIS ET PAR LES SUEDOIS POUR SALTHOLM EN 1985 (1973)

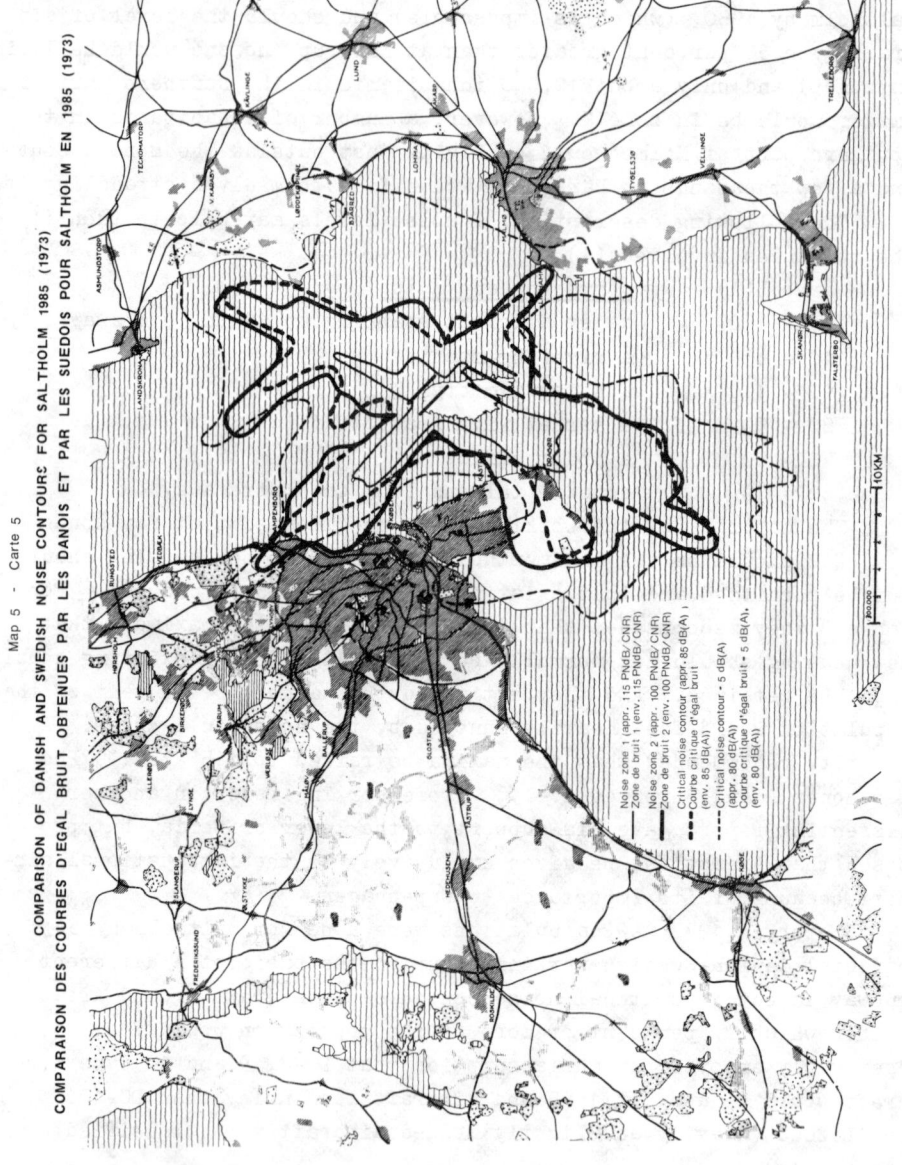

Noise zone 1 (appr. 115 PNdB/CNR)
Zone de bruit 1 (env. 115 PNdB/CNR)

Noise zone 2 (appr. 100 PNdB/CNR)
Zone de bruit 2 (env. 100 PNdB/CNR)

Critical noise contour (appr. 85 dB(A))
Courbe critique d'égal bruit
(env. 85 dB(A))

Critical noise contour + 5 dB(A)
(appr. 90 dB(A))
Courbe critique d'égal bruit + 5 dB(A),
(env. 80 dB(A))

critical noise contour is comparable to the Danish zone 2 contour.
The reason for the expectation that the spread of noise will be reduced by the year 2000 is that the use of bigger and quieter aircraft
is expected to outweigh increases in air traffic.

Map 6 shows another 1985 noise contour for Saltholm based on a
method developed by the Swedish Nature Conservation Authority. The
contour delimits areas within which more than 10 per cent of the
population might be expected to feel "very annoyed" if the most
disadvantageous take-off and landing routines were to be used by the
noisiest planes in use such as heavily loaded DC-8-63s. Contours
for the year 2000 are considerably less far flung since by then the
noisiest aircraft is expected to be the DC-10.

This method treats flights and noise levels independently, distinguishing between areas with high, medium and low frequencies of
overflight and relates annoyance to the noisiest types of aircraft
in use. Thus noise levels of up to 90 dB(A) are considered acceptable in areas of low exposure to flights but only 70 dB(A) in areas
of high exposure. The theory is based upon interviews among people
living near several Scandinavian and foreign airports. Similar investigations in the United States, France, Japan and the Netherlands
have produced comparable results.

ENVIRONMENTAL FACTORS OTHER THAN NOISE

Air pollution from aircraft has not been the subject of any
special investigation in Denmark. Soot and nitrogen compounds ori-
ginating from burnt kerosine do occur in considerable quantities at
airports and along flight paths to and from them but this is generally
thought to be only a minor problem compared with air pollutants from
motor cars, chimneys and domestic oil burners.

Any new airport site will destroy wildlife and change landscapes. Saltholm contains only a few farms raising sheep and cattle
and is seldom visited by people from Copenhagen or elsewhere so the
effects of an airport there would be confined to sea gulls and other
birds. An airport on South Amager would destroy a small wood and
interfere with birds living on reclaimed land. Land reclamation
at Saltholm or South of Amager is expected to have little effect on
water flows and fish, though shrimps may be reduced in number, because it will affect only very shallow waters. Any inland site would
mean a larger destruction of landscapes and wildlife. This is especially true of sites in the middle of Sealand. A site at
Lammefjorden would cause fewer invonveniences than other
possibilities.

Bird strikes are a matter of some importance at both Kastrup
and Saltholm. Collisions with either seagulls or migrating birds

Map 6 - Carte 6

NOISE CONTOURS FOR SALTHOLM 1985 AND 2000 (RYLANDER & AL. 1973)
(10 % « very annoyed » inside contour)

COURBES D'EGAL BRUIT POUR SALTHOLM EN 1985 ET 2000 (RYLANDER ET AUTRES, 1973)
A l'intérieur de la courbe, 10 % de la population est « très gênée »

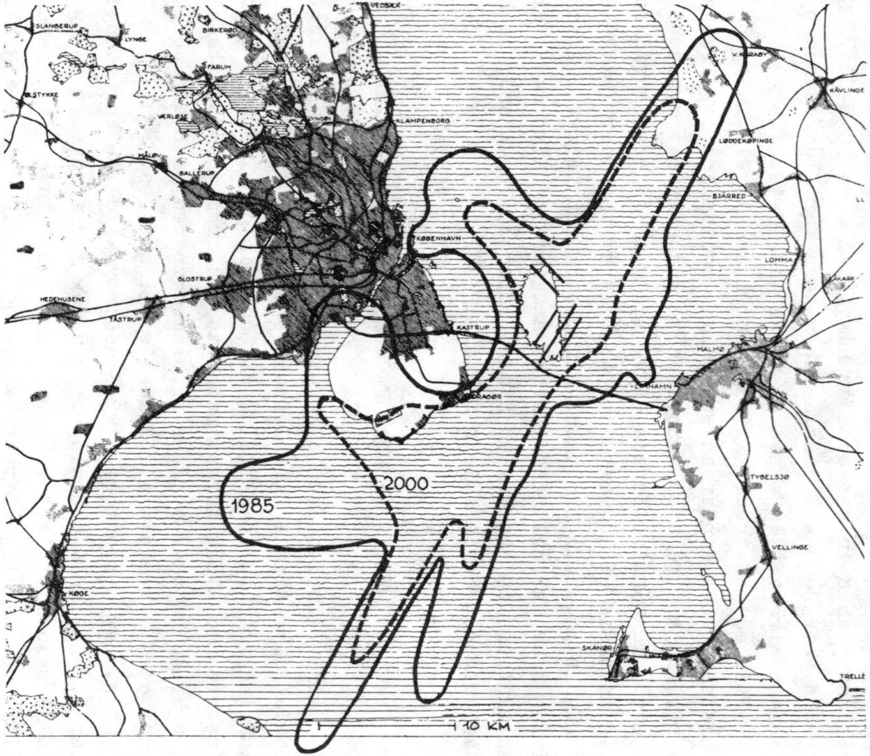

are possible. Danger from seagulls will probably diminish if the airport is moved to Saltholm since the hatching of large numbers of these birds would be frustrated. Bird migration between Scandinavia and the European continent is intense in the areas in question though it has not yet been the cause of any fatal accidents at Kastrup. The risk is greatest between the southwest corner of Sweden and the Danish coast along Køge Bay, South of Amager. The danger of collisions with migratory birds would therefore be greater for a South Amager airport than for one at Saltholm.

The risk of bird collisions at any inland site would be negligable.

An airport at Saltholm would not involve the destruction of any buildings of historical interest since none exist there, but one at South Amager would necessitate the clearing of a few villages of which Store Magleby contains some houses and other signs of 17th century Dutch influence. Most inland sites would involve the destruction of many historically valuable buildings though this is not the case at Lammefjorden which is on land reclaimed during this century.

Development towards the Southwest and West are the first priorities of the regional planners in Copenhagen. A major airport in these parts of the region is therefore unacceptable and even the secondary airport near Roskilde is in conflict with regional development aims.

An airport at South Amager would create no direct conflict with regional development objectives though the resulting noise would greatly disturb newly urbanised districts along Køge Bay, and would frustrate the development of a proposed new town of 25,000 households and a Scandinavia trade centre on South Amager. Co-ordinating a South Amager Airport with Roskilde would also be difficult.

The continued use of Kastrup will be destructive to large parts of Amager and central Copenhagen and will preclude realisation of the Western Amager plan. An airport at Saltholm would be in accord with regional planning aims and promote the integration of the Danish and Swedish sides of the Sound. Runway directions and operating procedures may require alteration in the interests of the Western Amager Plan and some areas in Sweden.

An airport at Lammefjord would not conflict with Copenhagen regional planning but would disrupt the large numbers of Summer houses and bathing resorts in Northwestern Sealand. The wide arrows on Map 2 show the conflicts raised by all the possible sites.

ECONOMIC EFFECTS

Kastrup has, and any future international airport will have, an immense influence on the economy of the region and some effect on the national economy. Ten thousand persons were employed at Kastrup in 1972, giving rise to a total of about 50,000 jobs. The airport is also a gateway for many foreign visitors - the total in 1972 was about two million - and provides business connections with the rest of the world. By the 1980s it is estimated that there will be about 20,000 employees at Saltholm giving an overall total of five times as many jobs and a gross annual income of about 8,000 million Danish crowns. The international airport will thus be the biggest single influence on the labour market, the foreign exchange balance and tourism.

The more accessible the airport is, the more impetus will it give to the economy of the region. Minor differences between the time to travel to and from different sites may not be decisive, but remote sites will definitely generate less traffic than ones as near to Copenhagen as Kastrup or Saltholm. Saltholm will moreover be more attractive to Swedish travellers than any other site. On the other hand the financial difficulties of the mid-1970s have led to a questioning of the expense of a new international airport and concern about energy has led to proposals to substitute less wasteful forms of transport for it.

THE COSTS AND BENEFITS OF THE COMPETING SITES

No attempt has yet been made to assess all the benefits and costs of the two different sites. Estimates of construction costs have been made from time to time but with varying assumptions. Several calculations have also been made about transport links. Thus in 1968 it was decided that a 16-lane motorway tunnel would be needed to connect Saltholm with Amager. Another report then recommended a six-lane motorway with special bus lanes that were to be replaced by a railway or tracked hovercraft after 1990.

Opponents of the Saltholm project - which competes with other transport investments such as a bridge or tunnel across the Great Belt - have repeatedly demanded that a benefit/cost analysis be undertaken in order to identify the best site. The objectors are mostly concerned about the cost of Saltholm and its implication for investment in transport projects in other parts of the country, about noise and the destruction of a bird sanctuary, and about the effects of prolonged uncertainty on long-term planning in the region and the city.

Swedish opponents are mostly concerned about noise from Saltholm though most objections are levelled against the proposed runway layout not the principle of an airport. Some interests fear that the new Sturup airport may suffer.

I am rather sceptical about the idea of expressing all relevant considerations including environmental factors such as noise nuisance, the destruction of recreational resources and risks of collision in financial terms so as to produce an overall "cost and disadvantage" account. I share the views on cost/benefit analysis voiced by Professor Colin Buchanan in his Note of Dissent in the Report of the Roskill Commission on the Third London Airport. He was uneasy about the basis of some of the figures and especially about the dominating role of travel times to and from the alternative sites. He had doubts about the meaningfulness of adding up all the costs to produce a "batting order". And he would have preferred to see the cost/benefit analysis used to illustrate alternative choices available within a land use plan formed by previously defined policies.

With this in mind, I have tried to list the direct costs and the most important planning and environmental factors that should be taken into account in assessing alternative sites for Copenhagen's international airport (Tables 1 and 2). The advantages and disadvantages of the various possibilities are all accounted for but without the use of any figures. It appears that the main advantages of Kastrup are its relatively low construction costs and its short distance from Central Copenhagen, while the main advantages of Saltholm are its potential capacity, its lack of noise problems and the contribution it makes to town and regional planning objectives and to joint Danish-Swedish planning in the Sound. On top of this it has travel distances and transport economics almost as good as those for Kastrup.

The South Amager solution would be somewhat cheaper than Saltholm and quicker to build but it is inferior on environmental and planning grounds. A solution involving large secondary airports seems to have many deficiencies and few advantages. The same is true in even greater degree for the Lammefjord site which has not been investigated in any detail.

The stand-still option has large financial advantages, at least in the short run, but does not meet the demand for future air travel. It leaves the noise problem unsolved, and it may be an unfavourable influence on export trades and tourism.

Weighing up the different factors is however a political matter and the Government and a majority of Parliament has clearly decided in favour of Saltholm. Nevertheless, a new political decision will have to be taken by the new Parliament after the election in January 1975.

Table 1

RELATIVE ADVANTAGES AND DISADVANTAGES OF ALTERNATIVE INTERNATIONAL AIRPORT SITES IN THE COPENHAGEN REGION

(The most important aspects are underlined)	Kastrup expanded	South Amager (+ Kastrup)	Kastrup restricted + larger secondary airports	Saltholm	Lammefjorden (+ Kastrup restricted)	Stand-still in Kastrup
1. Airport construction costs		-		--	?	++
2. Construction costs of road and rail access(x)		(-)		(-)	--	++
3. Economic profitability of operation (a) short term (b) long term	+ -	++ ++	- --	- +	- -	+
4. Exclusion of alternative land uses	--	--	--	+	-	--
5. Water, sewerage, etc., and private auxiliary services				-	?	
6. Length of period before start of operations will be possible	+	+	-	--	--	+
7. Capacity reserves at the site for later expansion	-	+	-	+	?	-
8. Possibility of co-ordinated operation with Kastrup	+	+	+	-	+	+
9. Distances between airport and population served	++	+	++	+	--	++
10. Land transportation economics	++	+	+	++	--	++
11. Probable number of passengers (and freight)	-	+	-	++	--	--

Legend: ++   large advantage
         +   considerable advantage
       (+)   minor advantage

--   large disadvantage
-   considerable disadvantage
(-)   minor disadvantage

(x)   excluding existing road and rail connections and connections already planned independently of the airport siting (Copenhagen-Malmo road connection).

Table 2

RELATIVE ADVANTAGES AND DISADVANTAGES OF ALTERNATIVE INTERNATIONAL AIRPORT SITES IN THE COPENHAGEN REGION

(The most important aspects are underlined)	Kastrup expanded (+ Kastrup)	South Amager (+ Kastrup)	Kastrup restricted + larger secondary airports	Saltholm	Lammefjorden (+ Kastrup restricted)	Stand-still in Kastrup
12. Meteorology					(+)	
13. Air space issues, air traffic control and safety		(-)	(-)			
14. Risks of birds collisions	(-)	-	(-)	(-)		(-)
15. Risks of crash in built-up areas	(-)	(-)	(-)			(-)
16. Noise annoyance	--	-	--		-	-
17. Conflicts with existing buildings and constructions	-	-	--		(-)	-
18. Destruction of wildlife, landscape and recreational areas		-	--		-	
19. Destruction of agricultural areas	(-)	-	--		--	
20. Accordance with regional development planning		-	-	+		-
21. Accordance with Copenhagen town and transportation planning	--	-	-	+	-	-
22. Possibilities for industrial and commercial development		+		++		-
23. Promotion of Danish-Swedish Sound Region planning		(+)		++		
24. Attractivity for Swedish passengers	+		+	++		--
25. Noise annoyances over Swedish territory			-	(-)		--

Legend:
++ large advantage
+   considerable advantage
(+) minor advantage

-- large disadvantage
-   considerable disadvantage
(-) minor disadvantage

115

Part 3

FINDING SITES FOR MAJOR AIRPORTS:
THE EXPERIENCE OF OSAKA

Masao Hirai,
Deputy Head of Kansai International Airport, Research Office,
Ministry of Transport, Tokyo and
Kazuo Yoda,
Deputy Head of City Bureau, City Planning Division,
Ministry of Construction, Tokyo

BACKGROUND

Kansai, a region that embraces Osaka, Kobe and Kyoto, is one of Japan's major economic centres. Osaka International Airport, its main focus of aviation, therefore plays an important role in the nation's air transport system but it cannot cater for the expected growth in air travel. A decision has consequently been taken to find a site and build a new international airport for the Kansai region. This paper indicates the issues that need to be considered in promoting such a project.

The demand for air transport in Japan has increased rapidly in recent years. Passengers departing and arriving on international flights in 1971 numbered 4.32 million with another 32.76 million making domestic trips. The corresponding figures for Osaka airport were 800,000 and 8.68 million or 18.5 per cent and 26.5 per cent respectively of all air passengers travelling to or within Japan.

Flight frequencies at Osaka have increased with the growth of passenger demand, reaching 158,000 movements in 1971. Forecasts of passenger demand and flight frequencies are shown in Figures 1 and 2. Flight frequency estimates are based on the assumption that aircraft with larger capacity will be introduced in the years to come.

It is estimated that the maximum capacity of Osaka airport is 175,000 movements a year. This suggests that a critical position has already been reached. The airport is surrounded by cities and there is no room for expansion. Moreover, aircraft noise creates a serious problem in nearby residential areas. Severe restrictions on flight frequencies, the introduction of a curfew and redesignation of flight routes seem inevitable unless a new airport is constructed. Realisation of this situation led the Ministry of Transport to start preliminary work on the new airport project in 1968.

Figure 1

THE TREND AND ESTIMATION
OF AIRO-PASSENGERS IN KANSAI REGION

TENDANCE ET ESTIMATION DES NOMBRES
DE PASSAGERS AERIENS DANS LA REGION DE KANSAI

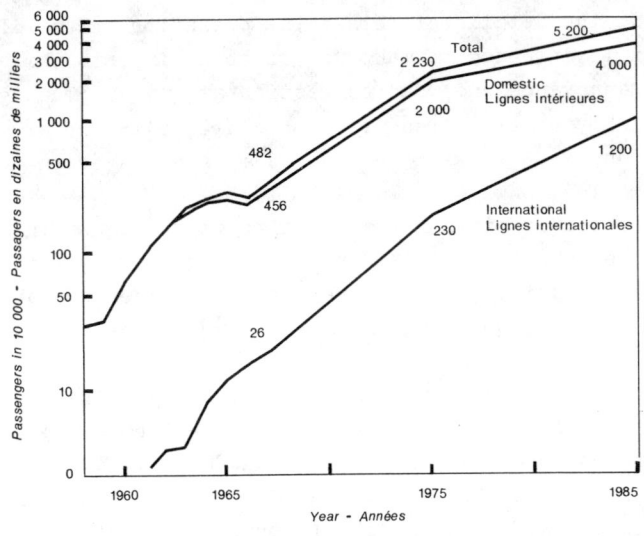

Figure 2

THE ESTIMATED NUMBER OF LANDING AND TAKING OFF IN
THE PEAK DAY AND THE ESTIMATION OF ONES IN A YEAR

ESTIMATION DU NOMBRE D'ATTERRISSAGES ET DE DECOLLAGES
POUR UN JOUR DE POINTE ET ESTIMATION ANNUELLE

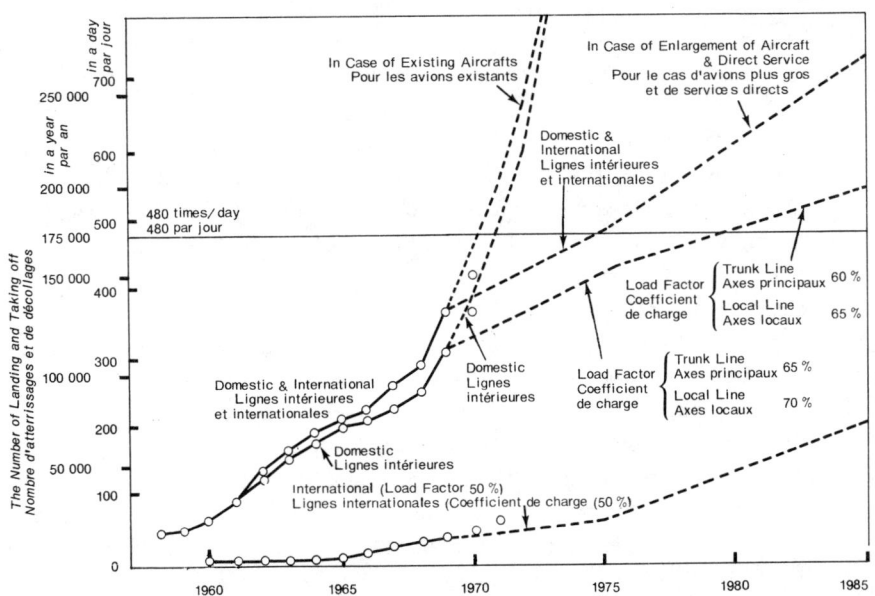

OUTLINE OF THE PLAN

The new site is intended to become the primary airport in Kansai and will handle all international and a considerable number of domestic flights. Osaka airport will be used as a supplementary airport but the details of this joint operation are still uncertain. However it is intended to make use of both airports while alleviating noise and annoyance and road congestion at Osaka. The new airport will initially have an area of 850 hectares with two 4,000 m close-parallel runways. It will be doubled in area later on and a second set of parallel runways could be built.

Four possible sites for a new airport are shown in Figure 3 and all have take-off and landing routes over the sea to minimise noise in residential areas. Nevertheless residents near the proposed sites are actively opposing the airport due to concern over airport noise.

Official concern to protect the interests of residents is shown by a Ministry of Transport enquiry into the "Scale and Location of Kansai International Airport". This was submitted to the Aviation Council on 13th October, 1971. The Council had established a sub-committee for Kansai International Airport consisting of 25 members, which met 24 times up to March 1973. In August 1972, a two-day public hearing was held to permit the governors, mayors and representatives of residents in the areas concerned to express their views on the proposed sites. More time will be needed before the final report is concluded.

ORGANISATION

The construction and the administration of a civil airport is normally entrusted to the Minister of Transport or to the appropriate head of local government. However Tokyo's new international airport is to be managed by a public corporation set up by the Central Government and this example has been followed by Osaka. The new airport will therefore be a public corporation financed by national capital, public investment, the debentures of the corporation, and local government finance. Local government, however, has not yet agreed to its share in the investment. Access roads to the airport except the final approach to the terminal, will be financed and constructed in the same way as other expressways (Hanshin Expressway Public Corporation operates in Kansai region at present). Railway links will differ depending on the site chosen. The offshore sites at Kobe and South Osaka would be served by existing or planned rapid transit routes. The offshore site at Harimanada and the site on

Figure 3

PROPOSED SITES OF KANSAI INTERNATIONAL AIRPORT
AND ITS ROUTES EXPECTED ON ARRIVAL AND DEPARTURE

SITES PROPOSES POUR L'AEROPORT INTERNATIONAL DE KANSAI
AVEC LES TRAJECTOIRES D'ATTERRISSAGE ET DE DECOLLAGE PREVUES

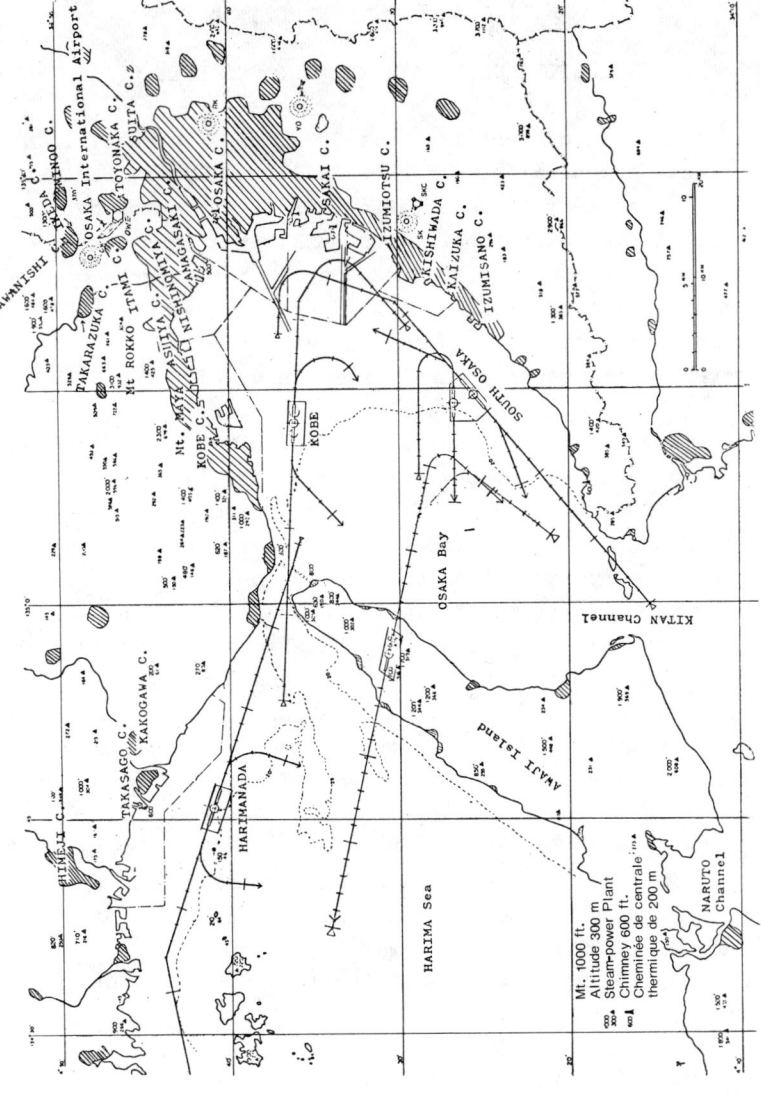

Awaji Island, on the other hand, will need specially constructed express railways. These links will br provided by private railway companies or by a local government supported body but there is no firm plan as yet.

BUILDING THE AIRPORT AND THE ROLE OF GOVERNMENT

When an airport is built in an urban area it is necessary to tie it into a general plan for roads and railways, regional development and environmental conservation. Administration has to be co-ordinated too. If the airport is to be built in a less-developed area, the affected residents will demand a regional development plan in return. Smooth relationships among the various governmental agencies concerned with airport development are therefore essential and local government must play a main role in development around the airport.

Tokyo's new international airport provides an example. The airport itself is constructed by the New Tokyo International Airport Public Corporation, the highways by the Japan Road Public Corporation, the railways by the Keisei Railway Company (private industry) and by the Japan National Railway. As the airport is inland, farmers have had to be resettled and alternative roads and waterways built. On 4th March, 1966, the Cabinet Ministers Conference on the New Tokyo International Airport was established so that this work could be performed smoothly. The members are the Ministers for Finance, Commerce and Industry, Transportation, Labour Construction and Home Affairs, the Executive Director of the Prime Minister's Office, the Chief Commissioner of the National Public Safety Commission, the Chairman of Tokyo Metropolitan Region Development Committee, the Director of the Economic Planning Agency and the Chief Secretary of the Cabinet.

On 21st July, 1967 an Executive Headquarters of the New Tokyo International Airport Construction, consisting of the directors of each Ministry and Agency, was established for the purpose of executing the policies agreed upon by the Ministers Conference. The programme for the development of the Tokyo Airport was divided as follows:
   a) Projects to be financed by the central government:
      3 inter-city expressways
      2 urban railways
      1 occupational training centre
   b) Projects to be financed jointly by central and local government:
      Highways (national and local)
      River improvement
      Water supply

Sewerage

Parks and greens

Nursery, elementary, middle and high schools suitably
equipped to combat noise

Fire brigade

Improvement of farms

New town

The total amount of investment is expected to reach approximately 264 billion Yen.

c) The development of Narita New Town.

In order to accommodate some of the employees of the New
Tokyo International Airport and their families, Narita New
Town is being developed. The new town is situated to the
West, about 8 km from Narita City and approximately 50 km
from central Tokyo.

Planning for Kansai International Airport has not yet reached
this stage but it is considered necessary to establish an administrative body consisting of central and local government officials. At
present Vice-Ministers from the Ministries of Transportation, Finance,
Home Affairs, Construction and Environment and the Vice-Chairman of
Kinki Region Development Committee and the presidents of the Fishery
Agency, the Maritime Safety Agency and the Meteorological Agency have
been assigned as temporary members of the Kansai International Airport division of the Aviation Council. The governors of Osaka and
Hyogo prefectures and the Mayors of Osaka and Kobe sit as observers.

THE SELECTION OF A SITE

The costs and benefits of the four proposed sites for the new
airport are being investigated by the Aviation Council. Items considered are as follows:

a) Convenience for users: time and distance to travel from
the centre of Osaka; scope for using existing and planned
road and rail routes.

b) Natural conditions: meteorological conditions, wave height
and tide level.

c) Aircraft operation and air traffic control techniques:
degree of difficulty in establishing arrival and departure
routes; arrivals and departures capacity.

d) Environmental conditions: noise, air pollution, influence
on tidal currents and the dispersion of pollution at sea.

e) Construction techniques: technical problems, time and cost;
scope for extension; maintenance.

f) Conflicts with existing interests such as fishing rights,
maritime traffic and existing land-owners.

121

g) Arrangements for regional land use, and railway planning.

h) Effects of development on regional structure and investment.

i) Acceptability to local community.

Each of these items is given a weight that is taken into account by the Aviation Council in the site-selection process. The following criteria have also been established: the selected site must be compatible with the continued operation of the existing airport; it must not cause a public nuisance; and it must be near to the centre of Osaka. Needless to say feedback of other viewpoints into the selection process is considered to be essential. One of the Council's main tasks is to ensure that the site chosen minimises environmental costs while still being convenient for users. A location in the sea therefore seems desirable and the resulting increase in costs should be regarded as a social necessity.

EFFECT ON THE ENVIRONMENT

Areas around the airport subject to serious noise annoyance will be purchased by the Government if land owners so desire. Future noise annoyance has been estimated by flying aircraft over each proposed site and taking on-the-spot measurements. Data on annoyance has also been drawn from the plans for the new Tokyo airport. Zoning will be changed where necessary in accordance with the insights gained in this way. Measurements have also been made of air pollution around the Tokyo and Osaka airports and its patterns investigated. Experiments have been made using a large scale model (horizontal scale 1/2,000, vertical scale 1/200) to identify the influences that an airport would have on tides in Osaka Bay and on pollution of the sea. Measures will be taken to control these undesirable environmental impacts.

ECONOMIC EFFECTS OF THE PROPOSED AIRPORT

In the discussion that follows the effects of three different airport locations are considered:

a) in a big city

b) in the suburbs of a big city

c) in a less developed area near a big city.

Consumer's expenditure by airport employees is estimated as follows in 1985:

	(persons)
Employees	approx. 52,000
Members of employees families	" 135,000
Total	" 187,000

	(Billion Yen per year)
Income of employees	approx. 160
Consumption level	" 108

(Consumers' expenditure by employees and their families is expected to be static in the long term.)

Financial effects on the local authorities concerned

An increase in tax revenue among the local authorities concerned has been estimated using data from the international airport proposals.

Tax revenues would vary depending mainly on the number of the inhabitants employed at the airport itself. The amount is estimated as follows:

	(Billion Yen per year)
Real estate taxes	approx. 1.35
Other taxes	" 1.82
Total	" 3.17

Investment effects, although only short-run, are important

They are expected to be as follows:

	(Billion Yen)
Investment expected by 1985:	
a) Airport within a big city	approx. 340
b) Airport in the suburbs of a big city	" 290
c) Airport in a less-developed area near a big city	" 620

Multiplier effects

Multiplier effects would result from population growth and the attraction of industry to the airport region.

- A. Estimates of the percentages of employees who will live in the area close to the airport are as follows:
    1. Airport within city   88 per cent
    2. Airport in suburbs   64 per cent
    3. Airport in less developed site   93 per cent

  Should the airport be sited in the suburbs of a big city, the number of employees living close by would be fewer than in the other cases due to easier access and shorter travel times.

B. Estimates of levels of consumers' expenditure within the
boundaries of the local authorities near the three types of
site are as follows:
1. 86 per cent
2. 58 per cent
3. 87 per cent
C. The estimated population in the areas close to each type of
site would be as follows:

	Population	(in 1,000 persons)	
	City	Suburb	Rural
1970	1.253	310	185
1985	1.368	387	147

Employment would be divided as follows among the primary,
secondary and tertiary sectors:

	City: Case 1			Suburb: Case 2			Rural: Case 3		
	Primary	Secondary	Tertiary	Primary	Secondary	Tertiary	Primary	Secondary	Tertiary
1965	3.1	38.1	58.6	8.1	54.5	37.4	43.2	22.3	34.3
1985	1.0	43.0	56.0	1.0	53.0	43.0	7.0	25.0	68.0

The ultimate population associated with the airport is expected
to be greater in Cases 1 and 2 due to the tendency of population
growth to concentrate in or near big cities. If, on the other hand,
the airport is located in a rural area, it is expected that the
total population will decrease in spite of the new development. A
new airport is expected to have little influence on the location of
industry in Case 1 but a considerable effect if it is in the suburbs.
If the airport is in a rural area, the potential for the development
of manufacturing industries is considered low.

EFFECTS OF A NEW AIRPORT ON URBAN DEVELOPMENT

Case 1: Little change in population is expected if the airport
is located in a big city. A new airport would, however,
strengthen sea and air transport within the Kansai metropolitan area, and could heighten its importance as a
distribution centre if an urban development scheme were
carried out.

Case 2: Suburbs which have been developed as residential areas
change as service industries move in. Affected local
authorities will need to improve the infrastructure and
control urban growth.

Case 3: In less developed areas the most important problem to
be solved would be to increase the area's attractiveness

for industrial development. The setting up of a regional goods distribution centre is one possible
solution. Tertiary industries set up in the wake of
the new airport would undoubtedly contribute to the
development of the region.

Chapter 8

A PROJECT UNDER CONSTRUCTION: PARIS

F. Levy,
Director, Division des Etudes et Programmes, Service
Régional de l'Equipement de la Région Parisienne

THE INTEGRATION OF CHARLES-DE-GAULLE AIRPORT
AND ITS SURROUNDINGS

The origin of Charles-de-Gaulle airport goes back to studies which began in 1957. The decision to proceed was made under a Ministerial Order of June 1964 and it then lay with the Paris Airport Authority to carry out the project. The Authority was set up in 1945 and is responsible for creating, developing and operating aerodromes within 50 kilometres of Paris.

Charles-de-Gaulle airport lies 20 kilometres north-east of the capital in an area with very little urban development (the acquisition of 3,000 hectares required the pulling down of only one farm building) and will not take on its final shape before 1985-1990. However the first facilities came into service in 1974. No. 1 air terminal and No. 1 runway will initially cater for some seven million passengers per annum, as against an estimated 40 to 50 million per annum when the airport is completed. By way of comparison, nearly 13 million passengers went through Orly in 1972. An undertaking on the scale of Charles-de-Gaulle airport inevitably raises awkward problems. These range from the economic repercussions caused by the direct or "induced" creation of jobs and the physical development of housing and transport links to the constraints due to the nuisances from air traffic generated by the airport.

These problems faced the "Paris-North Working Party" which was set up in October 1969.

THE MAIN PROBLEMS

Jobs

A survey was conducted in 1972 amongst future employers of airports in order to refine the Paris-North Working Party's

forecasts of employment in 1985. This survey showed that firms at
the airport would be recruiting some 6,800 employees during 1974-75
and that the jobs available during this initial phase would fall
within a fairly narrow range of skills, the more highly rated of
which would be taken by staff transferring from Orly.

These labour requirements account for approximately 0.6 per
cent of the labour force within a radius of 20 km of the airport.
Compared with a level of unemployment which ranges from 1.5 to 3 per
cent in various parts of this area, and compared with the 100,000
workers that will have settled there between 1968 and 1975, the
6,800 employees to be recruited for the airport represent only a
small drain on the labour market.

The Paris Airport Authority is nevertheless actively concerned
with aiding local recruitment. A branch of the National Employment
Agency has been set up at Charles-de-Gaulle and some publicity has
been directed to neighbouring communes. In addition all the problems
relating to employment were set out at a meeting at Charles-de-Gaulle
on 28th June, 1973, attended by almost all known future employers at
the airport. In addition to this the Regional Directorate of the
National Employment Agency will be provided with employers' recruitment forecasts.

Housing

Government directives of May 1970 contained two main points
about housing. One was the need to provide accommodation for households connected to the airport. The second was the need to have due
regard for the nuisances spread by aircraft over a wide area and for
the consequences that this has for building. The number of houses
needed to meet the needs of Charles-de-Gaulle airport accounts for
a very small proportion of the programme for the Paris Region in the
VIth Plan and although this proportion will be bigger under future
Plans, it poses no real problem (Table 1).

Thus the labour force transferring from Orly and seeking
accommodation can be estimated at a maximum of 5,000. However the
number of dwellings which will be completed under projects adopted,
or under way, within a radius of 20 km of the airport, amounts to
some 23,000 in 1974 and approximately as many in 1975. The housing
requirements generated by the opening of Charles-de-Gaulle will
therefore barely exceed one-tenth of the new dwellings put on the
market during this period. Hence it can reasonably be assumed that
the additional demand occasioned by the opening of the airport will
not generate any pressure on the housing market. Furthermore Air-
France, which is the largest employers, has already reserved 700
houses for rent under the employers' "contribution scheme".

Table 1

AREA SURROUNDING CHARLES-DE-GAULLE AIRPORT

Housing Forecasts in the Lachaize Report
compared with those concerning the Paris Region
in the Report of 16th March, 1972

	Lachaize Report		March 1972 Report	
	Dwellings to be built between 1970 and 1985 to meet airport requirements	Total number of new dwellings over the same period	Forecasts in the VIth Plan with regard to the number of projects launched	
Secteur Survilliers-Fosses-Saint-Witz	3,500	10,500	3,315	1,000 survilliers 1,170 Fosses 550 Marly-la-Ville 460 Puiseux 135 St-Witz
Zone Luzarches-Domont	3,000	7,000	860	400 Domont 300 Domont 160 Belloy
Vallée de Montmorency	4,000	55,000	7,930	4,000 Ermont-Franconville 930 Montmagny 2,000 Saint-Leu 1,000 Taverny
Secteur Dammartin-Saint Mard	2,000	5,000	1,943	600 Dammartin 1,000 Othis 200 St Pathus 143 Moussy-le-Neuf
Secteur Jablines	5,000	13,000	VIIth Plan	
Meaux	2,000	7,000	4,300(1)	
Vallée de la Marne	15,000	68,000	9,000 approximately	
Aulnay-Sevran-Tremblay-Villepinte	7,000	19,000	7,250	850 Aulnay 2,400 Sevran 2,000 Tremblay 2,000 Villepinte

1) The total for the Z.U.P. is 8,500.

An analysis of the choice of housing of the Orly labour force, based on assumptions that accessibility, proximity to Paris, quality of the environment and avoidance of exposure to noise would also guide the choice of workers at Charles-de-Gaulle, enabled "preference zones" to be identified. However these houses and their associated amenities will not be available until after 1975.

Hotels

The growth of air travel for business and pleasure generates an ever-increasing demand for hotel rooms that has to be taken into account in airport planning.

Until recently both the Paris Airport Authority and the big hotel companies held the view that the main demand to be catered for came from business travellers. (According to Air-France 70 per cent of passengers are on business.) Furthermore only business travel was thought capable of justifying large-scale hotel investment. The best returns were believed to be given by three or four-star hotels. The most popular locations were reckoned to be the airport precincts, Paris or La Défense.

Thus a market survey carried out by the Airport Authority recommended the provision of 100 rooms per million passengers within the airport precincts. In the light of this, contracts for 700 three-star hotel rooms have been awarded to the Société Borel. This accommodation will be provided near the No. 1 air terminal at Charles-de-Gaulle and will meet expected demand up to 1977-78. Experience during the initial stages of operation of the new airport will make it possible to adjust the subsequent programme for hotels in the central complex.

In Paris itself, apart from the recently completed Méridien-Maillot and P.L.M. Saint-Jacques four-star hotels, which mainly cater for Orly, and the Concorde-Maillot hotel and a 1,000-room four-star hotel near Montparnasse for the Sheraton group, projects include a 700-room four-star hotel on the Quai de Grenelle for Japan Air Lines, and a 500-room hotel being built by a Canadian company at La Défense.

There can be no doubt, however, that the growth of mass tourism will make it necessary to provide hotels in the middle price bracket. Two sites in the vicinity of Charles-de-Gaulle seem promising for this use. One is at Le Bourget which is being developed as an exhibition centre. The other is at an urban development project at Sevran, near a station on the future Roissy-Paris railway line.

Other large hotels also seem likely to be sited along the approaches to the Route Nationale 3 in Villeparisis and Claye-Souilly.

Lastly, there is a well-advanced Holiday Inns project for a 125-room hotel at Charles-de-Gaulle.

NOISE

A joint circular of 26th October, 1970, drawn up by the Ministries for Transport and Equipment, provided an analysis of a problem which, though not entirely new, had not previously been fully appreciated by all concerned. Witness the pressure exerted by certain local councillors to frustrate the first restrictions on building stemming from Government instructions in 1953.

This circular defined three noise zones covering decreasing levels of noise exposure and surrounding the airport at progressively greater distances.

In Zone A new buildings are only authorised if they are essential to the operation of the aerodrome or to industrial establishments whose activities depend on the proximity of the aerodrome. Adequate sound-proofing is essential.

In Zone B built-up areas cannot be extended and the construction of public buildings is restricted to those essential to the life of existing communities.

In Zone C built-up areas can be slightly extended on certain conditions, but comprehensive development schemes and public building should, as far as possible, be avoided.

At Charles-de-Gaulle two 1972 ministerial directives provide for a complete ban on housing construction in zones A and B. Detached houses can be built in zone C subject to certain conditions. Compensation for noise disturbance was the subject of official studies and led to a decree of 13th February, 1973. This provides that the Paris Airport Authority should levy a charge of one franc per passenger travelling to an airport in Metropolitan France and three francs for all other destinations. Rules for allocating the proceeds of these charges to sufferers from noise are covered by two ministerial orders dated March 1973.

ACTIVITIES

Within the airport

Forecasts for employment at Charles-de-Gaulle airport are given in Table 2. They are comparable, though slightly smaller, than those drawn up by the Paris-North Working Party in 1970.

Table 2

FORECASTS OF JOBS AT CHARLES-DE-GAULLE AIRPORT UP TO 1985

	1975	1980	1985
Ground Staff	14,600	between 26,000 and ·30,000	between 40,000 and 48,000
Aircrews based at the Airport	3,800	between 5,500 and 8,000	between 7,800 and 13,000
Directly "induced" industrial employment	2,000	about 7,000	about 15,000
Total	20,400	between 39,000 and 45,000	between 63,000 and 76,000

In the neighbourhood of the airport

Industrial jobs in areas near the airport are expected to number from 15,000 to 20,000 in 1980 and 30,000 in 1985.

Though the list of approvals granted in 1969, 1970 and 1971 did not indicate any great demand for industrial sites near the future airport, a different trend became apparent in 1972 (Table 3). Eighty-eight hectares of land for warehousing at Marly-la-Ville sanctioned in 1971 attracted sufficient interest for a further 30 hectares to be allocated to this use in 1973.

At the beginning of 1972 the area remaining available for industry in the neighbourhood of Charles-de-Gaulle up until the end of the VIth Plan amounted to some 220 hectares. The largest tract, 100 hectares of which were provided under the VIth Plan, is in the Paris North development zone but this does not include the nearby site of the Citroën plant.

Further away from the airport six industrial zones covering some 140 hectares in the Marne valley are at present committed under the VIth Plan. Other sites are available in the southern part of Oise.

It should be emphasized that when these zones were first mapped out the object was to bring work close to new residential areas. The opening of Charles-de-Gaulle airport cannot but help to achieve this aim.

Table 3

APPROVALS GRANTED IN THE AREA SURROUNDING CHARLES-DE-GAULLE AIRPORT

Square metres of useable floor space

Communes	Year 1972			1st half 1973		
	Industry	Offices	Stores	Industry	Offices	Stores
Aulnay-sous-Bois(1)	14,164	10,416	5,330	3,167	6,130	32,910
Bobigy	8,500	44,287	2,572	1,540	1,570	16,108
Le Blanc-Mesnil	1,400	2,142	1,230	2,700	290	4,600
La Courneuve	-	1,620	-	720	2,400	48,600
Fosses-Saint Witz	-	150	14,870	-	-	-
Garges-les-Gonesse	-	318	3,738	-	-	-
Gonesse	600	5,390	75,010	-	-	-
Goussainville	-	189	446	-	5,634	25,360
Marly-la Ville	-	-	-	960	14,180	20,000
Meaux	6,850	1,346	2,130	1,590	410	1,250
Mitry-Mory	970	2,130	6,865	960	200	47,500
Lagny	3,180	1,020	3,600	-	-	7,130
Neuilly-Plaisance and Neuilly-sur-Marne	2,800	2,500	3,100	3,220	-	-
Noisiel	13,300	2,026	4,177	1,010	450	150
Noisy-leGrand	-	-	-	5,140	295	940
Sarcelles	1,550	2,650	11,350	5,840	4,590	3,740
Torcy	-	-	-	-	300	1,060
Tremblay-les-Gonesse	-	-	-	-	720	5,390
Villepinte	1,900	430	1,500	1,930	1,300	15,240
Total	55,210	76,610	135,920	28,780	38,470	229,980

1) Not including Citroën which obtained approval for 180,000m² of useable floor space on 14th December, 1972.

By 1975-76, the capacity of No. 1 Air Terminal will be 10 million passengers per year or between 25 and 30,000 passengers per day. By 1985-90 the daily figure will have risen to between 120,000 and 140,000, since the forecasts are for 40 to 50 million passengers per year. By that time, between 70,000 and 80,000 employees will be commuting to the airport.

These figures underline the importance of access, by road and rail. An inter-ministerial committee in May 1970 gave special attention to this topic and the joint report presented by the Préfets of the Picardy and Paris Regions in March 1972 reviewed possible solutions. One possibility would be to try and cater for all journeys to and from the airport to be made by car. This would result in about 300,000 trips a day and about 36,000 in peak hours and necessitate motorways with 21 lanes, an altogether unrealistic proposition. This indicates the need for alternative means of access, and in particular fixed-track mass transit.

Roads

As things stand virtually the only access to Charles-de-Gaulle in its initial stages will be the A1 motorway. As there are risks of congestion on this route, a new operating procedure will be introduced. The slip roads will be closed when the motorway is congested. This makes it essential to bring the B3 motorway into service as soon as possible so as to "irrigate" the whole north-eastern sector of the city.

As far as roads are concerned, motorway B3 is the principal means of access to the airport and it came into service in 1974.

Railways

The first objective of the rail planners is a branch line between Charles-de-Gaulle and the S.N.C.F. station at Aulnay on the Paris (Gare du Nord) to Soissons line. Later on, a connection will be made between the Soissons line and the Regional Express Metro being tunnelled under Paris, thereby linking the airport with the main economic centres of the capital.

A decree recognising this line as being in the public interest was issued in June 1973, and the Chairman of the S.N.C.F. was subsequently asked to ensure that the line is opened in April 1976 instead of 1977 as originally planned.

The cost of the rail link is estimated at 324 million francs of which the Paris Airport Authority will probably pay 70 million francs for about five kilometres of track from the airport boundary to the air passenger terminals.

subsequently asked to ensure that the line is opened in April 1976 instead of 1977 as originally planned.

The cost of the rail link is estimated at 324 million francs of which the Paris Airport Authority will probably pay 70 million francs for about five kilometres of track from the airport boundary to the air passenger terminals.

The 28 kilometres from the Gare du Nord to Charles-de-Gaulle will take nineteen minutes by through train and twenty-eight minutes by stopping train. Both services will run every fifteen minutes. Airport employees will thus be provided with mass transit from the large residential areas being developed in the north-east suburbs of Paris.

The Paris Airport Authority estimates that when the rail link comes into service in 1976, the quality of service to Charles-de-Gaulle should be similar to that now provided to Orly, and that traffic on the A1 motorway should be at present levels.

In the more distant future a high-speed aerotrain link may be provided between Charles-de-Gaulle and Orly. The importance of such a service was underlined by the Paris Chamber of Commerce and Industry in 1973.

CONCLUSIONS

No real problems are expected to be raised by demands for housing when the airport opens or in the years immediately afterwards. However some senior staff transferring from Orly may find it difficult to find the quality of accommodation they are accustomed to. The potential of the airport to stimulate economic activity means that it will be necessary to regulate companies locating within it and to ensure that their activities are related to air traffic. Firms sited at neighbouring industrial estates will need controlling too. The importance of doing this does not yet seem to have been grasped in neighbouring communities.

A mass transit system is even more necessary at Charles-de-Gaulle than at Orly as there is no way of catering for air passengers and airport employees by road transport alone. It is therefore imperative that the deadline for the completion of the Aulnay-Charles-de-Gaulle railway be kept. Failure to do so will jeopardise the development of the airport. Regulations restraining building in areas affected by air traffic noise must be observed, notwith-standing the damage they may cause to the economic development of some towns. The recent government measures involving financial aid should help the worst hit places to adapt.

CHAPTER 9

A PROJECT SUBSEQUENTLY ABANDONNED: LONDON

Stanley Smith
Principal Planner, Third London Airport Directorate,
Department of the Environment, London, England

INTRODUCTION

Maplin is not simply the story of an airport. The project
involves the relocation elsewhere of defence establishments sited
in the hitherto relatively remote Maplin area. It comprises a
major land reclamation scheme, the building, manning and operation
of an international airport and deep-sea port, the provision of new
motorways and railways, and the rapid building up of a new town
within a regional planning framework. The implementation period
for the project as a whole will extend into the next century.

This paper describes the general scope of the project, identi-
fies some of its likely impacts and lists the main objectives.

THE BASIS OF THE MAPLIN DECISION

Following the Government's decision, after a public inquiry,
not to go ahead with the development of Stansted as London's
third airport the Roskill Commission was set up to inquire into the
timing of the need for a four runway airport to serve the London
area and to recommend a site. The Commission concluded that the
first runway at a new airport should be brought into operation
during 1980 and narrowed down the possible sites to four including
Maplin, then known as Foulness. The Commission's final preference
for Cublington emerged from a painstaking analysis of a wide range
or factors. Considerable weight was attached to the value of air
travellers' time and to the argument that a site which was convenient
and financially attractive to users could most readily draw traffic
away from airports where there were environmental problems. The
Government took a different view, implicitly placing a higher value

on the environment of places where people lived and on regional planning considerations than on air-travel time. Their decision in April 1971 was in favour of a coastal site - Maplin.

The decision meant that the new airport would not spread the problem of aircraft noise to yet more existing or potential residential areas. As a corollary to this the Government's future policy for London's airports, announced in July 1971, was designed to secure that Maplin's capacity would be used so as to give the maximum benefit to those around existing airports who suffer from noise. Thus no new runways are to be constructed in the foreseeable future at Heathrow, Gatwick, Luton or Stansted. It is expected that, when Maplin is operational, stricter limits on air traffic movements and other restraints to reduce the impact of noise will be imposed at Heathrow and Gatwick. It is possible that Stansted will then be closed altogether and that Luton will not continue in use as a major public transport airport.

The extensive land reclamation scheme needed for Maplin provided opportunities for sea-port developments which could take advantage of the motorway, rail links and urban infrastructure which an air port would need in any case. Government approval in principle has been given for the Port of London Authority to prepare detailed plans for a deep-water oil terminal and container port.

An airport at Maplin was seen as an essential component of a regional plan for the South East. This had been in preparation during the course of the Roskill Commission's studies and proposed that South Essex - the area to the landward of the Maplin Sands - should be developed as a major regional growth area. The main reasons behind this proposal were:

a) South Essex is conveniently located to provide new housing and jobs to relieve housing stress in East London;

b) it is an area with generally less local employment opportunities than other parts of the region and, traditionally, large numbers have had to face long journeys-to-work, mainly to relatively low-paid clerical jobs in London;

c) South Essex is fairly extensively developed, with an existing population of about 600,000, but many of its urban and semi-urbanised areas have a poor layout derived from periods of haphazard land-sales dating back to past agricultural depressions. Since the War, much has been done by Basildon New Town Corporation and the local authorities to consolidate and improve the urban areas but there is still a basic need for improvement and expansion of the urban infrastructure.

The airport will provide the area with the necessary new employment base and bring a massive improvement in road and rail communications which will help redress the imbalance between South Essex and the hitherto more-favoured parts of the region particularly those to the north and west of London. The Government's acceptance of the regional plan as a framework for guiding the broad future distribution of population and employment changes in the South East was announced in October 1971.

The Maplin decision, therefore, encompassed a range of inter-related planning policies. Reflecting this, the Government's arrangements for planning and implementation are co-ordinated by the Secretary of State for the Environment. They are designed to secure close and effective co-operation between central Government and the main executive agencies on all aspects of the project.

PRESENT STATUS OF THE PROJECT

The Maplin Development Act received Royal Assent on 25th October, 1973: it provides powers and sets up the Maplin Development Authority to reclaim land at Maplin and to make areas available for the airport and seaport. It does not deal with any of the supporting transportation or urban infrastructure.

Section 2 of the Act requires that, before reclamation can begin at Maplin, a report on the project shall be laid before Parliament and an Order authorising the date at which reclamation can be commenced shall be obtained. The report, upon which work is now in hand, will incorporate the results of a wide ranging reappraisal by Government, after consultation with the executive agencies involved, of the need for and timing of the whole Maplin project. It will embrace a review of the existing forecasts of air traffic demands and will look forward to 1990. Airport solutions alternative to building a third London airport at Maplin will be examined together with their associated transportation and planning implications. The Government have, however, made clear their view that Maplin currently appears the best solution.

In parallel with this reappraisal, planning of the Maplin pro - ject, including the transportation and urbanisation elements, is being pushed ahead though no construction contracts will be let un- less and until the Section 2 Order is obtained. The shift from a 1980 to a 1982 planning date for airport opening announced by the Secretary of State for the Environment on 12th September, 1973 was consequent upon increasingly detailed development of the network for the project. This showed that the job could not be done by 1980; there was no decision deliberately to postpone the project

by two years. In fact any let-up in investigatory planning and
design work could soon close the option for a 1982 opening.

THE MAPLIN PROJECT

The Maplin Sands themselves are about 12,000 hectares in extent
located at the eastern end of the Southend peninsula - a geographical
fact which immediately restricts the catchment area for the airport's labour and urban support facilities. The sands are covered
with water to depths varying between roughly 2 m and 6 m at high-
water of ordinary spring tides and have been used for many years as
an artillery range and for cockling and fishing. They are also rich
in bird-life being particularly well-known as a winter feeding and
roosting area for Brent Geese which migrate from Siberia. The adjoining rivers and creeks are important for sailing, with an inter-
nationally-known centre at Burnham-on-Crouch, and for oysters.

The first-stage reclamation will provide about 2,200 hectares
for a two-runway airport and 1,000 hectares for the deep-sea oil
terminal and container berths. If the airport is ultimately developed to four runways, a second-stage reclamation could bring the
total reclaimed area to about 7,500 hectares. The necessity to
create a hydraulically acceptable shape at both stages will produce
areas surplus to specific airport and seaport requirements. This
extra land will be available for a variety of recreational, commercial or other purposes but there is no intention of establishing
heavy industries such as steel and petro-chemicals which could be
better located in less-prosperous regions of the country. The reclamation process will involve construction of a sea-wall behind
which levels will be raised by the use of sand. Part of this material will be obtained by dredging the proposed deep channel to the
seaport. This will accomodate 300,000 ton - and ultimately 500,000
ton - tankers which, through the new oil terminal, will help supply
the Thames estuary refineries.

The ecological aspects of the reclamation operations are re-
ceiving specially close attention. The basic hydraulic effects -
possible changes in tidal currents, water levels, siltation, etc -
are being investigated for different reclamation shapes on a recently
completed purpose-built hydraulic model. This is a large-scale
(1/1000 horizontal) model and is essentially a detailed design tool,
the feasibility of the project having already been established by
earlier hydraulic studies. It will also be used to test the effects
of possible future dredging of aggregates needed for construction
purposes; methods of discharging treated sewage effluents both from
the airport and from the existing and new urban areas; and the

feasibility of leaving open a channel to the sea for pleasure boating. Two complementary research programmes are in train on the effects of the reclamation on wildlife, the one aimed at conservation objectives and the other at possible bird-strike hazards at the airport. They include intensive studies of bird behaviour - feeding habits and movement patterns - and experiments in transplanting the Zostera upon which the Brent Geese feed. The intention is to establish new nature reserves elsewhere on the east coast and in North Kent and to develop management techniques for increasing their wildlife carrying capacity. Scientific liaison arrangements on fisheries, water and air pollution have been set up and the need to mount specific research efforts in these fields is being kept under continuous review.

Construction of the airport control tower and the first runway and terminal buildings will begin as soon as the requisite areas of reclaimed land are available and suitably consolidated. The siting of the airport within the general location of the Maplin Sands was determined after a large-scale public participation exercise on the choice of sites for the runways. A consultation document(1) was published showing four options each costed in respect of reclamation and air passenger and journey-to-work travel times. The site eventually selected was not the cheapest: extra costs were accepted in the interests of reducing the numbers of houses affected by the predicted noise shadow.

When fully developed the airport could be handling upwards of 100 million passengers a year and will become a substantial employment generator. There are therefore major movements problems to be solved. Studies are now well in hand embracing:

a) air passenger movement by means of a high-speed rail link connecting directly to a nodal point (King's Cross) in London's rail, underground and road transport systems;

b) air passenger and air and sea freight movements by means of a new motorway linking with London's existing and proposed primary road system and with the regional strategic road network, including a proposed lower Thames crossing;

c) journey-to-work movements by proposed new roads, by an extention of the existing London-Southend electrified commuter railway (which will also handle port container traffic and air freight) and by possible new public transport systems serving proposed urban areas;

d) internal airport movements including inter-terminal movements of inter-lining passengers.

1) Maplin Airport: Choice of sites for runways, Department of the Environment: London, April 1972.

The objective is to devise a compatible set of movement facilities involving the minimum of inter-changes and making the new airport especially convenient for passengers and as a place to which to travel to work. As regards a possible route for the London-Maplin motorway and high-speed rail link, which are to be built side-by-side, an investigation of feasible corridors, covering civil engineering, traffic, and environmental factors, has been completed and the possible options were the subjects of public consultations[1] carried out between July and October 1973. The results of those are now being studied and a decision on the choice of route for further detailed survey and design will be announced early in 1974.

Effects on population and employment growth and on journey-to-work patterns will begin to be noticeable as construction work commences on the airport, seaport, motorway, high-speed link, and on the new urban roads and utility services that the area will need. Air passenger and cargo traffic at the airport is expected to build up rapidly and so will employment for which year-by-year estimates have been made related to forecast air passenger traffic and aircraft movements. The most likely estimate, taking account of factors discussed in the Civil Aviation Authority 1973 report[2] on air traffic in the London area, is that by about 10 years after opening date direct employment could be around 50,000. The labour requirements for the seaport will be much smaller even when fully developed. In addition to direct employment at the airport there will be jobs in a variety of ancillary industries such as hotels and freight forwarding and in firms supplying the airport with goods and services, e.g. catering and cleaning. A special study of how far Maplin airport will also attract new industrial and commercial enterprises and encourage the expansion of those existing concerns which could benefit from a near-airport location has been carried out for the Department of the Environment by Economic Consultants Ltd. Their investigations of a number of major airports, including Heathrow and foreign airports, suggested that there are very few firms, other than airport ancillary businesses, who actually need to be sited near an international airport. They concluded that the airport itself would have only a marginal effect, but that the area would become more attractive to industry and commerce because of major improvements in communications and the general upswing in building and population growth. Subject to the Government's regional policies, the key factor which will determine the future growth rates both in airport

1) The Maplin Project: Surface Access Corridor. A consultation document, Department of the Environment: London, July 1973.

2) Forecasts of Air Traffic & Capacity at Airport in the London Area, Civil Aviation Authority, London, May 1973

ancillary and induced employment and in the area's existing industries will be labour availability - as indeed is very much the position in other favoured locations in South East England. Present
indications are that Maplin will mean that some 250-300,000 additional people may have to be provided for in South East Essex,
broadly during the last two decades of the century.

Thus an essential requirement in implementing the Maplin proposals will be to monitor and influence the area's economic and
social system so as to keep its various component sub-systems in
reasonable balance in what could become a relatively highly-charged
growth situation. There are a number of ways in which public sector
intervention can help in this:

a) the Government's powers over the location of industry and
    offices can, if necessary, be used to constrain labour de-
    mand by restricting new building to those developments
    which have essential ties to the area;

b) land-use controls and public investment in roads and public
    transport can be aimed at encouraging ripple-effect changes
    in journey-to-work patterns so that the impact of a rela-
    tively highly-localised labour demand at Maplin can be
    spread over a much wider area - including London itself;

c) immigration into the area can be encouraged by the provision
    of new housing for sale and to rent and by investment in an
    attractively high-level of services.

There are existing powers for policy action in these fields but
the two main Government-financed executive agencies which are being
specially set up will have important roles. Firstly, the new Maplin
Development Authority, which was formally set up on 6th November,
under the Maplin Development Act 1973, will not only reclaim the
Maplin Sands and make areas available to the British Airports
Authority and the Port of London Authority for building the airport
and seaport but it will have landlord functions over other potentially large areas of reclaimed land. It also has powers, for
example, to contribute to the expenses of local authorities and
statutory undertakers occasioned by the requirements of Maplin.
Secondly, a substantial area of South East Essex is to be developed
by a new town corporation which is to be set up under the New Towns
Act as an integral part of the Maplin project. Consultations(1) on the
extent of the area to be designated for this purpose took place at
the same time as consultations on route options for the London-Maplin
motorway and high-speed link. The new town corporation will provide

1) The Maplin Project: Designation Area for the New Town, a con-
    sultation document, Department of the Environment: London,
    July 1973.

141

an organisation with a comprehensive, detailed design capability and with landlord functions in the field of urban management. Specifically in the Maplin context, it will be able to build houses to rent both to assist the rapid recruitment of airport labour and, through London's existing new and expanded town arrangements, to provide new jobs and homes for London families in housing need.

SUMMING-UP

As now constituted the Maplin project embraces the largest group of developments currently being planned in this country. From the outset the Government's approach has been that the project as a whole - the airport and related developments, the road and rail links, urban development - must be tackled within an imaginative and coherent overall operational plan and carried through with the central objective of creating a first-class environment for living.

"On 21st March, 1974 the Secretary of State for Trade announced that he had set in train a re-appraisal of the Maplin project for a Third London Airport. The report(1) of this reappraisal was published on 18th July, 1974.
In the light of the findings that emerged, the Government considered that the case for a new airport at Maplin had not been established and it was decided to abandon it".

---

1) Maplin: Review of Airport Project, Department of Trade, London HMSO July 1974.

Chapter 10

Part 1

THE EXPANSION OF EXISTING AIRPORTS: FRANKFURT

K. Dehn,
Flughafen Frankfurt Main Aktiengesellschaft and
J. Meise
Battelle-Institut, Frankfurt-Main

INTRODUCTION

This paper surveys the effects of Frankfurt airport on economic
and urban development. It gives only a first appraisal of the issue
and is written from the point of view of the airport authority. The
first part contains a description of the airport's development up to
1973 and the expansion that is expected during the next five to ten
years. The second part contains a discussion of the airport's location within an air transport network, its market area, its economic
influence as a large centre of employment and a focus of high quality
of transport services, and its influence on urban development. A
third section assesses the effects of the expansion of the airport on
traffic, employment, revenue, and urban development. Reference is
also made to the complex of political institutions involved in airport planning.

THE GROWTH OF THE AIRPORT

Civil aviation began in the Rhein-Main region in 1924. In 1937
an airport was opened on a 300 hectare field on the site of the present Rhein-Main airport. Since then further expansion has followed
increases in transport demand (Figures 1 and 2).

After World War II the development of the airport proceeded at
a remarkable pace. One million passengers were handled in 1957, two
million in 1960, four million in 1965, and finally, in 1972 more than
11 million. Parallel increases occurred in airfreight and airmail
(Table 1). Increases in employment followed a similar growth curve
and today some 25,000 people work for firms and institutions clustered around the airport (Table 2).

Figure 1

DEVELOPMENT 1937 - 1946 - EVOLUTION DE 1937 A 1946

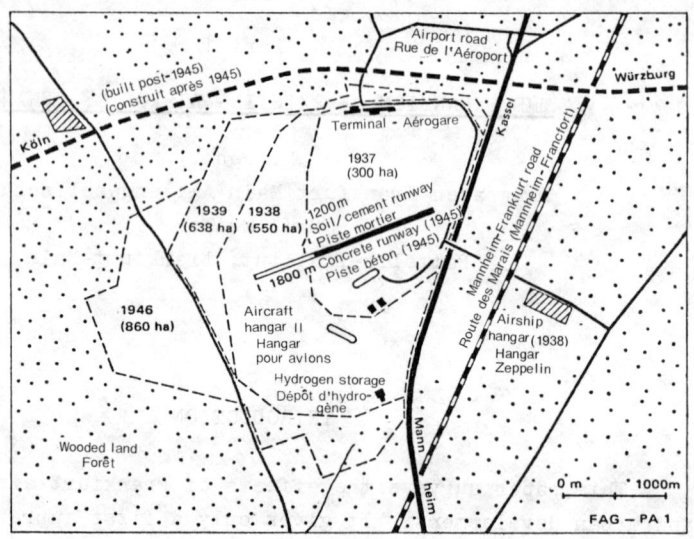

Figure 2

DEVELOPMENT 1946 - 1971 - EVOLUTION DE 1946 A 1971

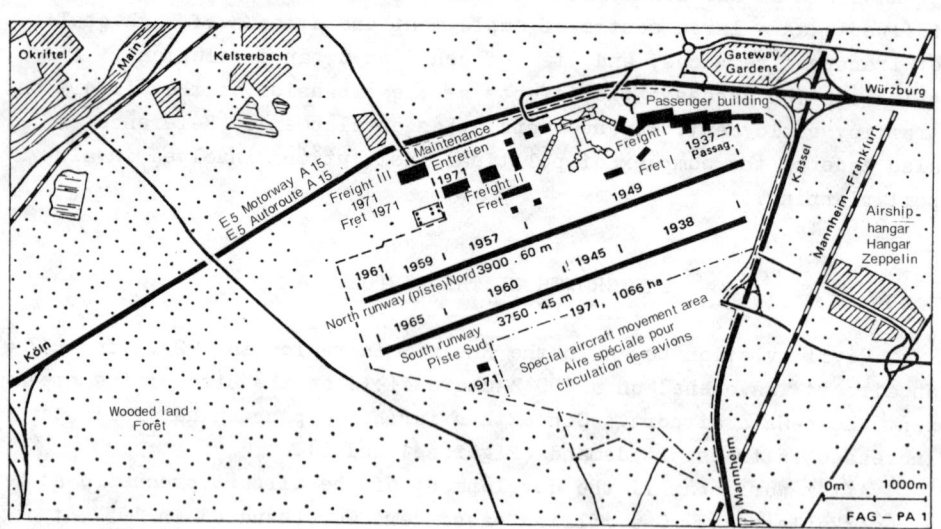

144

Table 1

DEVELOPMENT OF AIRTRAFFIC AT FRANKFURT INTERNATIONAL AIRPORT
(1950-1972)

In millions

	Development Data			
	Passengers (pers.)	Freight	Mail (t)	Movements (mov.)
1950	0.195(1)	0.004	0.002	0.013(2)
1953	0.525	0.011	0.004	0.027(2)
1956	0.997	0.017	0.006	0.047(2)
1960	2.172	0.047	0.012	0.108
1963	3.454	0.087	0.031	0.115
1966	5.663	0.159	0.043	0.149
1970	9.402	0.327	0.059	0.216
1971	10.585	0.353	0.063	
1972	11.611	0.398	0.066	0.227

1) 1950 without transit.
2) Special services excluded.

Table 2

DEVELOPMENT OF EMPLOYMENT AT FRANKFURT AIRPORT

In thousands

Year	Employment Groups					
	FAG-Airport Enterprise	Airtransport Companies	Other Commerical Enterpris.	Public Services	Others (1)	Total
1950	0.1	(2)				
1955	0.4					
1960	0.9	1.7	0.7	1.1	1.9	6.3
1965	1.6	4.4	1.2	1.5	1.6	10.3
1970	3.7	9.7	3.8	1.9	1.2	20.3

1) Except building firms.
2) No data available.

EXPANSION PLANS

The development of aviation at Rhein-Main Airport is foreseen
to be undertaken in three stages: from 1973-1980 the construction
of runway "West", the rearrangement of the existing runways, the
construction of a freight centre and the extension of the passenger
terminal.(1)

Figure 3

FUTURE DEVELOPMENT 1972 - 1985
EVOLUTION FUTURE, DE 1972 A 1985

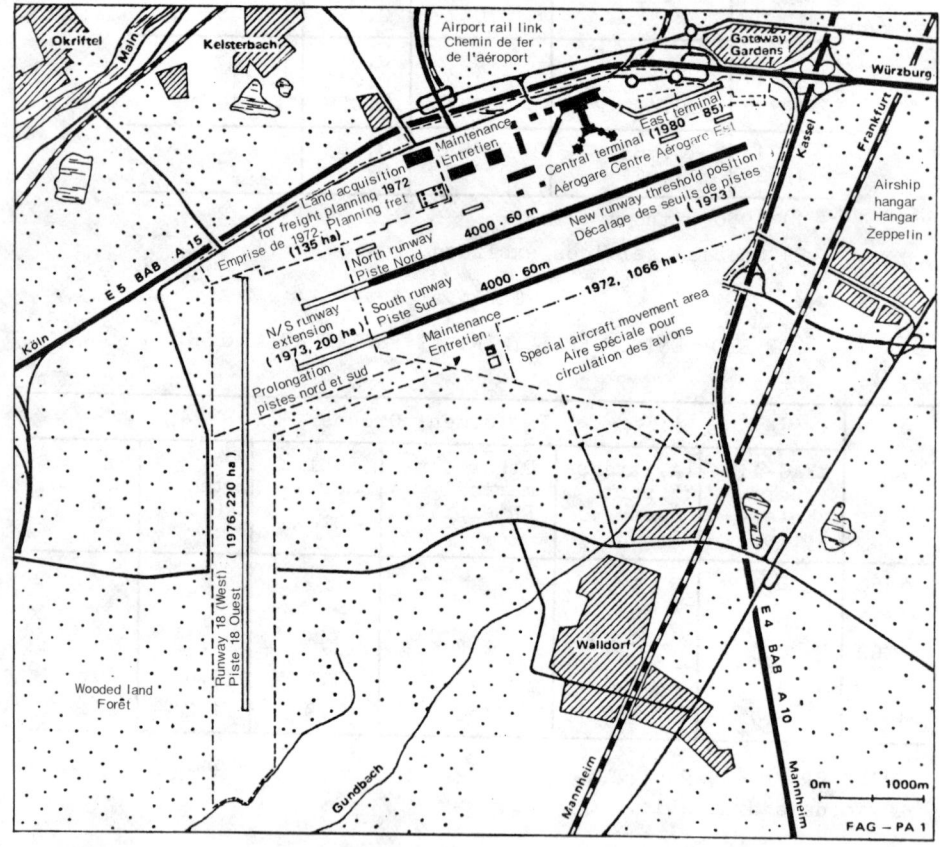

---

1) The details of this expansion are: a) rearrangement of the existing parallel runways would reduce the vulnerability of Frankfurt
airport to bad weather; b) the new freight centre would increase
the annual capacity of the airport by 380,000 tons; c) the new
runway "West" would increase the capacity of Frankfurt airport
from 45 to 75 movements per hour; and d) a new passenger terminal
would permit the number of people handled to rise from 30 million
to 45 million per year.

Existing expansion plans, though blocked by public opposition
are agreed upon by the legislators; and construction is expected to
begin in 1973-1974. The second and third stages are, however, neither
clearly defined nor in sight of realisation. This study is therefore
based on the first-stage expansion plan (Figure 3).

THE EFFECTS OF THE AIRPORT ON DEVELOPMENT

Frankfurt airport's rapid development is largely explained by
its location on international and national airways. It is not only
an important hub for international travel and a transit station for
40 per cent of its passengers but a depot for freight and airmail.
In European air traffic Frankfurt ranked third behind London-Heathrow
and Paris-Orly in 1972 in passengers, second in freight and first in
airmail. Among German airports Frankfurt's central location made it
first in national traffic with about 31 per cent of all passengers,
67 per cent of all freight and 54 per cent of all airmail in 1972.

Growth of air traffic at Frankfurt airport may be seen as a
stimulus and an effect of regional development. Rhein-Main has one
of the fastest rates of growth of population and gross product of all
German regions. It is a centre of industry and dominated by firms
in chemicals, electronics, machinery, optics, furs and leather producing high-value goods for export. It is also a centre for activities such as banking, administration, fairs and consultancy which
rely on good access and on information. No single set of regional
boundaries can be defined that would be meaningful for all these
effects. A region of about 12,000 square kilometres embracing four
million people and two million jobs and extending between 30 and 50 km
from the airport has however been used as a basis for discussion in
this paper (Figure 4 and Table 3). The largest and most populous
cities in this region are clustered around Frankfurt airport.

Table 3

EMPLOYMENT STRUCTURE AND POPULATION OF THE REGION

In million persons

Year	Popu-lation	Employment				
		Agricult.	Industry	Services	Others	Total
1961	2.93	0.05	0.74	0.31	0.34	1.44
1969	3.39	0.04	0.76	0.30	0.39	1.49

While this region provides a convenient reference for analysis,
neither the transport market nor the economic and urbanisation influences radiating from the airport are completely contained within it.

Figure 4

THE REGIONAL SITUATION

PLAN DE SITUATION REGIONAL

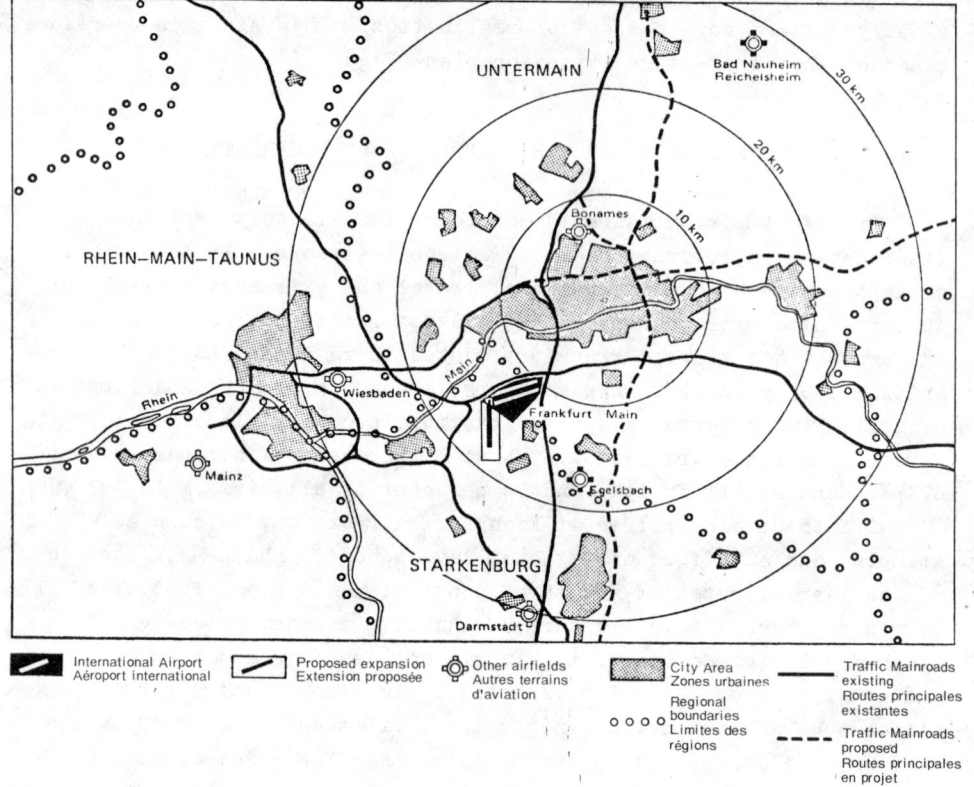

International Airport Aéroport international	Proposed expansion Extension proposée	Other airfields Autres terrains d'aviation	City Area Zones urbaines	Traffic Mainroads existing Routes principales existantes	
			Regional boundaries Limites des régions	Traffic Mainroads proposed Routes principales en projet	

THE AIRPORT'S MARKET AREA

Passengers with origins or destinations at Frankfurt airport comprised 58 per cent of all passengers passing through the airport in 1971. About 60 per cent of passengers going abroad originated in the region, predominantly in the city of Frankfurt. Nearly 80 per cent of arriving passengers were travelling to places within the region, again, most of them in Frankfurt.

Of all the freight passing through Frankfurt in 1970, 80 per cent originated or was consigned to the airport and about half of this had a trip end in the region. The special rates available for some goods mean that the market area of the airport extends as far as Austria to the south and to Scandinavia to the north.

The pattern of distribution of airmail is, as might be expected, much wider. Less than 50 per cent of the total amount handled at Frankfurt airport has its origins or destination within the region.

THE ECONOMIC INFLUENCE OF THE AIRPORT

An airport is an assembly of various firms and institutions. At Frankfurt their concentration in a relatively small locality creates an important employment centre comprising the airport authority, Flughafen Frankfurt Main AG (FAG), the airlines (including the home base of Lufthansa the German national airline), other commercial enterprises such as oil companies, freight forwarding companies, retailers, restaurants and taxi firms. In addition to this there are such public services as customs, police, post office, air traffic control and weather observation. With 21,162 employees in 1971, the airport complex was one of the four largest enterprises in the region, paying about DM.430 million in wages (Tables 2 and 4).

This wages roll provided the income of about 15,000 households or 40,000 people, so that together with the people required to serve them, the airport population is estimated to have comprised some 60,000 people in 1971. Furthermore over half of these people live near the airport in Frankfurt and its surroundings, a fact that underlines the dependence of some of the smaller communities on the airport (Table 5).

Employers at the airport buy goods and services and have to maintain and renew their buildings, and it is estimated that about 60 per cent of these expenditures are revenues of firms within the region (Table 6).

Other non-aviation related goods and services bought by firms at the airport were estimated to have generated an additional DM.225 million in revenues in 1970 of which 70 per cent may flow into the region.

Some revenues can neither be exclusively attributed to the existence of the airport nor fully accounted to the regional economy. Thus revenues collected in the region from passengers, freight and airmail departing from the airport are assumed to be distributed over a larger territory. However, it may be argued that such revenues express the airport's importance for the region. It may also be argued that tourist spending by air passengers staying in the region is not completely dependent upon the airport (Table 7).

All these revenues can be expected to release much larger money flows into the region. A multiplier of about two seems likely. Commercial firms, banks, consultants, stock markets and other central institutions that rely on fast access or exchange of information account for other less easily measured economic effects of the airport. The same is true of industry that exports by air. The importance of Frankfurt airport to such enterprises can be described only in very general terms. Yet many such firms would not be in the region and especially in the city of Frankfurt if an airport with a high level of service was not there too.

Table 4

WAGES AND SALARIES

	1970		1971(1)	
	million DM	%	million DM	%
Frankfurt Airport Company	73	21	94	19
Airlines	199	56	304	61
Commercial Enterprises	51	14	62	12
Public Services	32	9	42	8
Total Airport(2)	355	100	502	100

1) Estimates.

2) Excl. Special Benefits.

Table 5

DISTRIBUTION OF EMPLOYMENT AND "AIRPORT POPULATION" (1970)

Distance km	Airport Employment(1) in '000	"Airport Population" in '000
0-5	3.6	14.4
5-15	11.2	44.8
15-20	0.2	0.8
0-20(2)	15.0	60.0

1) Accounted in selected communities (1970).

2) Above 80 per cent of airport employment.

Table 6

EXPENDITURES FOR GOODS AND SERVICES (1970, 1971)

	1970		1971(2)	
	million DM	%	million DM	%
Frankfurt Airport Company				
Construction	220.6	50	372.9	63
Operation	72.2	16	72.5	12
Airlines				
Public Services	89.9(3)	20	102.9(3)	17
Commercial Enterprises				
Other Investments(1)	59.3	14	46.2	8
Total	442.0	100	594.5	100

1) Except FAG.

2) Estimations.

3) Airlines, Public Services and Commercial Enterprises.

Table 7

REVENUES OF COMMERCIAL ACTIVITIES AT THE AIRPORT (1971, estim.)

Revenues from	in million DM	in %
Passengers	770.0	49.2
Freight	511.0	32.7
Airmail	34.6	2.2
Tourism	140.0	8.9
Concessionaires	97.9	6.3
Personnel of Airlines (Lay-overs)	3.8	0.2
Cars sold to Foreigners	4.0	0.2
Transport to Airport	5.0	0.3
Total	1,566.8	100.0

THE AIRPORT AND URBAN GROWTH

The various firms at the airport, the airport itself, and its highway and public transit links make up a sub-regional centre. The effects of this centre on the environment extend as widely as 400 square kilometres and are potentially an influence on urban development. However despite the existence of noise-countour and building obstruction maps, the communities along the flight paths seldom restrict development.

The airport's influence on population distribution is shown in Table 5. People are gravitating towards it and causing development especially in the smaller neighbouring communities.

CONCLUSIONS

Frankfurt airport is an important pole in regional development and is vital to the economic life of the city of Frankfurt and its neighbouring communities.

The total of DM.2.3 billion that can be associated with the airport in 1970 was a significant contribution to the gross product of both the region (DM.44.1 billion) and the city of Frankfurt (DM.17.8 billion) in 1970-1971 (Table 8).

Expansion of the airport

As things stand the maximum capacity of Frankfurt airport is 250,000 air movements a year or 45 movements per hour. This is

151

Table 8

AIRPORT'S CONTRIBUTION TO GROSS PRODUCTS (1970, 1971)

In billion DM

	1970	1971
Airport:		
Wages + Salaries	0.4	0.5
Goods + Services	0.5	0.6
Commercial	1.4	1.6
Total:	2.3	2.7
Gross Products:		
State of Hesse	64.3(1)	69.0(1)
City of Frankfurt	17.8(1)	19.3(1)
Airport Region	44.1(1)	-

1) Preliminary data.

called "level 1". After expansion, capacity is expected to rise to 350,000 movements a year or 75 per hour. This is called "level 2" (Figure 5). Changes in scheduling air traffic control and aircraft size could affect these capacities but it has been assumed they will not change significantly.

Figure 5

IMPACT APPROACH

ESTIMATION DE L'IMPACT

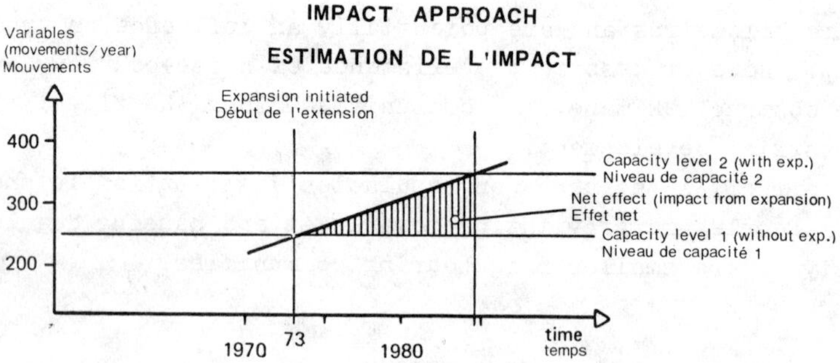

Effects of the expansion of air traffic

Passenger, freight and airmail movements will be forecasted separately on the assumption that there are no limits on capacity. Subsequent combination of these movements will provide rough estimates of the numbers of passengers, tons of freight and airmail to be expected and the times when levels 1 and 2 will be reached. It is assumed that in the period 1973-75-85 the growth of air transport in Germany will follow world trends; that Frankfurt airport will increase its share of national air traffic; that domestic air traffic will stagnate; that international traffic will increase; and that a growing proportion of flights will involve jumbo jets. Table 9 show forecasts of air traffic demand made on this basis in 1972.

Table 9

TRAFFIC DEMAND 1973-1985 (CURRENT IN 1972)

	1972	1973	1976	1980	1985
Movements (in '000s)	226.1	264.0	296.0	327.0	359.0
Passengers (in millions)	11.6	14.0	20.2	30.0	45.0
Freight (in '000 t)	397.8	500.0	825.0	1500.0	2600.0
Mail (in '000 t)	66.4	74.0	92.0	115.0	140.0

Effects of expansion on employment

Expansion is likely to affect airport associated employment located at the airport, airport associated employment located elsewhere and secondary airport associated employment in the region. No data is available for the second two categories but forecasts of the first are given in Table 10.

Table 10

AIRPORT ASSOCIATED EMPLOYMENT, "AIRPORT POPULATION"
AND VISITORS (1972-1985)

In 1,000 persons

	Airport Associated Employment					Total Airport Population (3)	Visitors
	Frankfurt Airport	Airlines	Other Companies	Public Services	Total (1)		
1972	4.8	10.0	4.4	2.0	21.2	63.6	1.2(2)
1973	-	-	-	-	28.5	85.5	2.5
1976-77	7.6	16.8	6.9	2.7	34.0	102.0	3.2
1980	-	-	-	-	41.0	123.0	3.5
1985	10.5	25.5	10.5	4.0	50.0	150.0	4.0

1) Except building firms and others.

2) Only March-September.

3) Average multiplier 3.0.

Economic effects of airport expansion

The four main employment groups are assumed to maintain their present relationships and a forecast of the gross wages and salaries attributable to each in 1977 is given in Table 11. It is expected that increases in the airport's gross productivity will follow the regional trends from 1973 to 1985 and that growth rates will be about 4.5-4.9 per cent per year.

Table 11

WAGES AND SALARIES OF AIRPORT EMPLOYMENT (1971-85)

In million DM

	Wages and Salaries(1)(2)				
	FAG-Airport Enterprise	Airlines	Commercial Enterprises	Public Services	Total
1972	94	304	62	42	502
1973 1977(3) 1980 1985	200	532	133	85	950

1) Increase in income following the trend 1965-70.
2) Price level 1970.
3) No change in share of employment groups.

It is assumed that the distribution of households and of their purchasing power will follow present trends (Table 5) but that there will be some shift towards those communities that are accessible by rapid transit.

The demand for goods and services by undertakings at the airport is a function of air traffic. The airport authority will be forced to build a new runway, freight and passenger facilities. Other firms will have to enlarge or replace their buildings too. For purpose of this study the share of expenditures on these goods and services within the region is expected to stay at 60 per cent with 60-75 per cent of this going to the city of Frankfurt.

Commercial activities will be generated at the airport and outside it. In this study it has been assumed that: the average revenue generated per commercial (airport) employee will be equivalent to 1971-1972 plus an increase for higher purchasing power; that there will be an increase in revenue due to commercial development; and that 70 per cent of total revenue will be distributed within the region.

Urban development

Further development is expected beyond a 1,000 bed hotel planned for 1973. Restaurants, conference rooms and office buildings are likely. However, lack of space within the airport site will force out developments that do not have to be within it.

Increases in air movements will increase noise nuisance along flight paths and make it necessary to restrict development in certain areas. This will cause conflict since the affected communities are experiencing rapid increases in population. Restricting their growth will increase pressure for development in adjacent areas.

Following earlier conclusions about the regional distribution of airport population, expansion will generate a significant demand for housing and related services especially in the smaller communities in the vicinity of the airport.

Uncertainty remains about the influence of airports on the distribution of commercial firms. It can, however, be assumed, that the airport will contribute to the further concentration of certain types of industries and tertiary activities in the Rhein-Main area.

Political-institutional impact

The number of planning institutions whose remit covers the airport or its surroundings is as follows:

the airport:
    two regional planning authorities
    two counties
    six communities

the airport region:
    two states
    three regional planning authorities
    six counties
    100 communities (approximately).

With a view to improving the quality of future decisions the airport authority has proposed a planning body that would help to bind together this galaxy of government institutions and co-ordinate regional and air transport planning.

Part 2

THE EXPANSION OF EXISTING AIRPORTS: ZURICH

V. Touzin,
Cantonal Planning Authority

INTRODUCTION

This study describes the relationship of Zurich airport to its surroundings. It has been limited to data that lends itself to statistical analysis except for the results of the referendum on the airport's expansion.

Although it is not easy to trace an airport's influence, the technique of organising data by successive geographical rings permits some insight to be gained into the complex relations linking an airport to the communities around it. In this case the surrounding communities have been divided into four rings, with a subsequent division within each ring (Map 1).

The first two rings were established mainly on the basis of distance from Kloten, whereas the third and outer rings were delineated to reflect their main functions, urban centres and commuting ties respectively.

LAND USE

The ratio between farm land, excluding woods and unproductive land, and built-up areas provides a useful index of land use in a developing region. Table 1 shows the changing basis of this relationship in the rings around Kloten. The same data is presented in a simplified form in Figure 1.

The statistics used correspond for the most part to actual land use during the second half of the 1960s though they do not include small, isolated areas. Despite these qualifications the data is

Map 1 - Carte 1

LIMITS AND SUBDIVISIONS OF THE REGION SURVEYED SURROUNDING THE KLOTEN AIRPORT
LIMITES ET SUBDIVISIONS DE LA REGION ETUDIEE ENTOURANT L'AEROPORT DE KLOTEN

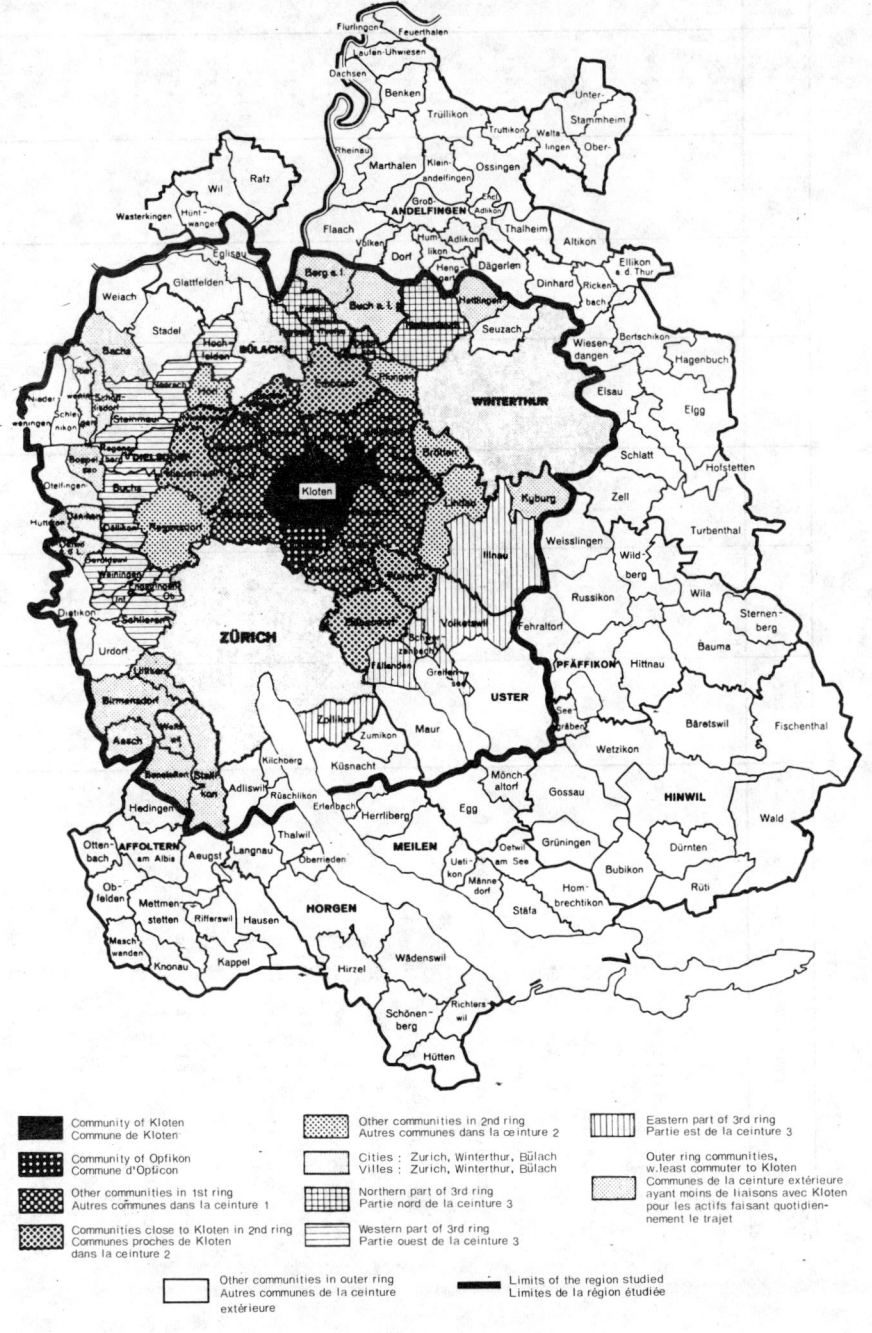

Community of Kloten Commune de Kloten	Other communities in 2nd ring Autres communes dans la ceinture 2	Eastern part of 3rd ring Partie est de la ceinture 3
Community of Opfikon Commune d'Opfikon	Cities : Zurich, Winterthur, Bülach Villes : Zurich, Winterthur, Bülach	Outer ring communities, w.least commuter to Kloten Communes de la ceinture extérieure
Other communities in 1st ring Autres communes dans la ceinture 1	Northern part of 3rd ring Partie nord de la ceinture 3	ayant moins de liaisons avec Kloten pour les actifs faisant quotidien-
Communities close to Kloten in 2nd ring Communes proches de Kloten dans la ceinture 2	Western part of 3rd ring Partie ouest de la ceinture 3	nement le trajet
	Other communities in outer ring Autres communes de la ceinture extérieure	Limits of the region studied Limites de la région étudiée

Table 1

LAND USE ACCORDING TO 1970 REGISTRATIONS (hectares)

Data provided by the Cantonal Planning Authority

Community or area	Agriculture	Woods	Unprod. Land	Compl. Blt. Ar.	Transp. + Ind.	Built Area	Total Area	Blt. + Transp. + Ind.
Kloten	836	487	40	246	283	529	1,942	0.60
Opfikon	259	99	1	187	19	206	565	0.80
Other communities in 1st ring	4,181	1,927	153	877	246	1,123	7,384	0.27
Total for 1st ring	4,440	2,026	154	1,064	265	1,329	7,949	0.30
Communities close to Kloten in 2nd ring	2,944	1,389	79	909	21	930	5,342	0.32
Other communities in 2nd ring	2,471	1,230	123	401	54	455	4,279	0.18
Total for 2nd ring	5,415	2,619	202	1,310	75	1,385	9,621	0.26
Cities: Zurich-Winterthur-Bülach	4,271	5,502	569	6,714	533	7,247	17,589	1.70
Northern part of 3rd ring	1,675	1,116	60	212	-	212	3,063	0.13
Western part of 3rd ring	3,158	1,654	263	727	99	826	5,901	0.26
Eastern part of 3rd ring	3,045	1,574	743	931	26	957	6,319	0.31
Total for 3rd ring excluding cities	7,878	4,344	1,066	1,870	125	1,995	15,283	0.25
Total for 3rd ring including cities	12,149	9,846	1,635	8,584	658	9,242	32,872	0.76
Communities with least commuter ties to Kloten	5,563	4,191	139	626	-	626	10,519	0.11
Other communities in the outer ring	8,441	4,832	1,492	2,539	78	2,617	17,382	0.31
Total for communities in the outer ring	14,004	9,023	1,631	3,165	78	3,243	27,901	0.23
Total for area surveyed, including Kloten	36,894	24,001	3,662	14,369	1,359	15,728	80,285	0.43
of which:								
Kloten and Opfikon	1,145	586	41	433	302	735	2,507	0.64
Kloten and 1st ring	5,326	2,513	194	1,310	548	1,858	9,891	0.35
Kloten and 1st and 2nd ring	10,741	5,132	396	2,620	623	3,243	19,512	0.30

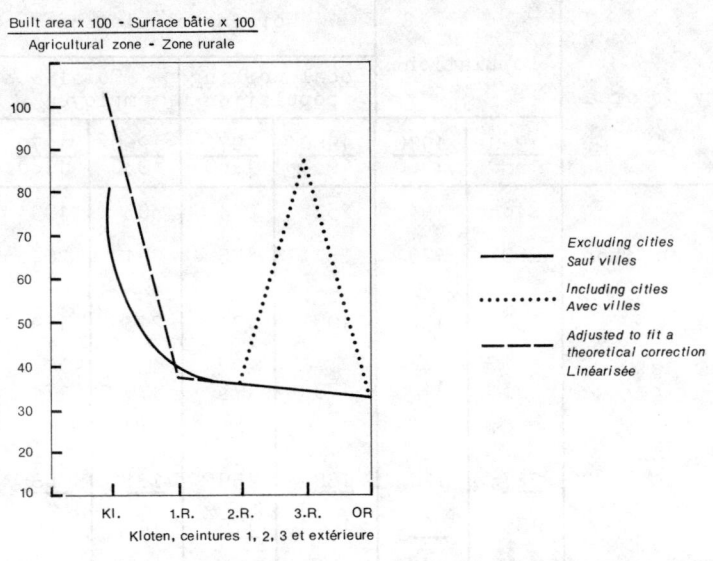

Figure 1

1970 LAND USE

UTILISATION DU SOL EN 1970

trustworthy enough to indicate the kind of relation that exists between land use and increasing distance from Kloten. If city influences are eliminated, the land used for building decreases noticeably
with distance from the airport, while within subsequent rings there
are more pronounced differences which can be explained either by the
distance or by their special roles.

GROWTH OF EMPLOYMENT

Increases in population and employment are shown in Tables 2,
3, 4, and 5. Figures from the last four censuses and their corresponding growth rates are given. A summary view of growth from 1941
to 1970 is provided in Figure 2. This shows that employment rose
faster than population in Kloten and in the first ring. In the other
rings, however, employment grew at a slower rate than population.
This cannot have been due to demographic changes alone. There is no
doubt that the airport played a significant part in it. The tables
give further proof that the airport's impact fell mostly on Kloten
and the first two rings. However certain shifts began to occur towards the end of the period under survey. Growth began to swell in
the outer rings. This is shown in the changing ratios for $\frac{1960}{1950}$ and
$\frac{1970}{1960}$.

Table 2

RATIOS OF POPULATION TO EMPLOYMENT

Community or area	Population		Working population			
			Local working population		Total employed	
	$\frac{1960}{1950}$	$\frac{1970}{1960}$	$\frac{1960}{1950}$	$\frac{1970}{1960}$	$\frac{1960}{1950}$	$\frac{1970}{1960}$
Kloten	246	194	252	214	303	199
Kloten and Opfikon	268	170	284	185	291	204
Kloten and 1st ring	230	134	199	171	213	179
Kloten and 1st and 2nd ring	193	148	179	173	179	174
of which:						
1st ring	227	120	188	159	181	168
2nd ring	155	169	160	175	146	166

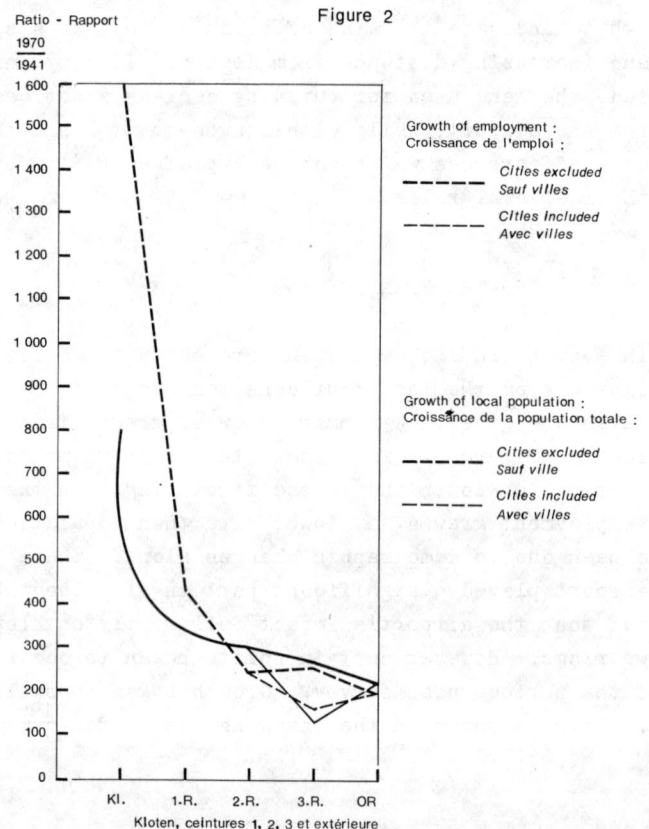

Figure 2

Ratio - Rapport

$\frac{1970}{1941}$

Growth of employment :
Croissance de l'emploi :

- - - - Cities excluded
Sauf villes

----- Cities included
Avec villes

Growth of local population :
Croissance de la population totale :

- - - - Cities excluded
Sauf ville

----- Cities included
Avec villes

Kl.   1.-R.   2.-R.   3.-R.   OR
Kloten, ceintures 1, 2, 3 et extérieure

Table 3

POPULATION AS OF VARIOUS CENSUS DATES

Data provided by the Cantonal Planning Authority

Community or area	1941	1950	1960	1970	1950/1941	1960/1950	1970/1960	1970/1941
Kloten	2,019	3,429	8,446	16,388	170	246	194	812
Opfikon	1,549	2,613	7,749	11,115	169	297	143	718
Other communities in 1st ring	11,292	13,737	29,303	33,255	122	213	113	295
Total for 1st ring	12,841	16,350	37,052	44,370	127	227	120	346
Communities close to Kloten in 2nd ring	10,832	13,064	20,274	35,020	121	155	173	323
Other communities in 2nd ring	5,688	6,265	9,682	15,695	110	154	162	276
Total for 2nd ring	16,520	19,329	29,956	50,715	117	155	169	307
Cities: Zurich-Winterthur-Bülach	399,155	461,579	528,710	526,405	116	115	99	132
Northern part of 3rd ring	4,289	4,403	4,686	4,959	103	106	106	116
Western part of 3rd ring	11,500	14,137	23,014	31,556	123	163	137	274
Eastern part of 3rd ring	12,712	14,681	20,548	42,882	115	140	209	337
Total for 3rd ring excluding cities	28,501	33,221	48,248	79,397	117	145	165	279
Total for 3rd ring including cities	427,656	494,800	576,958	605,802	116	117	105	142
Communities with least commuter ties to Kloten	7,590	8,602	10,886	15,984	113	127	147	211
Other communities in the outer ring	47,932	56,770	83,359	112,600	118	147	135	235
Total for communities in the outer ring	55,522	65,372	94,245	128,584	118	144	136	232
Total for area surveyed, including Kloten	514,558	599,280	746,657	845,859	116	125	113	164
of which:								
Kloten and Opfikon	3,568	6,042	16,195	27,503	169	268	170	771
Kloten and 1st ring	14,860	19,779	45,498	60,758	133	230	134	409
Kloten and 1st and 2nd ring	31,380	39,108	75,454	111,473	125	193	148	355

Table 4

LOCAL WORKING POPULATION

Data provided by the Cantonal Planning Authority

Community or area	1941	1950	1960	1970	1950/1941	1960/1950	1970/1960	1970/1941
Kloten	933	1,576	3,964	8,493	169	252	214	910
Opfikon	692	1,227	3,995	6,204	177	326	155	897
Other communities in 1st ring	5,246	6,378	10,273	16,539	122	161	161	315
Total for 1st ring	5,938	7,605	14,268	22,743	128	188	159	383
Communities close to Kloten in 2nd ring	5,073	6,014	9,886	17,570	119	164	178	346
Other communities in 2nd ring	2,852	3,027	4,558	7,690	106	151	167	270
Total for 2nd ring	7,925	9,041	14,444	25,260	114	160	175	319
Cities: Zurich-Winterthur-Bülach	204,785	232,124	272,388	278,232	113	117	102	136
Northern part of 3rd ring	1,974	2,027	2,185	2,447	103	108	112	123
Western part of 3rd ring	5,298	6,560	11,095	17,266	124	169	156	326
Eastern part of 3rd ring	5,863	6,803	9,601	20,116	116	141	210	343
Total for 3rd ring excluding cities	13,135	15,390	22,881	39,829	117	149	174	303
Total for 3rd ring including cities	217,920	247,514	295,269	318,061	114	119	108	145
Communities with least commuter ties to Kloten	3,567	3,861	4,928	7,504	108	128	152	210
Other communities in the outer ring	22,180	26,152	39,402	53,149	118	151	135	240
Total for communities in the outer ring	25,747	30,013	44,330	60,653	117	148	136	235
Total for area surveyed, including Kloten	258,463	295,749	372,275	435,210	114	126	117	168
of which:								
Kloten and Opfikon	1,625	2,803	7,959	14,697	172	284	185	904
Kloten and 1st ring	6,871	9,181	18,232	31,236	134	199	171	455
Kloten and 1st and 2nd ring	14,796	18,222	32,676	56,496	123	179	173	382

Table 5

TOTAL EMPLOYED AS PER COMMUTER BALANCE

Data provided by the Cantonal Planning Authority

Community or area	1941	1950	1960	1970	1950/1941	1960/1950	1970/1960	1970/1941
Kloten	822	2,192	6,644	13,206	267	303	199	1,607
Opfikon	548	998	2,632	5,711	182	264	217	1,042
Other communities in 1st ring	4,185	5,171	8,521	13,007	124	165	153	312
Total for 1st ring	4,733	6,169	11,153	18,718	130	181	168	395
Communities close to Kloten in 2nd ring	4,650	5,119	7,992	11,882	110	155	150	256
Other communities in 2nd ring	3,287	3,149	4,122	8,148	96	131	198	248
Total for 2nd ring	7,937	8,268	12,044	20,030	104	146	166	252
Cities: Zurich-Winterthur-Bülach	220,075	256,861	317,200	353,786	117	123	112	161
Northern part of 3rd ring	1,453	1,457	1,468	1,656	100	101	113	114
Western part of 3rd ring	5,392	6,421	9,732	15,089	119	152	155	280
Eastern part of 3rd ring	4,387	4,821	6,374	13,187	110	132	207	301
Total for 3rd ring excluding cities	11,232	12,699	17,574	29,932	113	138	170	266
Total for 3rd ring including cities	231,307	269,560	334,747	383,718	117	124	115	166
Communities with least commuter ties to Kloten	3,062	2,945	3,492	4,563	96	119	131	149
Other communities in the outer ring	11,877	21,884	29,836	39,677	117	136	133	211
Total for communities in the outer ring	21,839	24,829	33,328	44,240	114	134	133	203
Total for area surveyed, including Kloten	266,638	311,018	397,943	479,412	117	128	120	180
of which:								
Kloten and Opfikon	1,370	3,190	9,276	18,917	233	291	204	1,381
Kloten and 1st ring	5,555	8,361	17,797	31,924	151	213	179	575
Kloten and 1st and 2nd ring	13,492	16,629	29,841	51,954	123	179	174	385

INCREASING SEPARATION OF WORK PLACE AND HOME

A trend towards increasing separation of work place and home is noticeable in the area under inquiry. Table 6 shows relationships between all jobs and locally resident workers in the various parts of the area surveyed, using minimum, maximum and average percentages. The value of 100 corresponds to a balanced state. Values above 100 signify more jobs than locally resident workers, while values under 100 indicate the reverse, in other words, a residential area.

An increasing excess of jobs over residents is characteristic of the area under study. It was 3.1 per cent in 1941; it grew by 2 per cent until 1950; by 1.7 per cent in the 1950s and by 0.9 per cent during the following decade. Imbalances also became more extreme in some places. Between 1941 and 1960 jobs dropped from 39 to 31 per cent of local resident workers in one "bedroom community", while jobs increased from 190 per cent to 200 per cent of resident workers in the most concentrated "work communities". In the 1970s this separation of work place and home grew even more pronounced, with the lowest value sinking to 24 per cent and the highest rising to 237 per cent.

In the cities the excess of employment over local working population accelerated and reached 27.1 per cent in 1970. The construction of the airport, on the other hand, created an excess of jobs in Kloten as high as 39 per cent in 1950, a figure that rose to almost 68 per cent in 1960. Disregarding the development in the cities and a slight temporary excess of jobs in the Limmattal valley and in a few of the communities of the outer ring, it is clear that the heaviest concentration of jobs has taken place in Kloten and the second ring. The first ring continues to be more oriented towards living. A sharper separation took place within the second ring, where the communities close to Kloten had the lowest percentages of all, both for individual cases and on the average, thus meriting the designation of "bedroom communities".

This separation of work place and home is reflected in patterns of commuting (Table 7). Positive values indicate an excess of persons employed, negative ones, an excess of local working population. The figures confirm the picture already established and point to Kloten's importance as a major work place outside the cities. Under the impact of the airport, Kloten, an average out-commuter community, turned into one of the most important in-commuter communities, with a balance of almost 5,000 in-commuters and a larger relative excess of employment than the cities. Despite the different roles they play, both of the communities lying closest to the airport, namely Kloten and Opfikon, have either the same share of the commuter balance as the cities or an even higher one.

Table 6

TOTAL EMPLOYMENT EXPRESSED AS MINIMUM, MAXIMUM AND AVERAGE PERCENTAGES OF LOCAL WORKING POPULATION

Data provided by the Cantonal Planning Authority

Ø = average

Community or area	1941	1950	1960	1970	Ø 1941	Ø 1950	Ø 1960	Ø 1970
Kloten	88	139	168	156	88.1	139.0	167.6	155.5
Opfikon	79	81	66	92	79.1	81.3	65.8	92.0
Other communities in 1st ring	59-96	63-100	60-96	49-97	79.7	81.0	82.9	78.6
Total for 1st ring	59-96	63-100	60-96	49-97	79.7	81.1	78.1	82.3
Communities close to Kloten in 2nd ring	65-130	64-96	43-86	24-77	91.6	85.1	80.1	67.6
Other communities in 2nd ring	61-170	56-152	66-130	37-126	115.2	104.0	90.4	105.9
Total for 2nd ring	61-170	56-152	43-130	24-126	100.1	91.4	83.3	79.2
Cities: Zurich-Winterthur-Bülach	107-111	108-111	99-117	99-131	107.4	110.6	116.4	127.1
Northern part of 3rd ring	39-110	35-105	39-101	51-82	73.6	71.8	67.1	68.2
Western part of 3rd ring	50-132	44-130	31-121	33-135	101.7	97.8	87.7	87.3
Eastern part of 3rd ring	71-85	68-94	63-141	50-109	74.8	70.8	66.3	65.5
Total for 3rd ring excluding cities	39-132	35-130	31-141	33-135	85.5	82.5	76.8	75.1
Total for 3rd ring including cities	39-132	35-130	31-141	33-135	106.1	108.9	113.3	120.6
Communities with least commuter ties to Kloten	65-105	61-101	53-90	47-115	85.8	76.2	70.8	60.8
Other communities in the outer ring	54-189	51-202	43-191	48-237	84.6	83.6	75.7	74.6
Total for communities in the outer ring	54-189	51-202	43-191	47-237	84.8	82.7	75.1	62.7
Total for area surveyed, including Kloten	39-189	35-202	31-191	24-237	103.1	105.1	106.8	107.7
of which:								
Kloten and Opfikon	79-88	81-139	66-168	92-156	84.3	113.8	116.5	128.7
Kloten and 1st ring	59-96	63-139	60-168	40-156	80.8	91.0	97.6	102.2
Kloten and 1st and 2nd ring	59-170	56-139	43-168	24-156	91.2	91.3	91.3	92.0

Table 7

COMMUTER BALANCES (Total employed (TE) - local working pop.
= in-commuters - out-commuters)

Data provided by the Cantonal Planning Authority

Community or area	abs. 1941	abs. 1950	abs. 1960	abs. 1970	% TE 1941	% TE 1950	% TE 1960	% TE 1970
Kloten	-111	+616	+2,680	+4,713	-13.5	+28.1	+40.3	+35.6
Opfikon	-144	-229	-1,363	-493	-26.2	-22.9	-51.7	-8.6
Other communities in 1st ring	-1,061	-1,207	-1,752	-3,532	-25.3	-23.3	-20.5	-27.1
Total for 1st ring	-1,205	-1,436	-3,115	-4,025	-25.4	-23.2	27.9	-21.5
Communities close to Kloten in 2nd ring	-423	-895	-1,964	-5,688	-9.0	-17.4	-24.7	-47.8
Other communities in 2nd ring	+435	+122	-436	+458	+13.2	+3.8	-10.5	+5.6
Total for 2nd ring	+12	-743	-2,400	-5,230	+0.15	-8.9	-19.9	-26.1
Cities: Zurich-Winterthur-Bülach	+15,290	+24,737	+44,820	+75,554	+6.9	+9.6	+14.1	+21.3
Northern part of 3rd ring	-521	-570	-717	-791	-35.8	-39.1	-48.8	-47.7
Western part of 3rd ring	+94	-139	-1,363	-2,177	+1.7	-2.1	-14.0	-14.4
Eastern part of 3rd ring	-1,476	-1,982	-3,227	-6,929	-33.6	-41.1	-50.6	-52.5
Total for 3rd ring excluding cities	-1,903	-2,691	-5,307	-9,897	-16.9	-21.1	-30.1	-33.0
Total for 3rd ring including cities	+13,387	+22,046	+39,505	+65,657	+5.7	+8.1	+11.8	+17.1
Communities with least commuter ties to Kloten	-505	-916	-1,436	-2,941	16.4	-31.1	41.1	-64.4
Other communities in the outer ring	-3,403	-4,268	-9,566	-13,472	-18.1	-19.5	-32.0	-33.9
Total for communities in the outer ring	-3,908	-5,184	-11,002	-16,413	-17.8	-20.8	-33.0	-37.0
Total for area surveyed, including Kloten	+8,175	+15,269	+25,668	+44,702	+3.0	+4.9	+6.4	+9.3
of which:								
Kloten and Opfikon	-255	+387	+1,317	+4,220	-18.6	+12.1	+14.1	+22.3
Kloten and 1st ring	-1,316	-820	-435	+688	-23.6	-9.8	-2.4	+2.1
Kloten and 1st and 2nd ring	-1,304	-1,593	-2,835	-4,542	-9.7	-9.6	-9.5	-8.7

Further light on commuting is given by Figure 3 and Table 8. Kloten's increase of in-commuters is seen to be way ahead in relative figures and only the cities or entire rings have higher absolute figures. Table 9 shows where Kloten's in-commuting comes from and how the flow has grown. Table 9 summarises the data by sub-areas though flows of fewer than five out-commuters have been omitted.

Figure 3

GROWTH OF IN-COMMUTERS TO THE COMMUÑITIES
according to 1970/ 1941 growth rate

AUGMENTATION DU NOMBRE MIGRANTS-ENTRANTS
suivant le taux de croissance 1970/ 1941

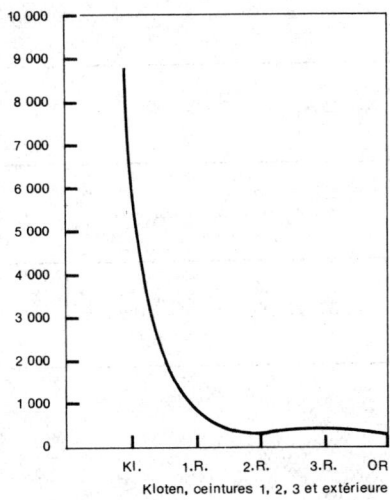

Whereas the first ring has steadily furnished one-third of Kloten's in-commuters, half of them came from the cities in the 1950s and 1960s. The inflow from the cities continued to grow in absolute terms until 1970 but its relative share grew less, probably on account of housing shortages in the cities and Zurich's loss of population. The significant commuter relationship between the second ring communities around Kloten and Kloten itself is confirmed by Table 9. Flows of commuters from the eastern and western parts of the third ring, and then from other communities in the outer ring, are also notable. Favourable locations and the existence of good transport explain these linkages.

Table 8

IN-COMMUTER TOTALS

Data provided by the Cantonal Planning Authority

Community or area	1941	1950	1960	1970	1950/1941	1960/1950	1970/1960	1970/1941
Kloten	90	955	3,814	7,865	1,061	399	206	8,739
Opfikon	136	417	975	3,111	307	234	319	2,288
Other communities in 1st ring	782	1,318	3,186	5,713	169	242	179	731
Total for 1st ring	918	1,735	4,161	8,824	189	240	212	961
Communities close to Kloten in 2nd ring	961	1,098	2,336	3,736	114	213	160	389
Other communities in 2nd ring	1,055	903	1,442	3,357	86	160	233	318
Total for 2nd ring	2,016	2,001	3,778	7,093	99	189	188	352
Cities: Zurich-Winterthur-Bülach	20,745	32,727	59,938	99,585	158	159	166	480
Northern part of 3rd ring	223	229	343	452	103	150	132	203
Western part of 3rd ring	1,699	2,374	4,332	6,898	140	182	159	406
Eastern part of 3rd ring	467	616	1,353	4,535	132	220	335	971
Total for 3rd ring excluding cities	2,389	3,219	6,028	11,885	135	187	197	497
Total for 3rd ring including cities	23,134	35,946	65,966	111,470	155	184	169	482
Communities with least commuter ties to Kloten	233	245	550	1,109	105	224	202	476
Other communities in the outer ring	2,952	4,706	7,595	11,574	159	161	152	392
Total for communities in the outer ring	3,185	4,951	8,145	12,683	155	165	156	398
Total for area surveyed, including Kloten	29,343	45,588	85,864	147,935	155	188	172	504
of which:								
Kloten and Opfikon	226	1,372	4,789	10,976	607	349	229	4,857
Kloten and 1st ring	1,008	2,690	7,975	16,689	267	296	209	1,656
Kloten and 1st and 2nd ring	3,024	4,691	11,753	23,782	155	251	202	786

Table 9
OUT-COMMUTERS INTO KLOTEN

Data provided by the Cantonal Planning Authority

	1950	1960	1970	% 1950	% 1960	% 1970	1960/1950	1970/1960	1970/1950
Kloten									
Opfikon	123	682	1,065	14.5	19.3	14.6	554	156	866
Other communities in 1st ring	142	478	1,332	16.7	13.6	18.3	337	279	938
Total for 1st ring	265	1,160	2,397	31.2	32.9	32.9	438	207	905
Communities close to Kloten in 2nd ring	134	222	788	15.8	6.3	10.8	166	355	588
Other communities in 2nd ring	–	50	130	–	1.4	1.8	–	260	–
Total for 2nd ring	134	272	918	15.8	7.7	12.6	203	338	685
Cities: Zurich-Winterthur-Bülach	409	1,840	2,893	48.2	52.1	39.7	450	157	707
Northern part of 3rd ring	–	18	45	–	0.5	0.6	–	250	–
Western part of 3rd ring	5	24	118	0.6	0.7	1.6	480	492	2,360
Eastern part of 3rd ring	12	85	338	1.4	2.4	4.7	708	398	2,817
Total for 3rd ring excluding cities	17	127	501	2.0	3.6	6.9	747	394	2,947
Total for 3rd ring including cities	426	1,967	3,394	50.2	55.7	46.6	462	173	797
Communities with least commuter ties to Kloten	–	2	–	–	–	–	–	0	–
Other communities in the outer ring	24	130	577	2.8	3.7	7.9	542	444	2,404
Total for communities in the outer ring	24	132	577	2.8	3.7	7.9	550	437	2,404
Total for area surveyed, including Kloten	849	3,531	7,286	100.0	100.0	100.0	416	206	858
of which:									
Kloten and Opfikon									
Kloten and 1st ring	265	1,160	2,397	31.2	32.9	32.9	438	207	905
Kloten and 1st and 2nd ring	399	1,432	3,315	47.0	40.6	45.5	359	231	831

The tendency for commuting to increase is explained only in part by changes in urban geography. The development of "tertiary" services and the decline of farm employment are responsible too. Thus Table 10 shows sharp drops in employment in some areas and, in particular, the decline in agricultural jobs.

In Kloten, the development of the airport was accompanied by an above average decline in farming jobs but this divergence from the norm was not great. Furthermore Kloten is a community with one of the largest acreages of farms in the canton. If this particular is adjusted by combining the data for Kloten and Opfikon, then the rate of decline is the same as for the region as a whole. From this it may be deduced that the airport did not cause any significant decrease in primary sector employment apart from that attributable to the taking over of farm land for the airport.

It is on the secondary and, above all, on the tertiary sector that the airport's impact has been greatest (Tables 11 and 12 and Figure 4).

Figure 4

SECTORAL DEVELOPMENT OF LOCAL WORKING POPULATION (CITIES EXCLUDED)

DEVELOPPEMENT SECTORIEL DE LA POPULATION ACTIVE (VILLES EXCLUES)

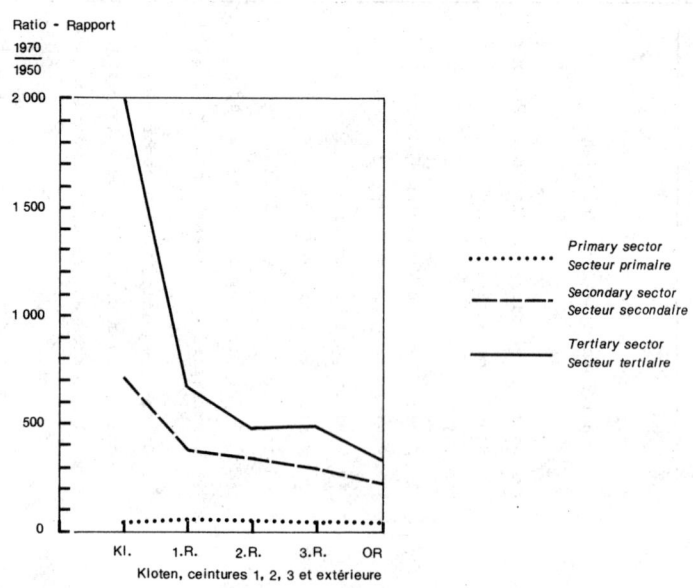

Table 10

LOCAL WORKING POPULATION EMPLOYED IN PRIMARY SECTOR (Agriculture, market gardening etc.)

Data provided by the Cantonal Planning Authority

Community or area	1941	1950	1960	1970	1950/1941	1960/1950	1970/1960	1970/1941
Kloten	296	211	193	153	71	91	79	52
Opfikon	123	75	92	72	61	123	78	59
Other communities in 1st ring	1,486	1,158	990	848	78	85	86	57
Total for 1st ring	1,609	1,233	1,082	920	77	88	85	57
Communities close to Kloten in 2nd ring	1,103	806	869	665	73	108	77	60
Other communities in 2nd ring	790	651	568	396	82	87	70	50
Total for 2nd ring	1,893	1,457	1,437	1,061	77	99	74	56
Cities: Zurich-Winterthur-Bülach	3,886	1,324	2,679	1,929	34	202	72	50
Northern part of 3rd ring	596	487	391	307	82	80	79	52
Western part of 3rd ring	1,286	943	938	656	73	99	70	51
Eastern part of 3rd ring	1,257	970	973	693	77	100	71	55
Total for 3rd ring excluding cities	3,139	2,400	2,302	1,656	76	96	72	53
Total for 3rd ring including cities	7,025	3,724	4,981	3,585	53	134	72	51
Communities with least commuter ties to Kloten	1,775	1,449	1,298	1,051	82	90	81	59
Other communities in the outer ring	3,469	2,534	2,561	1,860	73	101	73	54
Total for communities in the outer ring	5,244	3,983	3,859	2,911	76	97	75	56
Total for area surveyed, including Kloten	16,067	10,608	11,552	8,630	66	109	75	54
of which:								
Kloten and Opfikon	419	286	285	225	68	100	79	54
Kloten and 1st ring	1,905	1,444	1,275	1,073	76	88	84	56
Kloten and 1st and 2nd ring	3,798	2,901	2,712	2,134	76	93	78	56

Table 11

LOCAL WORKING POPULATION EMPLOYED IN SECONDARY SECTOR

Data provided by the Cantonal Planning Authority

Community or area	1941	1950	1960	1970	1950/1941	1960/1950	1970/1960	1970/1941
Kloten	358	667	1,364	2,553	186	204	187	713
Opfikon	408	680	1,914	2,590	167	281	135	635
Other communities in 1st ring	2,340	3,029	5,514	8,268	129	182	150	353
Total for 1st ring	2,748	3,709	7,428	10,858	135	200	146	395
Communities close to Kloten in 2nd ring	2,504	3,081	5,593	8,882	123	182	159	355
Other communities in 2nd ring	1,298	1,499	2,600	4,366	115	173	168	336
Total for 2nd ring	3,802	4,580	8,193	13,248	120	179	162	348
Cities: Zurich-Winterthur-Bülach	90,712	103,834	119,548	108,003	114	115	90	119
Northern part of 3rd ring	1,105	1,165	1,362	1,490	105	117	109	135
Western part of 3rd ring	2,687	3,685	6,344	8,792	137	172	139	327
Eastern part of 3rd ring	2,326	2,672	4,056	8,460	115	152	209	364
Total for 3rd ring excluding cities	6,118	7,522	11,762	18,742	123	156	159	306
Total for 3rd ring including cities	96,830	111,356	131,310	126,745	115	118	97	131
Communities with least commuter ties to Kloten	1,058	1,398	1,939	3,000	132	139	155	284
Other communities in the outer ring	11,039	13,512	21,210	25,445	122	157	120	231
Total for communities in the outer ring	12,097	14,910	23,149	28,445	123	155	123	235
Total for area surveyed, including Kloten	115,835	135,222	171,444	181,849	117	127	106	157
of which:								
Kloten and Opfikon	766	1,347	3,278	5,143	176	243	157	671
Kloten and 1st ring	3,106	4,376	8,792	13,411	141	201	153	432
Kloten and 1st and 2nd ring	6,908	8,956	16,985	26,659	130	190	157	386

Table 12

LOCAL WORKING POPULATION EMPLOYED IN TERTIARY SECTOR

Data provided by the Cantonal Planning Authority

Community or area	1941	1950	1960	1970	1950/1941	1960/1950	1970/1960	1970/1941
Kloten	279	698	2,407	5,787	250	345	240	2,074
Opfikon	161	472	1,989	3,542	293	421	178	2,200
Other communities in 1st ring	1,420	2,191	3,769	7,423	154	172	197	523
Total for 1st ring	1,581	2,663	5,758	10,965	168	216	190	694
Communities close to Kloten	1,466	2,127	3,424	8,023	145	161	234	547
Other communities in 2nd ring	764	877	1,390	2,928	115	158	211	383
Total for 2nd ring	2,230	3,004	4,814	10,951	135	160	227	491
Cities: Zurich-Winterthur-Bülach	110,187	126,966	150,161	168,300	115	118	112	153
Northern part of 3rd ring	273	375	432	650	137	115	150	238
Western part of 3rd ring	1,325	1,932	3,813	7,818	146	197	205	590
Eastern part of 3rd ring	2,280	3,161	4,572	10,963	139	145	240	481
Total for 3rd ring excluding cities	3,878	5,468	8,817	19,431	141	161	220	501
Total for 3rd ring including cities	114,065	132,434	158,978	187,731	116	120	118	165
Communities with least commuter ties to Kloten	734	1,014	1,691	3,453	138	167	204	470
Other communities in the outer ring	7,672	10,105	15,631	25,844	132	155	165	337
Total for communities in the outer ring	8,406	11,120	17,322	29,297	132	156	169	349
Total for area surveyed, including Kloten	126,561	149,919	189,279	244,731	118	126	129	193
of which:								
Kloten and Opfikon	440	1,170	4,396	9,329	266	376	212	2,120
Kloten and 1st ring	1,860	3,361	8,165	16,752	181	243	205	901
Kloten and 1st and 2nd ring	4,090	6,365	12,979	27,703	156	204	213	677

A comparison of the most recent and the most remote periods of development shows marked differences in the growth curves for the tertiary and secondary sectors. The former far surpasses the latter, especially in Kloten and, to a lesser extent, also in Opfikon. Changes in local working populations in the tertiary and secondary sectors in 1970 confirm well-known trends in urban employment. Thus for every ten residents employed in the secondary sector there were 16 in the tertiary sector in the cities of Zurich, Winterthur and Bülach, 23 in Kloten and 18 in Kloten-Opfikon.

Until 1960 this development was largely the result of a rearrangement of the sectors with both of them maintaining approximately equal growth. But after 1960 a slowing-down of growth took place in the secondary sector, whereas the tertiary sector's growth rate increased steadily throughout the region. However the fastest rate at Kloten, and more noticeably at Opfikon, took place in the 1950s.

DEVELOPMENT OF IMPORTANT SECTORS

A picture of how the various branches of the economy have developed in Zurich may be obtained from two business surveys carried out by Prognos AG of Basel(1). In this paper attention will be confined to an analysis of the structure and distribution of the more important branches of the economy (Table 13).

A point to note is the large and increasingly concentrated share of transport and hostelry business in Kloten and its declining or static state elsewhere. Table 14 shows that between 1955 and 1965 Kloten's share more than doubled even though its share of secondary sector employment increased by only half.

The Table also shows that the surroundings of Kloten had a relatively small share of the region's employment on account of the influence of the cities.

Table 15 shows how firms in three branches of the economy grew in number.

LAND VALUES

Insufficient data is available on land sales to show how the airport has affected values. Conclusions may however be drawn from the average prices for land in the first two rings and in the cities

---

1) "The Zurich Region in the Context of the Swiss National Economy", 1972.

Table 13

EMPLOYMENT STRUCTURE IN THE SECONDARY AND TERTIARY SECTORS 1955 AND 1965, BY BRANCH (TOTAL FOR EACH YEAR = 100)

Data provided by the Cantonal Planning Authority

Community or area	Ind. + Build.		Trade + Bank.		Trans. + Hostelry		Remain. Tert. Sec.	
	1955	1965	1955	1965	1955	1965	1955	1965
Kloten	19.9	15.1	5.3	6.9	73.8	76.2	1.0	1.8
Opfikon	67.9	67.9	17.8	21.9	7.3	6.1	7.0	4.1
Other communities in 1st ring	81.3	81.2	9.2	10.9	7.2	5.0	2.3	2.9
Total for 1st ring	78.4	77.9	11.0	13.6	7.3	5.3	3.3	3.2
Communities close to Kloten in 2nd ring	80.3	73.4	10.5	13.1	7.4	6.1	1.8	7.4
Other communities in 2nd ring	87.3	77.5	3.9	15.0	7.0	4.8	1.8	2.7
Total for 2nd ring	82.9	75.1	8.0	13.9	7.3	5.6	1.8	5.4
Cities: Zurich-Winterthur-Bülach	53.2	49.4	27.0	30.3	13.7	12.3	6.1	8.0
Northern part of 3rd ring	84.2	80.8	5.4	6.5	7.2	7.3	3.2	5.4
Western part of 3rd ring	86.1	72.2	6.8	16.0	5.7	5.6	1.4	6.2
Eastern part of 3rd ring	63.0	64.6	14.0	15.6	10.7	7.3	12.3	12.5
Total for 3rd ring excluding cities	78.6	70.3	9.0	15.3	7.4	6.3	5.0	8.1
Total for 3rd ring including cities	54.2	50.5	26.3	29.5	13.5	12.0	6.0	8.0
Communities with least commuter ties to Kloten	77.7	76.9	6.0	7.3	15.1	13.4	1.2	2.4
Other communities in the outer ring	76.2	72.1	10.5	12.6	8.1	7.0	5.2	8.3
Total for communities in the outer ring	76.3	72.5	10.1	12.2	8.7	7.5	4.9	7.8
Total for area surveyed, including Kloten	56.4	53.2	24.2	26.7	13.5	12.5	5.9	7.6
of which:								
Kloten and Opfikon	33.8	30.3	9.0	11.2	54.5	56.0	2.7	2.5
Kloten and 1st ring	58.5	54.0	9.1	11.0	29.9	32.3	2.5	2.7
Kloten and 1st and 2nd ring	67.9	61.9	8.7	12.1	21.1	22.3	2.3	3.7

Table 14

GEOGRAPHIC DISTRIBUTION OF EMPLOYMENT IN THE SECONDARY AND TERTIARY SECTORS 1955 AND 1965, BY BRANCH

Data provided by the Cantonal Planning Authority

Community or area	Ind. + Build.		Trade + Bank.		Trans. + Hostelry		Remain. Tert. Sec.	
	1955	1965	1955	1965	1955	1965	1955	1965
Kloten	0.4	0.6	0.2	0.5	5.9	12.5	0.2	0.5
Opfikon	0.5	1.0	0.3	0.7	0.2	0.4	0.5	0.4
Other communities in 1st ring	2.4	3.9	0.7	1.0	0.9	1.0	0.7	1.0
Total for 1st ring	2.9	4.9	1.0	1.7	1.1	1.4	1.2	1.4
Communities close to Kloten in 2nd ring	1.8	2.5	0.6	0.9	0.7	0.9	0.4	1.8
Other communities in 2nd ring	1.1	2.0	0.1	0.8	0.4	0.5	0.2	0.5
Total for 2nd ring	2.9	4.5	0.7	1.7	1.1	1.4	0.6	2.3
Cities: Zurich-Winterthur-Bülach	79.4	73.5	94.0	90.0	85.5	77.8	89.0	83.1
Northern part of 3rd ring	0.5	0.5	0.05	0.1	0.2	0.2	0.2	0.2
Western part of 3rd ring	3.2	3.6	0.6	1.6	0.9	1.2	0.5	2.2
Eastern part of 3rd ring	1.3	1.7	0.7	0.8	0.9	0.8	2.4	2.2
Total for 3rd ring excluding cities	5.0	5.8	1.3	2.5	2.0	2.2	3.1	4.6
Total for 3rd ring including cities	84.4	79.3	95.3	92.5	87.5	80.0	92.1	87.7
Communities with least commuter ties to Kloten	0.7	0.8	0.1	0.2	0.5	0.6	0.1	0.2
Other communities in the outer ring	8.7	9.9	2.8	3.4	3.9	4.1	5.8	7.9
Total for communities in the outer ring	9.4	10.7	2.9	3.6	4.4	4.7	5.9	8.1
Total for area surveyed, including Kloten	100.0	100.0	100.0	100.0	100.0	100.0	100.0	100.0
of which:								
Kloten and Opfikon	0.9	1.6	0.5	1.2	6.1	12.9	0.7	0.9
Kloten and 1st ring	3.3	5.5	1.2	2.2	7.0	13.9	1.4	1.9
Kloten and 1st and 2nd ring	6.2	10.0	1.9	3.9	8.1	15.3	2.0	4.2

Table 15

NUMBER OF FIRMS IN THE BRANCHES SELECTED

Data provided by the Cantonal Planning Authority

Community or area	1955 Share of area total				1965-1955 Index			
	Ind. + Build.	Trade + Bank.	Trans. + Hostelry	Total	Ind. + Build.	Trade + Bank.	Trans. + Hostelry	Total
Kloten	0.6	0.4	1.2	0.7	158	180	160	164
Opfikon	0.8	0.4	0.4	0.6	130	165	171	145
Other communities in 1st ring	2.5	1.4	2.0	2.0	126	133	150	133
Total for 1st ring	3.3	1.8	2.4	2.6	127	140	154	136
Communities close to Kloten in 2nd ring	2.1	1.2	1.6	1.7	114	113	158	122
Other communities in 2nd ring	0.9	0.5	0.9	0.7	139	156	141	143
Total for 2nd ring	3.0	1.7	2.5	2.4	121	124	152	129
Cities: Zurich-Winterthur-Bülach	77.1	86.3	79.4	80.9	83	97	114	95
Northern part of 3rd ring	0.6	0.3	0.6	0.5	77	91	98	85
Western part of 3rd ring	2.3	1.5	2.0	1.9	123	123	149	128
Eastern part of 3rd ring	2.5	1.6	1.9	2.1	107	113	137	114
Total for 3rd ring excluding cities	5.4	3.4	4.5	4.5	110	116	137	117
Total for 3rd ring including cities	82.5	89.7	83.9	85.4	85	98	115	96
Communities with least commuter ties to Kloten	1.2	0.5	1.3	1.0	125	118	127	124
Other communities in the outer ring	9.4	5.8	8.6	7.9	98	105	120	105
Total for communities in the outer ring	10.6	6.4	9.9	8.9	101	106	121	107
Total for area surveyed, including Kloten	100.0	100.0	100.0	100.0	89	100	118	99
of which:								
Kloten and Opfikon	1.4	0.8	1.6	1.3	141	172	163	155
Kloten and 1st ring	3.9	2.2	3.6	3.3	132	148	156	142
Kloten and 1st and 2nd ring	6.9	3.9	6.1	5.7	127	138	154	136

177

of Zurich and Winterthur. The figures cover all parcels of land sold
on the open market, including farms and woods (Table 16).

The figures in Table 16 are subject to various distortions. They
depend on the extent to which the land in question was sold for building, on location, access, local land policies and other influences.
The lower averages for 1971 should not therefore be interpreted as
a drop in prices. Where two values are given, the maximum ones, and
all those that are underlined, reflect prices paid for sites in urban
areas. Values for the canton as a whole (broken underlining) reflect
large land deals in rural areas and protected zones.

Table 16

AVERAGE PRICE PER SQUARE METRE OF LAND IN SWISS FRANCS: 1970-1971

Community or area	1970	1971
Kloten	106.55	86.63
Opfikon	152.68	221.47
Other communities in 1st ring	5.99-154.04(1)	28.91-159.04
Communities close to Kloten in 2nd ring	52.53-159.41	39.95-100.19
Other communities in 2nd ring	40.32-73.12	32.07-108.23
Cities of Winterthur and Zurich	53.04-376.13	58.49-319.96
Average for country communities	40.97	48.09
Average for the entire canton	50.08	57.86

1) Where two figures are given they indicate minimum and
   maximum sale prices.

REFERENDUM ON EXPANDING THE AIRPORT

Any inquiry into the impact of an airport would be incomplete
if it did not include the voice of the people. In Zurich's case a
referendum was held that enabled this voice to express itself.

The result was that the communities of the Unterland plain and
the Furttal valley, which suffer most from noise, voted against the

proposal. A second group of scattered agricultural and mountain communities voted against the plan too. Their interests were not directly threatened by the airport but they were opposed to the huge scale of public expenditure involved in its expansion. Of the 171 communities in the canton of Zurich, 133 approved the proposed loan while all of them endorsed the noise legislation. Map 2 shows the pattern of voting for the loan.

Map 2 - Carte 2

RESULTS OF THE REFERENDUM ON EXPANSION OF THE AIRPORT
Tages-Anzeiger (Daily Herald), Monday, September 28, 1970, p. 17

RESULTATS DU REFERENDUM SUR L'EXTENSION DE L'AEROPORT
« Tages Anzeiger » du lundi 28 septembre 1970, p. 17

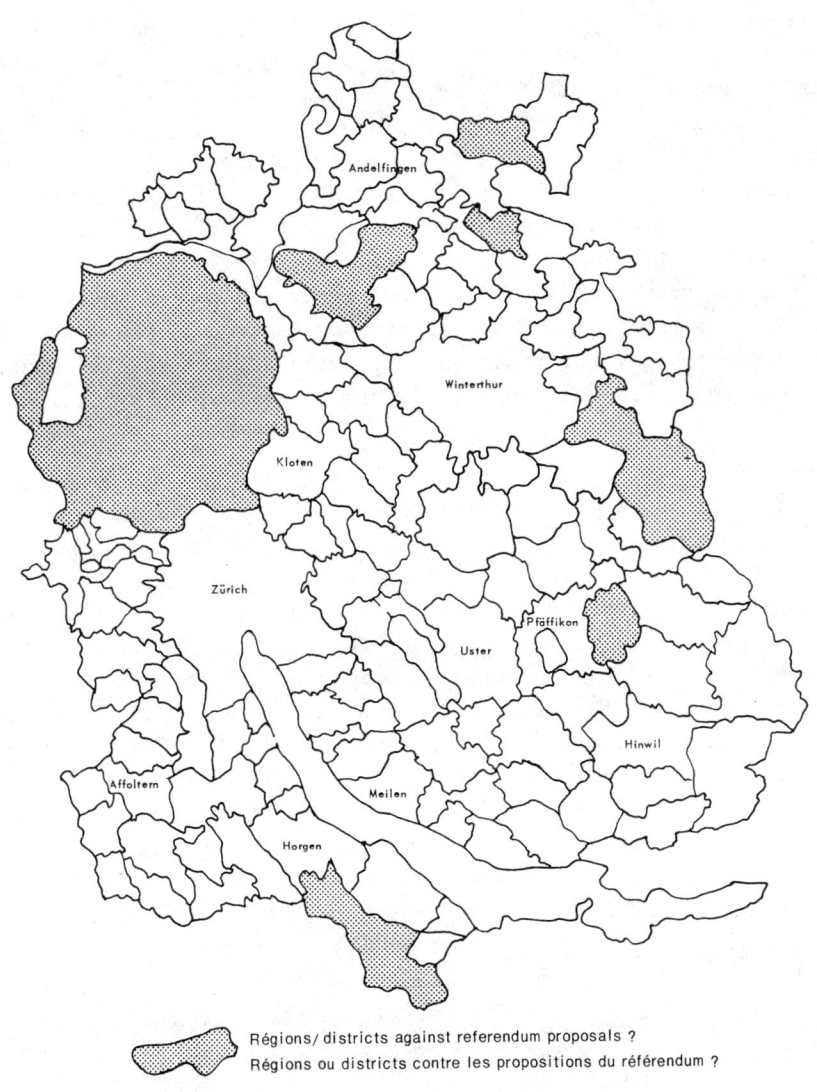

Régions/ districts against referendum proposals ?
Régions ou districts contre les propositions du référendum ?

CONCLUSIONS

Zurich's airport has a significant impact on land use in Kloten and a lesser effect in other nearby communities. The airport's most noticeable effects are on employment and commuter traffic. Its development has led employment to grow faster than both the inhabitants and the working population of Kloten and has led to a cleavage between work place and home.

Commuting

In the early stages of the airport's development its influence was limited to the actual airfield. Then, step by step, its influence stretched out to the neighbouring and outlying communities. Throughout this process the communities lying in the first ring continued to serve as "homes", as did the communities close to Kloten in the second ring remain "work places", like the cities whose employment role continued to grow. Although the cities, or entire rings of communities, are in the lead in absolute numbers of in-commuters, Kloten is way ahead in relative increase. Almost a half of Kloten's in-commuters came from the cities until the 1960s, and almost a third have continuously come from the first ring. In recent years the in-commuter flow has been fed in addition by the more distant communities in the outer ring. Thus the airport's effect is felt throughout the largest and most important part of the canton of Zurich.

The economy

Apart from the farms needed for the airfield the airport has had no substantial impact on farming. Its impact fell rather on the secondary and, principally, the tertiary sectors of the economy, with growth in the tertiary sector becoming more varied than in the secondary one. The relationship between local residents employed in the secondary and tertiary sectors is reminiscent of city conditions. Kloten's value for this index is almost half again as high in the cities. The tertiary sector's highest growth rate occurred in the 1950s in Kloten and Opfikon, mostly as a result of a reshuffling of the two sectors area by area, since their growth in the region as a whole was approximately equal.

Kloten was the only part of the area studied which increased its share of jobs in "transport and hostelry". In the decade up to 1965 the community more than doubled its share of the region's total for this kind of work, whereas its share for the secondary sector increased by only half. In addition, Kloten has a larger share of firms than of employed persons in the secondary sector and in "trade and

banking". This indicates that the airport attracts smaller firms
than in other sectors. During the same ten-year period the number
of firms in the "trade and banking" category in Kloten and in the
second ring grew faster than those in "transport and hostelry".
Decrease in growth with distance from Kloten was strongest for firms
in the secondary sector, followed by trade and banking firms in the
first two rings.

The environment

Mounting concern to protect people from industrial nuisances
will change the effect of the airport on housing and economic growth.
Restrictions on night flights are one example of this. On the other
hand, the inescapability of some air transport nuisances will in turn
result in restrictions on residential development and economic growth
in places such as Unterland and Furttal. This will then lead to
further specialisation in the role of different parts of the region.

Finally, a word of caution about the trends brought to light
in this study. It is not the airport alone which has made itself
felt on residential development and economic growth but also - and
especially - the city of Zurich.

Chapter 11

AN EXPANSION HALTED: KENNEDY AIRPORT, NEW YORK

Steven Ebbin,
Senior Staff Scientist, Programme of Policy Studies
in Science and Technology, George Washington
University, Washington D.C.

INTRODUCTION

The Jamaica Bay/Kennedy Airport Environmental Study was
commissioned by the Port of New York Authority and the Environmental
Studies Board of the National Academies of Sciences and Engineering
in 1970. It was intended to set a precedent for the kind of study
necessary to meet the requirements of the National Environmental
Policy Act of 1969.

A letter from Justin J. Tobin, Executive Director of the Port
of New York Authority (PNYA), spelled out the concerns of his agency
about a proposal to expand Kennedy Airport into Jamaica Bay: "... it
would be impossible to proceed with any expansion into the Bay without first knowing what effects such an action would have on the
viability of the Bay and on the people who live in its environs."
He wished to know: "... whether such an expanison could somehow be
made compatible with other plans for development of the Bay by the
City of New York and the federal government, and could be designed
in such a way as to upgrade the quality of the Bay's environment."

The study took ten months and entailed a multidisciplinary
group of natural and physical scientists, engineers and social and
behavioural scientists. The organisation of the study group into
five subcommittees reflected a judgment about the various impacts,
existing and prospective, of the airport on the Bay and its surroundings. Each member served on at least two subcommittees which were
organised along the following lines:

I. Ground and air transportation systems

   a) aircraft noise
   b) aircraft air pollution
   c) aircraft safety

d) aircraft traffic control

e) ground rail link

f) freight and passenger car links

II. Recreation and conservation

a) swimming

b) boating and fishing

c) shoreside parks and playgrounds

d) Gateway National Seashore Proposal

e) wildlife refuges

f) marine ecology

g) education

III. Land use and community needs

a) housing

b) industry and commerce

c) ground transportation

d) waste disposal

e) noise

f) traffic congestion

g) employment

h) political action

IV. Metropolitan needs and the expanding economy

a) central city needs

b) fourth airport problem

c) human need for air transport

d) regional development and growth

e) employment

f) alternative uses of sites

g) indirect costs

V. Water management

a) sewage

b) flood control

c) dredging

d) oil pollution

The object of the study group was not to decide the issue but to analyse the environmental impacts that could be expected from various airport developments generated by themselves and by the PNYA, the airlines, professional consultants and governmental bodies. Environment was defined by the group in its broadest possible sense,

183

and included not just aspects of the physical surroundings such as air, water, estuarine resources, noise, wildlife and fish, but the social, economic and political ambience. In fact the decision made by the PNYA was heavily influenced by the study.

BACKGROUND

Jamaica Bay, like most other natural resources which chance to lie near or within cities, is coveted by many competing users. It acts as a tertiary waste-treatment facility, a wildlife habitat, a sink for aircraft noise, an airport, a housing site, a place of recreation, a source of fill for building, a commercial centre, a pitch for fishermen, a solid-waste dump and, perhaps as important as any of the above, a political football. Though New York City designated it a park in 1948, almost nothing has been done to fulfil this promise. As far back as 1931, New York City grew concerned that the Bay was a hazard to health but only in the last decade has work started on upgrading the water in it to make it fit for swimming. Concern for the ecology of the Bay is more recent.

The single most dominant force in the bay's recent life is Kennedy International Airport. Kennedy was created from Jamaica Bay. Its 5,000 acres are composed of sand pumped mainly from the northest quandrant of the bay. The average depth of the bay has been increased from 3 to 16 feet and about 70 per cent of its volume results from dredging.

At its inception 35 years ago Kennedy Airport was thought to be a highly imaginative bit of planning. It lay near the city in a then thinly populated place. Few contested its construction during the mid 1940s and, due no doubt to the infrequency of flights and excitement with aero-technology, a period of grace prevailed until the introduction of commercial jets and the rapid growth of the region's population in the later 1950s.

A second airport was constructed in the early 1940s on Barren Island in the southwest quandrant of the almost-circular bay and served until recently as a naval air station. Several years ago this 2,800-acre installation was declared surplus and is soon to be diverted to other purposes. Competition for its future use, like that of the bay, has been heated. A federal decision to make Barren Island part of the Gateway National Seashore conflicts with the aim of the State Housing Authorities to use the site for housing despite its exposure to high levels (30NEF)(1) of aircraft noise.

1) NEF: an approximate conversion to NNI (Noise and Number Index) between the 30-60 NNI range is NEF $\simeq$ 1½ unit charge = 45 NNI.

An additional 4,000 acres along the western and north-western rim of the bay have been used as a tip for rubbish and solid wastes for nearly three decades. These conversions have reduced the bay from 25,000 to 13,000 acres.

Jurisdiction over Kennedy Airport and Jamaica Bay is exercised by 44 political or civil entities which in part explains why "everybody's business" was attended to by no one until 1972.

Jamaica Bay, though polluted and insulted by the technology, economics and politics of man, is the only significant estuary left to the people of New York City. And despite the insults poured upon it, the bay is still a reasonably healthy ecosystem and still serves as an efficient tertiary treatment system for 220 million gallons a day of partially treated sewage. Admittedly the bay shows signs of decay. It contains large numbers of coliform bacteria and has a low level of dissolved oxygen. Some species found in healthy estuaries are absent and others usually found in polluted ones are present. Nevertheless it still works. Some 60 species of fish and shellfish use the bay as a nursery and over 300 species of birds have been recorded at the sanctuary provided in 1954.

ENVIRONMENTAL IMPACTS

One of the first tasks of the study group was to consider the PNYA's claim that increased capacity was needed at the city's airports, even though short-term fluctuations in air travel pointed to the beginnings of a decline.

The group concluded that environmental damage would result whatever action was taken. The alternatives examined included administrative measures to reduce general aviation flights, the marrying up of competing flights, improved air traffic control, runway extensions, the construction of new runways into Jamaica Bay and the construction of a fourth New York jetport.

The study group concluded that a reduction of the noise impact was strongly dependent upon the technology of aircraft engines, while the environmental damage of runway construction depended on the amount and location of land and water needed. The latter was in turn closely related to improvements in air-traffic control.

The report went on to say that improvements in air-traffic control would make it possible for the gap between independently operated parallel runways to be cut by half to 2,500 feet or for dual runways to be spaced as little as 1,000 feet apart. In the cases considered the capacity would lie between today's 35 landings and a maximum of 100 landings per hour or more than twice the estimated demand of 45 in 1980.

Reductions in engine noise are possible through two recent developments. The first involves replacing existing nacelles with ones that reduce engine noise to levels closer to the Department of Transportation standards now in force for new aircraft(1). This treatment, costing about $500,000 per plane, could be fully implemented by 1975 if required. The second approach involves redesigned engines the noise level of which would lie 10 EPNdb (effective perceived noise level) below the present Transportation Department rule(2). Such engines, which could be available by 1975, would cost about $4 million to install in existing four-engine aircraft, but would raise the cost of new aircraft by only 10 per cent.

The noise effects of aircraft on people living near airports depend upon the characteristics of the aircraft being used, the number of flights and the runways used. Since engine technology can be advanced independent of airport operations, this improvement has been set in the context of the runway configurations and levels of usage predicted for Kennedy in 1980. This shows that larger numbers of people can be saved from excessive noise (above NEF 30) by modifying existing engines or fitting quiet ones than by building new runways farther out into the bay.

Construction of runways in Jamica Bay would require dredging and filling that would affect water quality and ecology. The area of water and marsh would be reduced, the tidal regime would be changed and existing patterns of surface drainage and water circulation interfered with. The acquisition and disposal of fill would raise other problems. Increased airport usage resulting from runway extensions would lead to further, indirect effects. Larger aircraft-fuel demands would increase the danger of oil spills. Demand at sewage treatment facilities would increase as would interference with water-based recreation, air pollution and bird-strike dangers.

The runway layouts considered would obliterate between 5 and 28 per cent of the water in the bay and from 1 to 26 per cent of the marshland. If the higher percentages were taken, the continuation of the marsh and of marine ecosystems would be endangered and water quality in the eastern end of the bay would be degraded. The relocation of sewage outfalls might be required.

---

1) FAR 36 (United States Federal Aviation Regulation 36 for aircraft noise). A new proposal will also limit average fleet noise by 1975 to FAR 36.

2) This would reduce noise footprints about ten times depending on the flight path and number of movements. EPNdb is about equal to PNdb $\pm$ 2 depending on duration and pure tone components. PNdb $\simeq$ dBA + 13.

Between 20 and 175 million cubic yards of fill would have to be obtained, and up to 18 million cubic yards of spoil disposed, outside the bay. This filling and dredging on circulation patterns in the bay require further study.

The more extensive of the runway layouts could lead to increases in bird strikes and raise questions of aircraft safety. At present there are more bird strikes at Kennedy than at any other United States airport. The number and size of birds being hit will increase as the runways intrude farther into the heart of the bay. Extensive filling of water and marsh areas near and between runways will be required to counter this tendency.

PRINCIPAL CONCLUSIONS AND RECOMMENDATIONS OF THE STUDY

The study group concluded: "Any runway construction will damage the natural environment of the Bay and reduce its potential use for conservation, recreation and housing. The degree of this impairment will be dependent upon the amount of Bay area taken. A sufficiently large land-taking, such as that proposed by the Port of New York Authority, could cause major irreversible ecological damage to the Bay.

"It is impossible to improve the Bay environment by technological means. Such improvements may be made independent of any airport expansion scheme, but any expansion would increase the economic costs or dilute the benefits of these improvements."

The study group recommended that: "The Port of New York Authority, in co-operation with the Civil Aeronautics Board and the Federal Aviation Administration, institute immediately a programme of landing fees, consolidation of flight schedules, and other administrative devices that will eliminate existing congestion and and allow for a more efficient utilisation of existing system capacity."

"If there is (still) a proven need in the future for increased runway capacity ... then additional runways might be considered, which would require minimal land-taking in the Bay. No new runways should be constructed ... unless it can be shown that the benefits exceed the costs, where benefits and costs include a full consideration of their impact upon people and the environment of the Bay area and the metropolitan region."

"... begin an intensive study of alternative systems for inter-city air and ground transport, such as vertical or short takeoff and landing aircraft and high-speed trains, which might affect future regional jetport needs."

"The Secretary of Transportation, ... appropriate state and local governmental agencies, should make an evaluation of the congestion problem, both at terminals and with respect to the ground access to the three major airports in the region, and propose plans to reduce this congestion."

"Aircraft noise, and, to a lesser extent, air and water pollution related to airport operation are perceived as major environmental hazards by residents in communities surrounding commercial airports. We have examined these effects in the environs of Kennedy Airport, and have concluded that: the construction of new runways will not significantly reduce the number of residents of nearby areas exposed to intense aircraft noise. Major reduction in noise exposure can come only from use of quieter aircraft."

"On both the local and federal level, measures need to be taken to reduce the impact of aircraft noise."

"Public authorities ... should establish and vigorously enforce building construction standards that protect the health and welfare of occupants against aircraft noise. These standards should apply to all new construction especially public buildings such as schools and publicly supported housing."

"In view of the present impact of noise on the community around the airport, all relevant public agencies, ... should press for the development and installation of quiet engines on aircraft."

"The Department of Transportation should: require the installation of acoustically treated nacelles on all existing aircraft by 1975 ... accelerate ... the development of quiet engines, and establish a regulation requiring that all new aircraft have engines that are quieter by 10 EPNdb (effective perceived noise level) below present standards by 1975."

"We have considered the many possible ways in which Jamaica Bay may be used to satisfy the need of the people of the New York area. With respect to some of these uses, we have concluded that: the permanent conversion of any estuarine area to airport or other commercial or industrial use diminishes a national environmental asset of great potential value to future generations. Although Jamaica Bay has been greatly altered by man's activities, its ecological viability can be maintained indefinitely into the future by environmental improvements only if no additional major incursions into the bay occur.

"To achieve this potential for sustaining a livable environment for millions of people near the bay we recommend the following actions: in the next ten years, the City of New York should develop Jamaica Bay extensively for conservation and recreational uses by its own citizens and for compatible housing. This requires completion of its existing sewage treatment programme, immediate termination of dredging and sanitary-landfill operations, and the extension of mass-transit connections to shoreside areas."

"The State of New York should establish a Jamaica Bay planning commission, composed of representatives of the bay communities, the Port of New York Authority and other relevent city, state and Nassau County agencies, which should be charged with developing a comprehensive long-range plan for compatible development of the bay and its contiguous land areas. The planning programme should provide opportunity for direct community participation in the formulation of proposals and decisions affecting the uses of the bay and its related land area, including airport improvements and operations that impinge on the quality of life in adjacent communities."

The study group then stated its concern that the issues might be seen by some in simplistic terms: "It is our hope that public understanding and discussion of these issues and the options that exist will eventually lead to wise decisions regarding actions to be taken. It is our fear that partisan debate will oversimplify the choices to 'birds versus planes' or 'jobs versus pollution.' In our experience, no environmental problem can be comprehended in such limited terms, nor do we expect that the environmental improvement so sorely needed by our nation can be secured through decisions so narrowly informed."

"The economic and political costs of implementing these recommendations may be large, but, they are bearable. These are the unavoidable costs of maintaining a livable environment for urban populations. For Jamaica Bay, the environmental bill is due now."

Chapter 12

AIRPORT AND NEW TOWN IN SWEDEN

C.L. Ahlberg and R. Persson
Stockholm County Council Regional Planning Bureau

INTRODUCTION

What happens when a major airport is developed near a big city? The most obvious effects can be observed in the vicinity of the airport. It is more difficult to identify any wider effects because of the complex interaction of factors influencing urban growth. This paper will therefore focus on the interplay between airport development and urban planning with special reference to Stockholm's Arlanda airport and the nearby town of Märsta. Such a process could be described in physical, economic or social terms but as the authors of this paper are physical planners at the regional level the main emphasis will be put on physical conditions and physical planning.

Arlanda and Märsta are examples of co-ordinated planning of airport and community development and as twelve years has elapsed since their inception it is possible to compare what was planned and what has happened. Perhaps the results will be useful for planners elsewhere.

Arlanda airport was built to receive jets which were too noisy to be allowed to use Bromma which is much closer to Stockholm. The town of Märsta was initially planned to provide homes and services for those working at the airport.

This paper will investigate the following aspects of the development of Arlanda:

a) the selection process and the criteria applied to evaluate potential sites;
b) the town planning process which led to a co-ordinated plan for the airport and its associated community;
c) how development followed or deviated from the plan;
d) the future.

THE SEARCH FOR A SITE

Stockholm's first airport was a basin for seaplanes temporarily established at Lindarängen just outside the city in 1921. It was extended and became permanent in 1929. That same year, the City Council reserved a site for "an airfield for landplanes" at Bromma, seven kilometres from the centre of the city. In 1935, Bromma was opened for scheduled flights and it is still in use today after many extensions (Figure 1).

During the Second World War, when aeronautical technique developed rapidly, the question of a new airport for Stockholm was raised and in 1944 the Government appointed a committee which proposed a site at Grillby about 65 kilometres north-west of the City. What finally fixed the choice of the location was the fact that aeronautical technique demanded a large, level area free from obstruction. The committee attached little importance to the airport's distance from Stockholm and to the poor capacity of the ground to support heavy structures. The proposal was subsequently rejected and the need for any new site to consist of solid ground established. After some deliberation a site was chosen at Halmsjön, about 40 kilometres north of Stockholm.

In 1946, Parliament agreed to build an airport at Halmsjön and a layout was proposed with runways in three directions. One of these, an east-west runway, was built whereupon work was discontinued. A study of community development possibilities led to sketches for a new town at Rosersberg about 10 kilometres from the airport (Figure 2).

Suggestions were then made that Bromma should be extended to become a major airport thus reducing the total investment in airport construction. Increases in air traffic and - no less important - the introduction of jets showed, however, that Bromma, surrounded as it was by buildings, was too confined. At that point renewed attention was given to the development of Halmsjön.

In 1956, a site at Jordbro about 25 kilometres south of central Stockholm was put forward as an alternative to Halmsjön and justified on grounds of access and cost. Its location to the south of the city rather than 40 kilometres to the north of it meant that most flights would have been shorter and thus less costly and that it would have been possible to save time and money on road improvements. The proposal was nevertheless rejected because it conflicted with military requirements and because of concern about noise. The proposal also led to the first serious stuides of aircraft noise in Sweden.

In 1957, yet another site was proposed at Ska Edeby about 25 kilometres west of Stockholm. It was considered acceptable from the point of view of noise and superior to Halmsjön in all other respects but was eliminated because the moist clay soil would not have been

Figure 1

SITES WHERE AIRPORTS HAVE BEEN BUILT OR CONSIDERED

SITES OU LA CONSTRUCTION D'AEROPORTS A ETE ENVISAGEE OU REALISEE

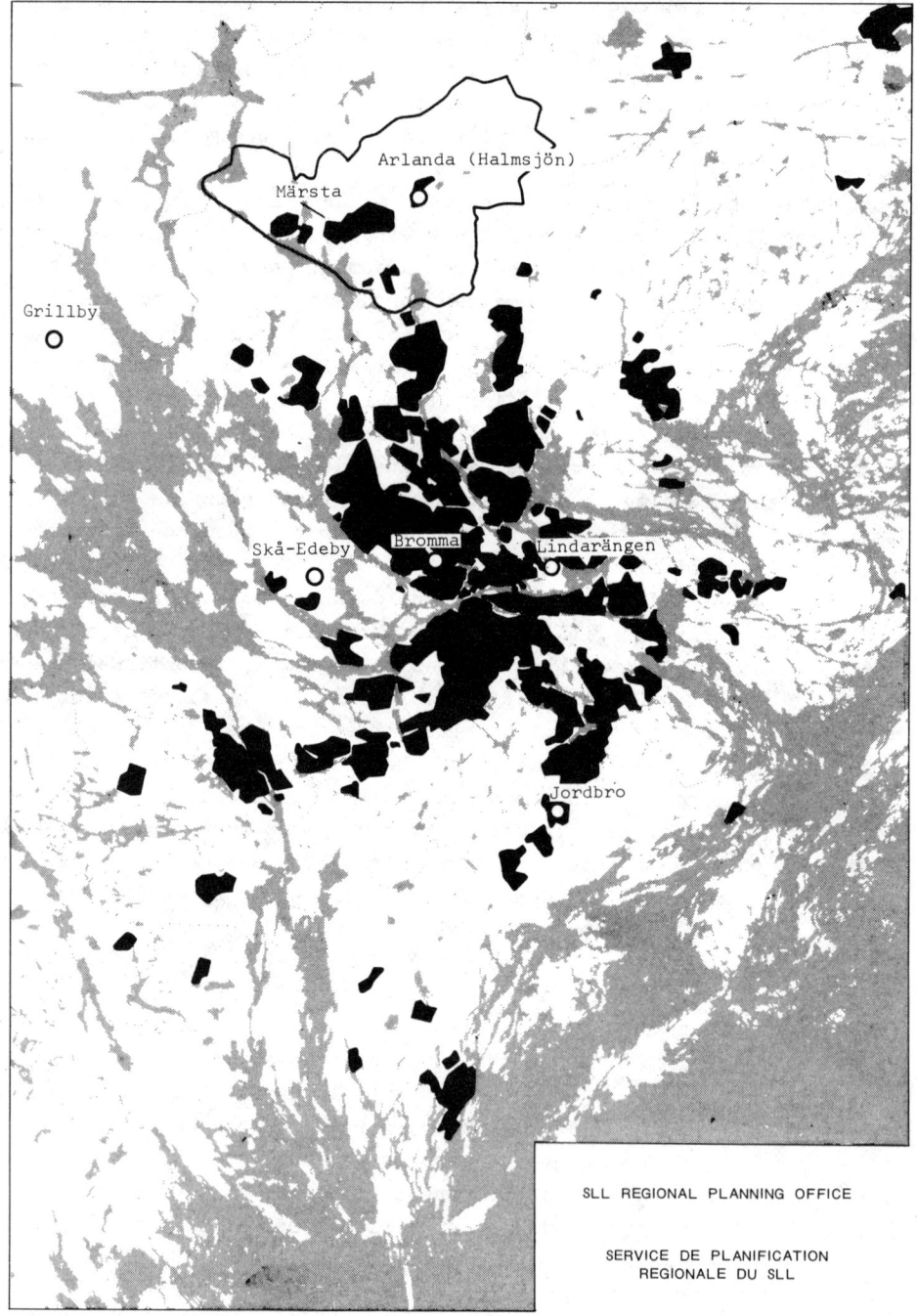

SLL REGIONAL PLANNING OFFICE

SERVICE DE PLANIFICATION
REGIONALE DU SLL

Figure 2

ARLANDA

DEVELOPMENT PROPOSED IN 1946 - PROJET DE DEVELOPPEMENT DE 1946

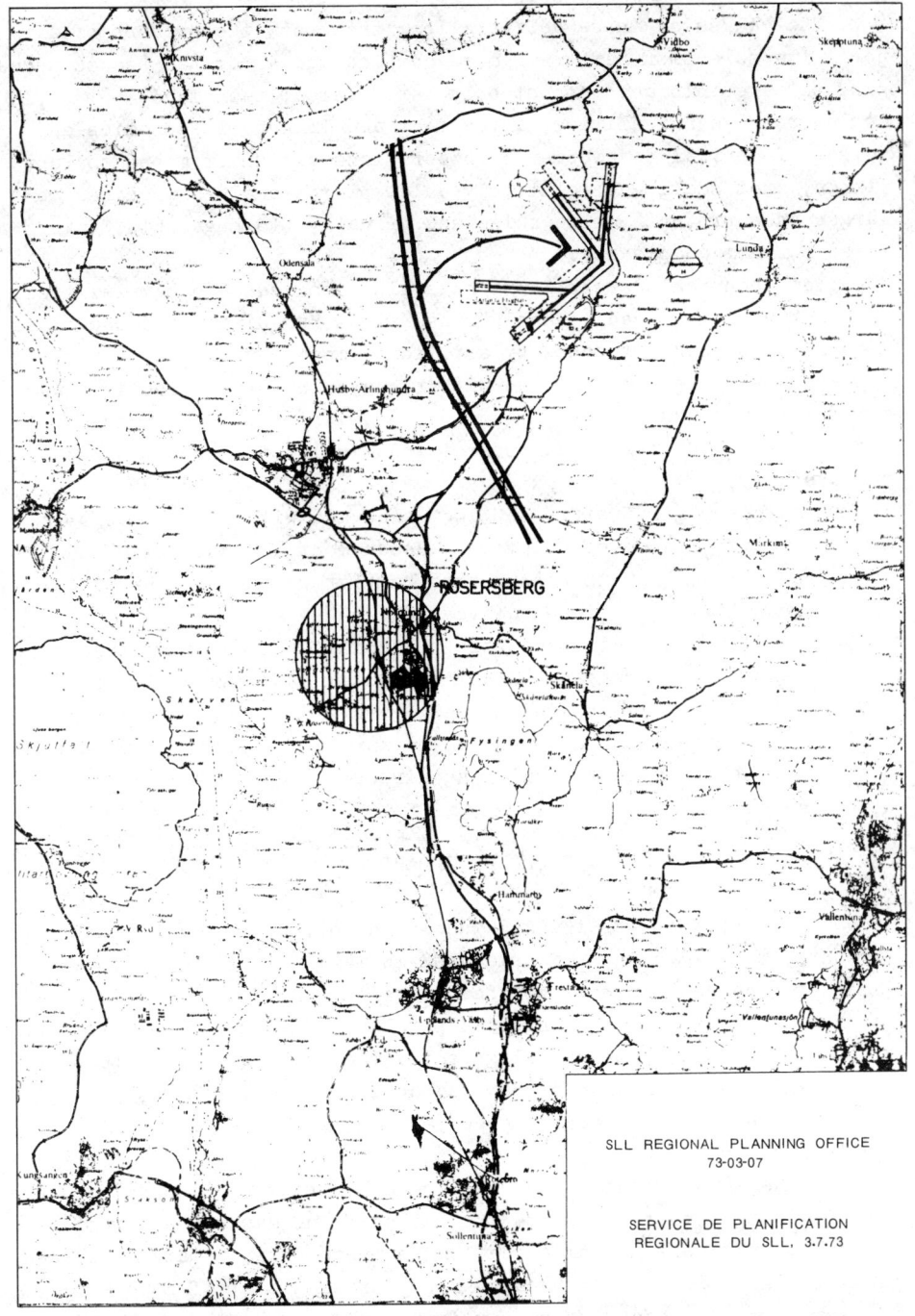

SLL REGIONAL PLANNING OFFICE
73-03-07

SERVICE DE PLANIFICATION
REGIONALE DU SLL, 3.7.73

able to support runways for heavy aircraft. A decision was therefore made in the same year to continue building up Halmsjön, which was named Arlanda.

The course of these deliberations shows how the process of airport site selection has grown more complicated as it has become necessary to take into account not only aeronautical technique, but civil engineering technicalities, investment and transport economics and noise. Technical developments in aeroplane design from sea to land planes, from small and relatively quiet piston-engined machines to larger ones producing more noise and, finally, to huge jets, have added further complexity.

Yet technical developments have also removed some complexities. For instance, the need to avoid cross winds has diminished and sites capable of being approached by air from almost any direction such as Grillby have given way to ones with runways in three directions as in the first Halmsjön project, then to ones with only two runways as in the second Halmsjön-Arlanda project and finally to ones with parallel runways only.

Meanwhile, air traffic has increased and with it the economic and social importance of aviation. Resentment against noise and demands to be freed of its disturbance have grown amongst the public and their political representatives too.

Gradually the factors considered decisive in choosing major airport sites have changed. A common denominator may be found in the need to find sites suited to new types of aircraft though in recent years attention has begun to be turned to finding aircraft that would be suitable for existing airports.

THE CHOICE OF ARLANDA

The first step was the 1957 decision to make Arlanda a major airport. What were the criteria used in making this selection and what were the consequences of that decision?

The proposed airport involved parallel north-south runways, and a third one on an east-west alignment. The new town was to be based on the existing community of Märsta, as it was realised that Roserberg, which had been proposed earlier, would be exposed to aircraft noise.

The Regional Planning Bureau of the District of Stockholm consequently decided to investigate the expansion of Märsta, a few kilometres further north. Communications between Arlanda-Märsta and central Stockholm were to be handled by up-grading part of European Highway 4 into a motorway, and by improving an existing railroad. Märsta already had a railway station. Arlanda was to be connected at a later stage by a branch from the main line.

In the decision it was declared that "the State in so far as possible, should promote the establishment of the necessary housing developments, schools and social facilities". Moreover, it was agreed that a specially appointed committee composed of local and national government representatives would participate in the planning of Märsta.

As yet little had been done except to make the decision to build the airport. The runway layout had been sketched and costs assessed, but noise estimates, as well as plans for the associated community development were lacking. The general feeling was that if a sufficiently remote site were selected (about 40 kilometres from the centre) problems from noise would not arise.

PLANNING THE AIRPORT AND ITS NEW TOWN

At one stage it was proposed to set up an English-style new town development agency to co-ordinate the build-up of the airport and its associated community but this would have been contrary to the deeply-rooted Swedish tradition of local self-government. It was therefore decided to leave the responsibility for expanding Märsta with the local authorities, while the Märsta committee already referred to was given advisory status. The task of this committee, which was composed of local and national government representatives under the chairmanship of the governor of Stockholm County, was to assist the local authorities in drawing up a master plan and with obtaining government finance.

The airport planning and the civil engineering work were done almost simultaneously. The existing east-west runway was obsolete and needed substantial improvements. The construction of the new main runway 01-19 was initiated. A temporary terminal building was built and by 1959 the airport was able to receive DC-8 aircraft.

A few years earlier, the Defence Department had convened a committee to study the problems associated with the introduction of military jet planes. The committee studied civil airports as well, and was instructed to focus on noise at Arlanda. The first estimates of aircraft noise were submitted to the Märsta committee in early 1958 and at the time they did not seem to pose any problems for the new town.

The 1958 Stockholm regional plan proposed development at Märsta (Figure 3) and the Regional Planning Bureau was instructed to prepare a master plan for the municipality. Forecasts were therefore made of direct and indirect employment at Arlanda, and used to calculate demand for houses (Tables 1 and 2).

The first draft of the master plan proposed four residential areas. These were to be located on the north, south, east and west

Table 1

FORECASTS OF EMPLOYMENT AT ARLANDA AND IN THE COMMUNITY OF MÄRSTA TO 1990

	1960	1963		1970		1980		1990	
		alt.I	alt.II	alt.I	alt.II	alt.I	alt.II	alt.I	alt.II
Scandinavian Airways System:									
Aircraft maintenance staff	185	530	700	1,750	1,750	3,700	5,000	5,000	5,000
Other staff	30	220	380	290	290				
Aviation management	90	220	220	40	40				
Other governmental authorites	10	30	30	150	150				
Other airline companies	--	100	100	150	150				
Aviation Service	--	100	150	220	220				
Industry	750	750	1,050	1,000	2,000	2,000	3,000	3,000	4,000
Construction enterprises	250	250	250	250	270	300	300	300	350
Intercommunication	75	200	370	275	630	500	950	750	1,300
Trade and other cons. services	70	210	530	500	1,150	2,500	3,100	3,500	4,400
Official services	140	296	420	500	1,250	1,700	1,900	2,500	2,600
TOTAL, about	1,700	2,900	4,200	5,000	7,750	10,700	14,250	15,000	17,600

Table 2

TOTAL POPULATION IN THE COMMUNITY OF MÄRSTA ON THE ASSUMPTION THAT
THOSE WORKING AT ARLANDA AND IN THE COMMUNITY ALSO SETTLE IN MÄRSTA

Year	Alt.I	Alt.II	Year	Alt.I	Alt.II
1959	2,900	2,900	1975	20,000	27,000
1963	7,000	10,000	1980	27,000	36,000
1965	9,000	13,000	1990	38,000	44,000
1970	12,000	19,000			

Figure 3

MÄRSTA IN THE 1958 REGIONAL PLAN FOR STOCKHOLM

MÄRSTA DANS LE PLAN D'AMENAGEMENT REGIONAL DE STOCKHOLM DE 1958

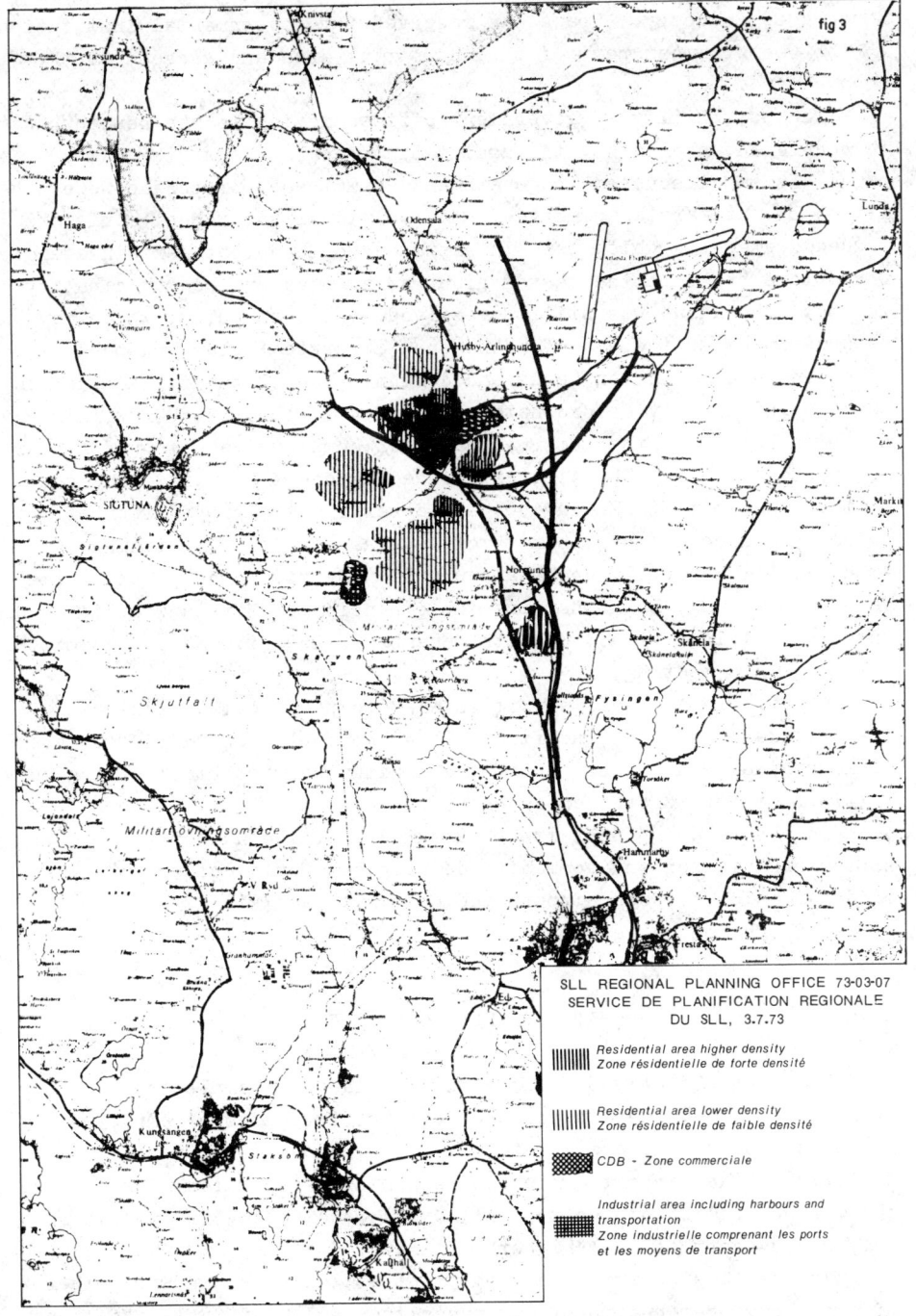

SLL REGIONAL PLANNING OFFICE 73-03-07
SERVICE DE PLANIFICATION REGIONALE
DU SLL, 3.7.73

Residential area higher density
Zone résidentielle de forte densité

Residential area lower density
Zone résidentielle de faible densité

CDB - Zone commerciale

Industrial area including harbours and
transportation
Zone industrielle comprenant les ports
et les moyens de transport

sides of a town centre. Later, when the new north-south main runway at Arlanda was proposed, calculations showed there would be a shift in the noise contours, and the eastern area had to be changed from housing to industry. Space was reserved for governmental institutions in the western-most part of the industrial area and closest to the town centre.

The possibility of government offices moving to the new town was to become an uncertainty throughout the preparation of the master plan. It was discussed in government committees, proposals were submitted by the Märsta committee, and individual government ministers issued statements which were interpreted to mean that certain agencies would move but when the master plan was adopted by the municipality in 1963, the issue was still unresolved. At that point, which may be considered as the end of phase one, a physical plan had been devised in which aviation needs and community development planning had been satisfactorily co-ordinated (Figure 4). About 2,500 dwellings had been built and the motorway had been completed as planned as far as Märsta in 1963. The Aircraft Noise Abatement Committee had submitted its report in March 1961 and described the propagation of noise annoyance in the vicinity of several airports, including Arlanda. It was still uncertain whether any governmental enterprises were to be moved, but otherwise the expansion of Märsta went in accord with the original plan. On 14th December, 1963, the Märsta committee held its last meeting.

Today, ten years later, it is easy to point out deficiencies in the original plan. In the first place, noise levels in the new areas of Märsta were only a bit below the maximum permissible, leaving very little room for unforeseen changes.

In the second place, it was assumed that the authorities responsible for aviation and community development would enforce the line of demarcation between airport and community activities as specified in the flight noise report.

WHAT HAPPENED THEREAFTER?

Were the objectives defined in the plan for completion by 1963 fulfilled? The answer is yes and no. The forecasts of employment turned out to be quite accurate. In 1970, about 2,500 persons were employed at the airport, which corresponds to estimates made in 1958 and the population of the town of Märsta rose to 16,800 by 1970 or only 2,200 short of the "higher" estimate.

Forecasts of travel and employment at the new town were wider of the mark. Fewer airport employees than expected, only about one third, live in Märsta and half of Märsta residents travel to work

Figure 4

MASTER PLAN FOR MÄRSTA - SCHEMA DIRECTEUR DE MARSTA

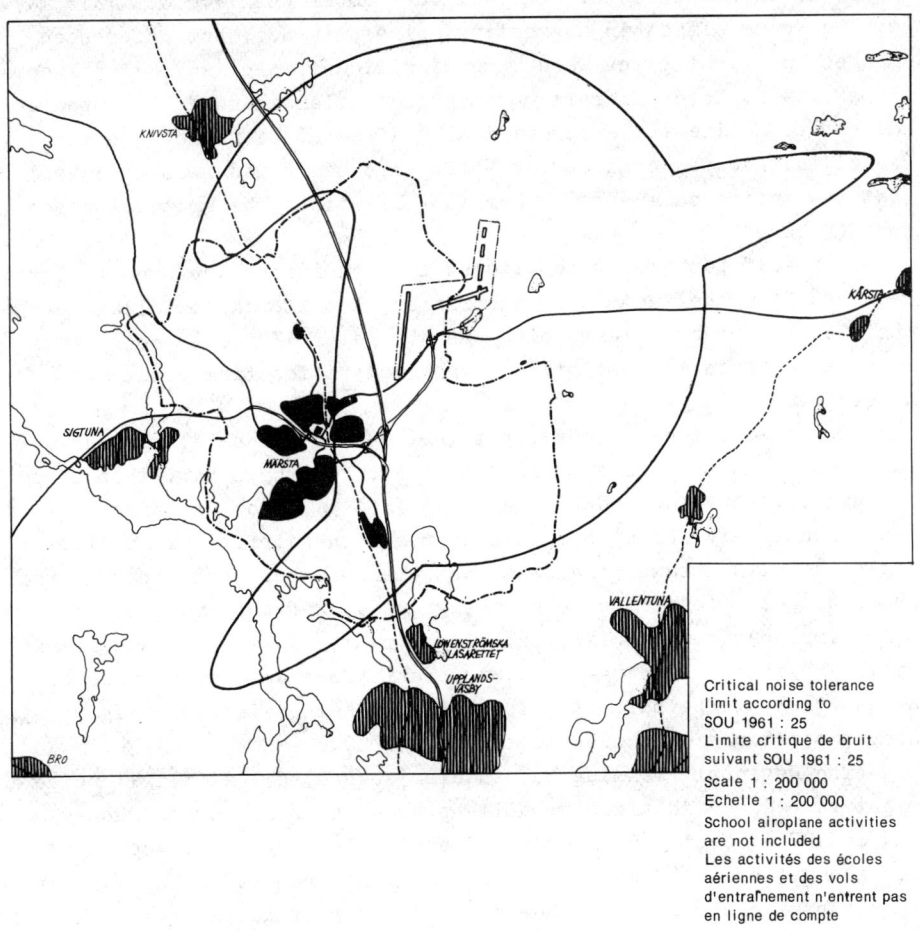

Critical noise tolerance
limit according to
SOU 1961 : 25
Limite critique de bruit
suivant SOU 1961 : 25

Scale 1 : 200 000
Echelle 1 : 200 000

School airoplane activities
are not included
Les activités des écoles
aériennes et des vols
d'entraînement n'entrent pas
en ligne de compte

No new residential should be planned inside the noise tolerance limit
Aucune zone résidentielle nouvelle ne doit être prévue à l'intérieur des limites critiques de bruit

REGIONAL PLANNING OFFICE 1960 - SERVICE DE PLANIFICATION REGIONALE DU SLL, 1960

outside the community. Many of them commute to Stockholm. The
situation might have been different had the expected decentralisation of government work taken place.

Estimates of air traffic were more accurate. In 1959, it was
forecast that the number of aircraft movements at Arlanda would increase to 62,000 by 1970. In fact the number was 77,000. This may
have had some effect in augmenting noise nuisance, but unforeseen
changes in flight paths were more significant. In 1967 a local committee re-examined aircraft movements at Arlanda and called upon an
advisor to define the area critically affected by noise. This revealed that 40 per cent of take-offs were being made westward and
that the entire community of Märsta fell within the critical noise
zone (Figure 5).

Take-off patterns were altered and conditions improved following
requests from the municipal authorities, but it was now clear that
the 1961 report on flight noise was obsolete. It could no longer
serve as a basis for isolating flight activities from urban
development.

There were two reasons for this. On the one hand, methods for
calculating noise annoyance had improved. On the other, technology
had not developed as had been assumed in 1961. For instance, it had
become customary for aircraft to approach the airfield at a flatter
angle and with greater engine thrust than had been anticipated, thereby leading to greater noise on the ground. Further study of the
noise implications of different flight patterns was then undertaken
by the Regional Planning Bureau to enable forecasts to be made of
areas likely to be subjected to "critical noise" in 1985 (Figure 6).
Some projections were made to the year 2000.

The Regional Planning Bureau also suggested that flight noise
might be reduced in already built-up areas by rearranging runways
and in 1971 the Stockholm County Council Planning Committee asked
for the matter to be studied. The resulting report, which was ready
by the beginning of 1972, showed that east-west runways were the only
alternative to the present north-south one taking into account the
position of Märsta and wind conditions (Figure 7). However, no decision had been made up to the middle of 1973 and uncertainty surrounded the future expansion of Arlanda and its surrounding
communities.

In the case of the airport, the choices facing the public authorities are the construction of a second north-south runway, a
change to east-west runways, or the construction of another airport
at some other site.

In the case of Märsta it is not clear whether future noise conditions will permit the south-west part of the town to be built. If

Figure 5

DEVELOPMENT BY 1985 - DEVELOPPEMENT PREVU POUR 1985

Aircraft noise from Arlanda
Bruit des avions provenant d'Arlanda

Estimated noise tolerance limit in 1967 excluding school airoplane activities
Limite critique du bruit estimé en 1967, vols d'entraînement non compris

SLL REGIONAL PLANNING OFFICE
SERVICE DE PLANIFICATION REGIONALE DU SLL

INGEMANSSONS ENGINEERING OFFICE - BUREAU D'ETUDES INGEMANSON

Residential area
Zone résidentielle
Employment area
Zone d'emploi

Figure 6

AIRCRAFT NOISE FROM ARLANDA BY 1985

BRUIT DES AVIONS, PROVENANT D'ARLANDA, EN 1985

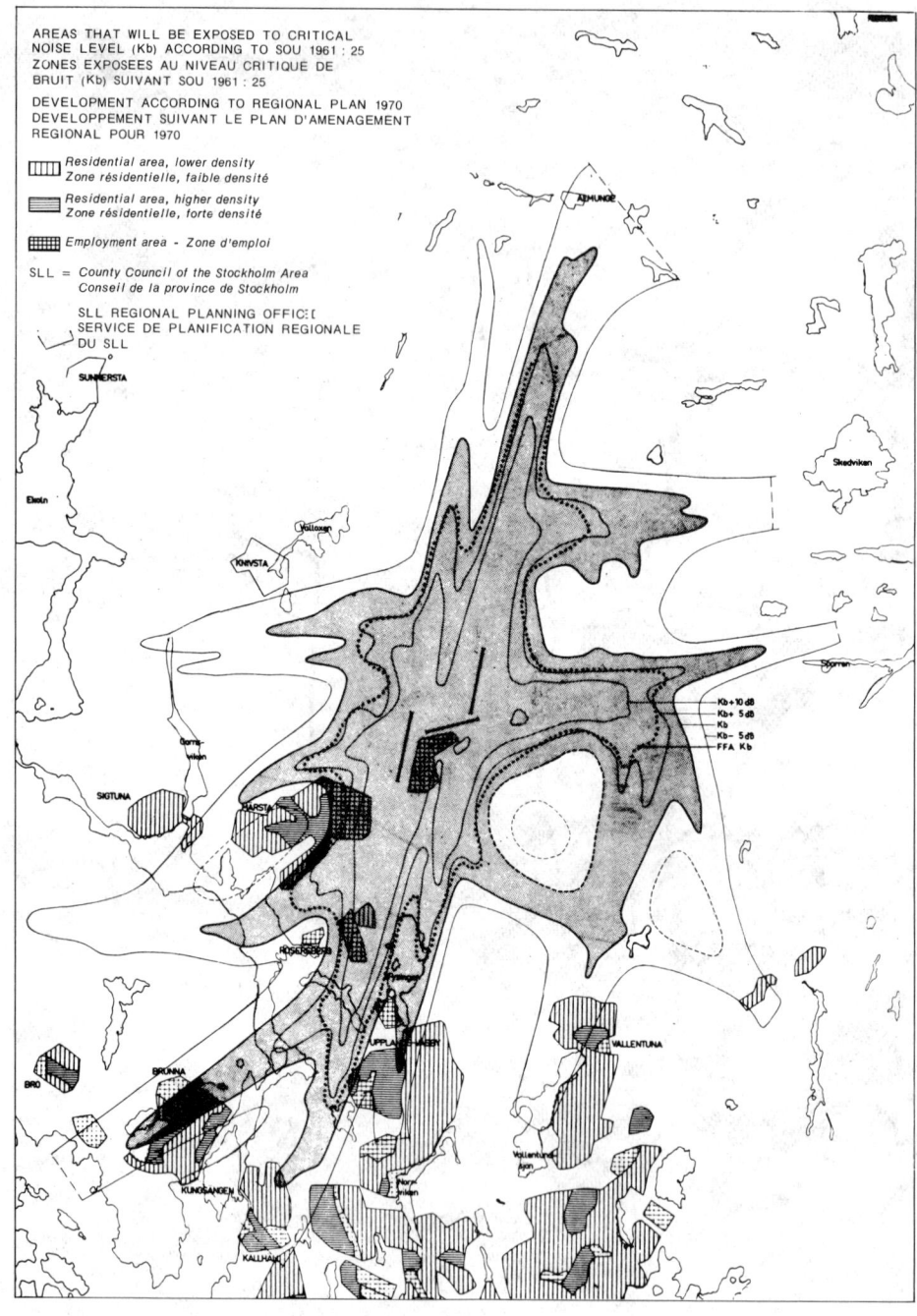

Figure 7

ALTERNATIVE RUNWAY SYSTEMS AT ARLANDA - LOCATION OF THE SECOND EAST-WEST RUNWAY
VARIANTE DE DISPOSITION DES PISTES A ARLANDA - POSITION DE LA SECONDE PISTE EST-OUEST

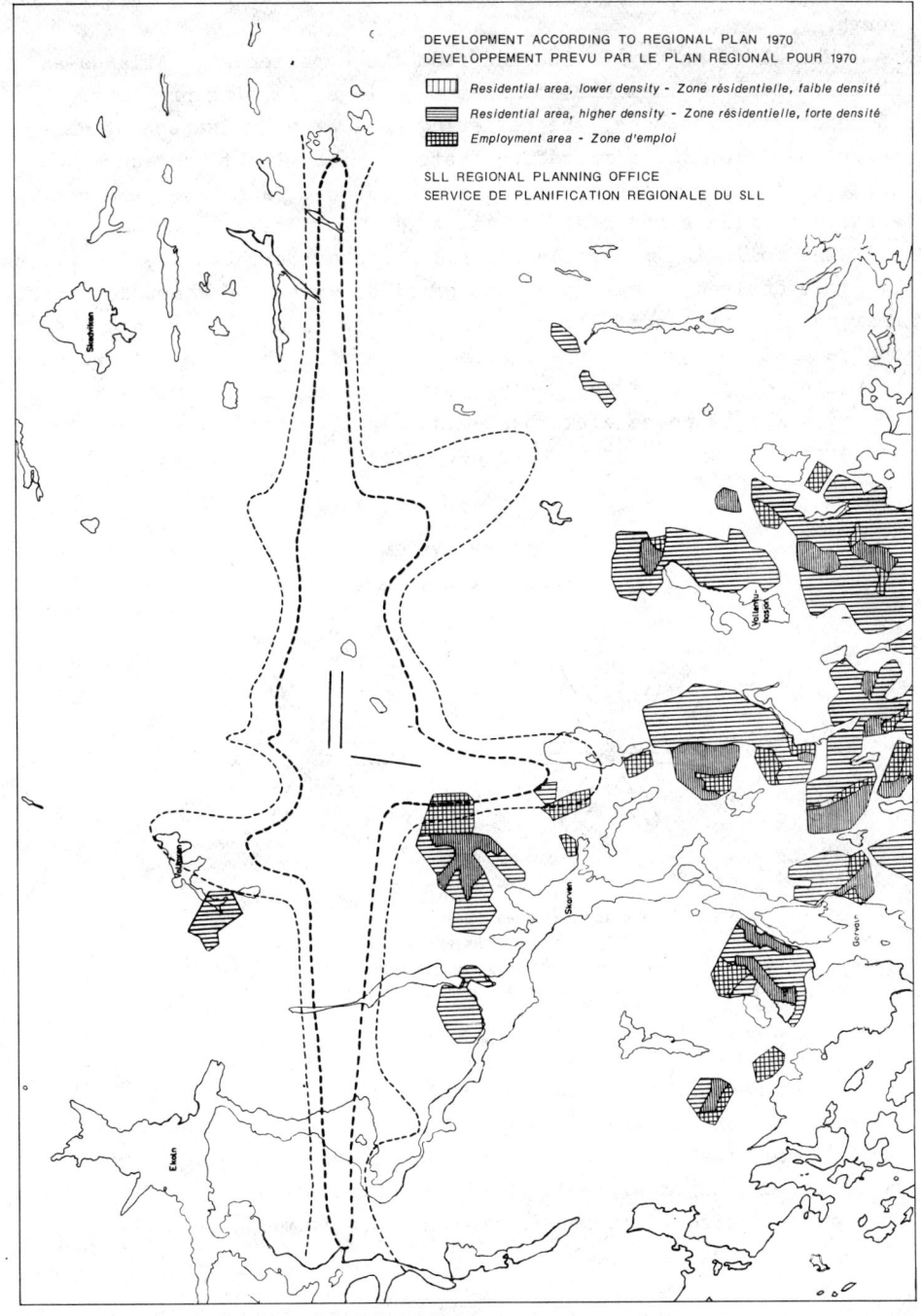

DEVELOPMENT ACCORDING TO REGIONAL PLAN 1970
DEVELOPPEMENT PREVU PAR LE PLAN REGIONAL POUR 1970

Residential area, lower density - Zone résidentielle, faible densité

Residential area, higher density - Zone résidentielle, forte densité

Employment area - Zone d'emploi

SLL REGIONAL PLANNING OFFICE
SERVICE DE PLANIFICATION REGIONALE DU SLL

it cannot, then the whole master plan will have to be revised. And pending a solution to the noise issue, development has even had to be discontinued in other parts of the Stockholm area that are further south.

What lessons may be learned from the experience of Arlanda and Märsta? Some of them are still at the stage of being problems. There is, for instance, the differing rate of amortization of different parts of the air traffic system - with flight procedures capable of being modified almost at the drop of a hat while a runway and its terminals may need to last 20 to 30 years.

The following principle for siting an airport can also be stated. If it is desired to make the most of sites with good communications near an airport, and full use of links between an airport and the centre of the city it serves, then the corridor between the two should be developed extensively. But to do so, it is imperative to restrict flight noise disturbance in this corridor. This may be achieved by placing the runways perpendicular or parallel to the corridor.

RUNWAY SYSTEM
DISPOSITION DES PISTES

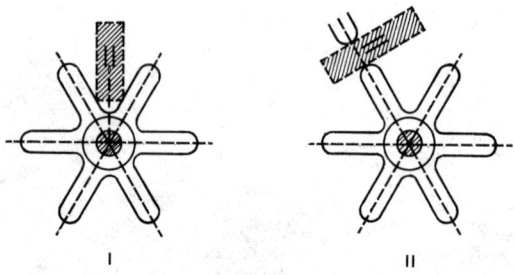

I. Parallel to Development Corridor
    Parallèlement à l'axe de développement

II. Perpendicular to Development Corridor
    Perpendiculairement à l'axe de développement

The Stockholm Regional Planning Bureau has clarified the array of studies necessary in order to gain insights into the likely development of an air traffic system. The Arlanda experience has also demonstrated the effect of a large airport on development and made it clear that major airports should be sited where they will help to promote desired patterns of regional development.

Chapter 13

ABATING NOISE: A SWISS APPROACH

Dr. Hans Reinhard
Zurich Cantonal Planning Authority

INTRODUCTION

Zurich airport, which was formerly an artillery range and a
forest, is ten kilometers north of the city centre. It came into
use in 1947 and has grown rapidly to provide access to Europe's
banking capital. Since 1960 passenger throughput has increased at
an average rate of 14 per cent each year and freight and cargo
tonnage at an average rate of 17 per cent each year. In 1972 the
airport handled 5.5 million passengers and 100,000 tons of freight.
It is estimated that by 1980 there will be 160,000 aircraft movements and that the airport will handle 12.5 million passengers and
300,000 tons of freight.

An expansion of the airport has been proposed to meet these
forecast demands. A new 3,000 meter runway, the extension of
existing cross-wind runways, a new terminal and a rapid transit
underground link to the city centre are involved. The airport is
however on the fringe of what has become a densely developed
suburb. As a result, there is concern that the expansion will increase noise annoyance and the need to bring the project through
the financial referendum made it essential to consider measures
to minimise this annoyance. The paper which follows outlines the
method proposed by the canton of Zurich for doing this. The
approach adopted is based on calculations of the noise contours
expected in 1980 and on the use of these contours for rezoning the
surroundings of the airport. This will involve redefining what
land uses are to be permitted. As rezoning will stop some landowners from using their property a method of compensating them
has been devised.

LEGAL ARRANGEMENTS

Measures to minimise the nuisance of noise from Zurich-Kloten airport are contained in legislation which was overwhelmingly supported by the voters of the canton in 1970. In addition to sanctioning the expansion of the airport, the new law gives the executive authority of the canton powers to lay down regulations prohibiting and restraining building and enforcing other noise protection on land owners. It also creates a fund out of airport operating profits to guarantee the means to give compensation. However as aviation is a federal responsibility in Switzerland the provisions of the law dealing with noise have no validity. Federal legislation on air travel is therefore having to be revised, and it is expected that new federal regulations will soon be announced.

A description follows of studies and plans produced by the canton of Zurich that are expected to be incorporated into the Swiss regulations.

DETERMINING NOISE ANNOYANCE

The Noise and Number Index (NNI) developed in England has been used to measure noise annoyance. This index is distinguished by its simplicity and comprehensibility and has been used extensively for psycho-sociological surveys.

It is defined as follows:

$$NNI = L_{PN} + 15 \log N - 80$$

where

L_{PN} = average value of noise peaks expressed in perceived noise decibels (PNdB)

N = number of flight movements.

The PNdB level to be used in this calculation is the peak noise of a flight and it is to be determined by a procedure that has not yet been worked out in detail. The number of flight movements considered are limited to those taking place between 6 a.m. and 10 p.m. (Annex 1).

But after a few trials it became clear that such measurements would not produce results uniform enough to be the basis of regulations for noise zones or land use. Too many variables such as flight frequency, climate, noise deflections and reflections were involved and made it unlikely that legal action based on such noise measurements would be successful.

In addition it was found that measurements of current noise were almost useless for designing land-use regulations with a long-term effect because noise from planned runways could not be accurately estimated by extrapolation.

A noise model based on a number of different ten-year fore-casts was therefore prepared (Annex 2). Forecasts of fleet composition and of the use made of the various types of aircraft were used to arrive at future flight conditions and the resulting noise data used to evaluate the first NNI factor (L_{PN}). The factor N was also taken from forecasts of the development of air transport. Using these data, various linear grids were calculated and inscribed with the curves for the same NNI values resulting from various types of future runway systems as well as the corresponding take-off and landing paths. However, a first rough optimisation of the increased capacity and its consequent noise annoyance showed that certain runway systems could not be considered until essential improvements had become generalised. These NNI curves are reliable only within $\pm$ 5 NNI but this uncertainty is encountered throughout the entire system and it is not caused by the randomness of individual cases. The calculated curves therefore offer landowners a better guarantee of justice than measurements which, as previously mentioned, may be changed by the forecasts. However the uncertainty becomes critical in the design of noise zones and precludes contour intervals of less than 10 NNI.

SETTING LIMITS FOR ACCEPTABLE EXPOSURE

The English study already referred to was used as a point of departure in setting limits for acceptable exposure to noise. It holds that aircraft noise of between 50 and 60 NNI represents an unreasonably high burden. Additional research suggested that 55 NNI be set as a limit beyond which no residential housing be permitted.

Comparison of this limit with one adopted by the Federal German Republic in 1968 and revised in 1971 showed the two to be in all respects identical despite the different measurement philosophies used. United States court decisions indicated further support for the Swiss assumption that compensation should be awarded to landowners only when their property was exposed to aircraft noise of 55 NNI or more.

Other limits were deduced from the 55 NNI baseline. Thus a zone extending from 55 to 65 NNI is to be assigned to industrial areas which are more tolerant of noise emissions. Beyond that, the only uses permitted are - with a few exceptions - those not requiring the constant presence of people. Moving in the opposite direction the construction of housing will continue to be allowed in existing built-up areas in zones subjected to between 55 and

45 NNI provided it is protected against noise. (Such protection may be afforded by walls and ceilings of above certain thickness and by regulating the size and construction of windows). Special types of buildings such as hospitals and schools are restricted to even quieter areas.

The full details of the noise code are:

Zone	Permitted Use
a) 66 NNI and above	agriculture
	warehouses
	military installations
	airport buildings
b) 56 - 65 NNI	industrial and commercial buildings
	stores and offices protected against noise
	temporary housing protected against noise
c) 46 - 55 NNI	stores and offices
	housing protected against noise

However, these regulations apply only to development in existing residential zones. New housing schemes will be limited to areas with less than 45 NNI.

IMPLEMENTING PLANS FOR NOISE ZONING

The inaccuracy inherent in noise measurements and calculations makes it impossible to translate acoustical data directly into land-use plans. Nevertheless the limits within which the various development restrictions apply must be set in complete accordance with the agreed standards. The use of every piece of property, perhaps even for parts of it, has to be laid down. General planning criteria will therefore be used to define the limits for each zone, and the NNI curves used as directives to be taken into account as far as possible. Wherever no topographical peculiarities affect the delineation of noise zones care should be taken to set limits that create useful development sites. Furthermore, there must be no overlapping of housing and industrial zones lest residents be exposed to the additional burden of noise from factories. In existing built-up areas, zone boundaries should coincide with main roads which more or less follow the noise curves. The width of the band delineated by the curve or the measurements will then leave a margin that is essential in land-use planning. This was another reason for using the NNI standard. The level of accuracy it gives is in keeping with the conventions of town planning. A more refined method of evaluation would therefore not noticeably improve the standard of control.

An example of this is the noise zone plan for Rümlang (Annex 3). The shaded areas represent the present extent of development. The lightly shaded areas will in the future be subject to Zone B provisions. The black shading indicates Zone C where only noise-insulated housing may be built in the future. Zone A has not been indicated since the community has not set aside any area for buildings of this type and hence the land-use regulations do not need to be changed. The designation of new residential zones in the areas under 45 NNI is for the communities themselves to decide and is therefore not shown on the map.

The prospective federal regulations are expected to make airport authorities responsible for dealing with noise as part of general land-use planning. Their plans, subject to supervision by relevant federal agencies, will have precedence over the land-use regulations of the municipalities responsible for overall planning. The remit of the municipal planning authorities will only apply to new plans for residential zones lying below the 45 NNI contour and new industrial zones below 65 NNI.

The new regulations have been designed to be lasting. Should the noise footprints forecast ten years hence turn out to be insufficient or wrongly shaped, it is assumed that the airport will be obliged to curtail its activities rather than inflict noise above the agreed levels. In view of the intense building that tends to go on in the immediate surroundings of airports, rapid utilisation of the under-45-NNI zones can be counted on. Developments of this kind would be irreversible.

FINANCIAL EFFECTS

The financial effects of reducing noise nuisance cannot yet be foreseen. Restrictions on development resulting from the establishment of noise zones could lead to requests for compensation on the grounds that restriction amounts to dispossession. The attitude of the courts to such requests cannot be known beforehand.

In principle, dispossession occurs whevever any and all construction is forbidden as is the case in Zones A. However, to the extent that such zones comprise land lying outside areas authorised for development, and taking into account federal legislation that limits the use of such land for development on water conservation grounds, compensation costs may not be high.

Landowners in Zones B are unlikely to be able to lay claim on public funds since assignment to a zone has not so far been recognised in the courts as grounds for compensation. In most cases the landowner will indeed suffer no monetary damage since land prices surrounding airports are practically the same for housing areas of average density and for industrial sites. However, it is conceivable that compensation will be granted exceptionally in order to maintain confidence. Noise protection is thus considered to be just one more responsibility placed on builders - no different from other responsibilities for health and safety for which no compensation is available from the government, though here too exceptional cases are not excluded.

The financing of all these measures is guaranteed by the fund mentioned in the beginning of this report. This fund is fed from the profits of airport operations and, in case of need, the State. The money available amounts to Sw.Frs.10 million a year. The fund may however contract debts provided that its yearly income covers interest on the sum borrowed. This is intended to ensure that enough money will be available to meet the high demands expected in the first years of the new noise measures.

Separate standards were originally proposed for night and day. However, this approach was not used at Zurich-Kloten because night-time noise will be reduced by a partial prohibition of flights.

What the Zurich measurements did show was that a wide scatter of noise is manifest especially in partly-built areas. At sites close to runways this is primarily a result of reflection off buildings. At points further from airfields, permissible deviations from flight paths cause additional scatter up to the order of the model's imprecision. Moreover, experience shows that it is only in very rare cases where the ground is flat and there are no obstacles or reflections that measurements can be achieved which might be considered relatively reliable in a court of law. Further-more attempts to divide plots and fit them into different noise zones proved to be useless. It is just not possible to measure different levels of noise exposure in plots averaging 30-40m in width. Another difficulty is the tremendous number of measuring points needed in order to delineate use zones. Such measurements could be carried out only little by little and over a period. Varying flight frequency and changing atmospheric conditions would meanwhile probably result in different results being obtained for different places around the airport.

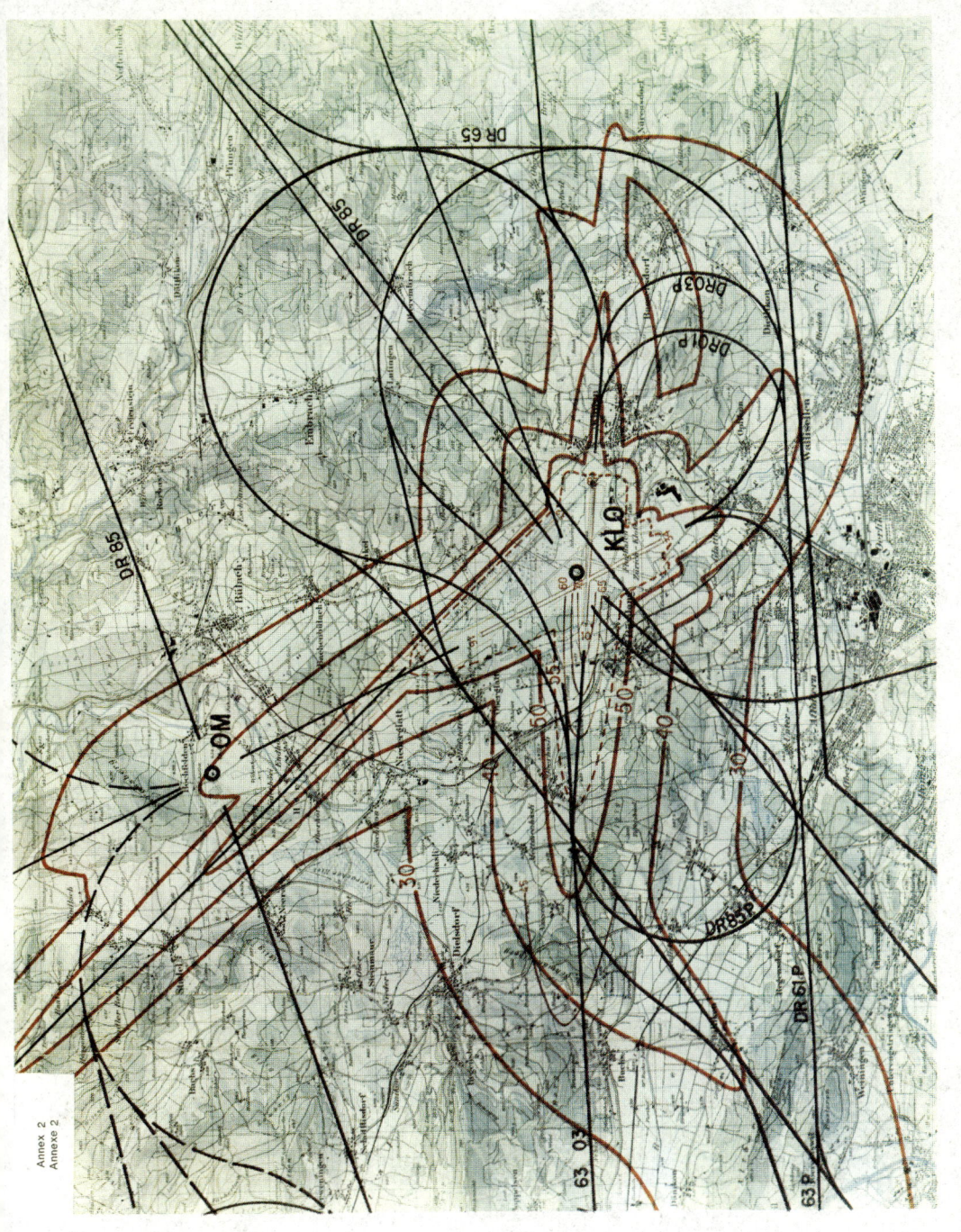

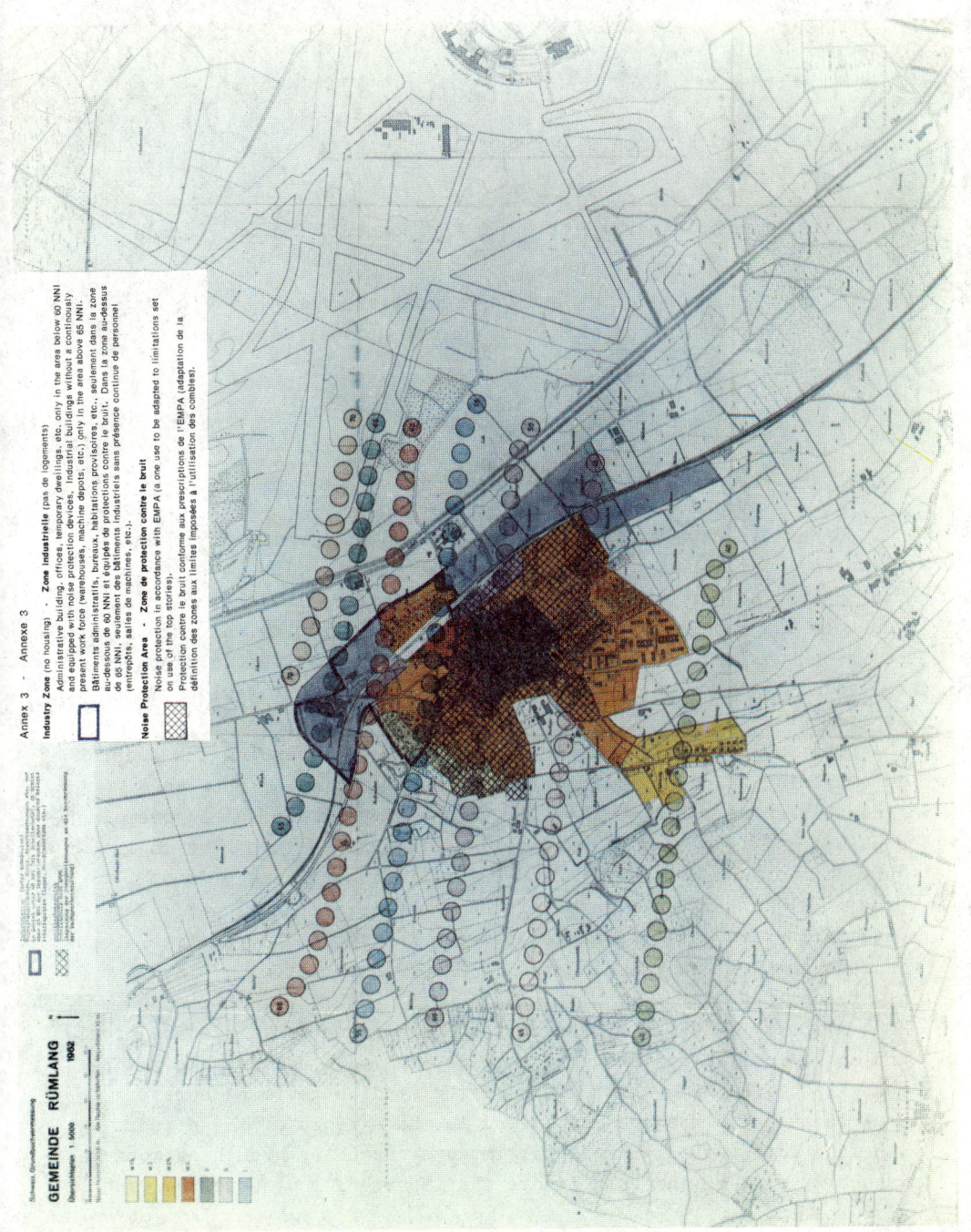

Annex 3 - Annexe 3

Industry Zone (no housing) - **Zone industrielle** (pas de logements)

Administrative building, offices, temporary dwellings, etc. only in the area below 60 NNI and equipped with noise protection devices. Industrial buildings without a continuously present work force (warehouses, machine depots, etc.) only in the area above 65 NNI.

Bâtiments administratifs, bureaux, habitations provisoires, etc., seulement dans la zone au-dessous de 60 NNI et équipés de protections contre le bruit. Dans la zone au-dessus de 65 NNI, seulement des bâtiments industriels sans présence continue de personnel (entrepôts, salles de machines, etc.).

Noise Protection Area - **Zone de protection contre le bruit**

Noise protection in accordance with EMPA (a one use to be adapted to limitations set on use of the top stories).

Protection contre le bruit conforme aux prescriptions de l'EMPA (adaptation de la définition des zones aux limites imposées à l'utilisation des combles).

GEMEINDE RÜMLANG 1962

215

Chapter 14

AIRPORTS AND ECOLOGY IN CANADA

Peter J. Marriot,
Policy Branch, Department of the Environment, Ottawa, Canada

Bryan D. Cook
Research Policy and Co-ordination Branch,
Department of the Environment, Ottawa, Canada

INTRODUCTION

Canada is constructing two new international airports, one at
Pickering near Toronto, and the other at Ste. Scholastique, near
Montreal. The airport at Ste. Scholastique is called Mirabel and
has been under construction since 1969. At Pickering only the site
has been acquired. Studies have been made of the impacts of both,
though after the sites had been chosen. This report reviews both
assessments.

The power to make laws is shared between provincial and federal
governments in Canada. Airports and the operation of them is a
federal responsibility but the Provinces have jurisdication over land,
highways and resources. Municipal governments in turn have their own
jurisdiction under provincial powers. Air quality and wildlife are
provincial matters and weather forecasting is a federal one. Responsibility for water is shared between the two. The political scene
is thus complex and planning has to involve the three levels of
government.

Airports affect air, water, land vegetation, wildlife and people
and do so indirectly through the roads, railways and urban development associated with them. Both of the studies reviewed here are
weak because their scope is limited to the effects of the airport
itself. Both neglect the larger impacts caused by growth and changes
in nearby cities, and both ignore the impact of routes to the
airports.

Despite these limitations both studies are effecting such aspects of the airports as runway location, neighbouring land uses,
drainage, waste disposal and bird hazard avoidance. In the case of
Pickering, the Federal Department of Environment will be able to

influence the design and construction of the airport as these phases are entered.

MIRABEL

The New Montreal International Airport, due to open in 1975, is 40 miles N.W. of the city. It will have two runways and one terminal and initially handle two million passengers a year. The airfield itself will cover 17,000 out of a total 95,000 acres of land expropriated by the Federal Government. The site was picked because it was available and it is part of a new centre of economic development. This growth area is being studied by the Centre de Recherches Ecologiques at the University of Montreal under the joint sponsorship of the National Research Council of Canada and the New Montreal International Airport Planning Office of the Federal Ministry of Transport.

The ecological investigations superimpose themselves upon numerous engineering, architectural, economic, and other studies. They began late in 1969, after construction had begun, and will be completed by April of 1973 at the cost of $460,000.

Map I shows the location of Mirabel airport. The dimensions of the expropriated land can be appreciated when one realises that Montreal Island, which is the home of 2.5 million residents is approximately the same size. The large area of land around the airfield is to serve as a buffer and its use is to be regulated to minimise adverse effects on man and nature.

The ecological studies cover the whole expropriated area and were designed to give basic data about the state of the ecosystem and to assess the likely effects of the airport on land use, water courses, air quality, wildlife and vegetation.

The results of these studies have already had an influence on land planning and on the types of vegetation that are to remain near the airport. Some changes have also been made to the location of fuel stores, methods of waste disposal, the use of aircraft de-icing fluids, and the layout of runways. Federal, provincial and municipal agencies are negotiating the future of the municipalities affected by the airport, and the use and management of the expropriated land around the airfield.

Present land use

The airport site lies in a plain with forest to the North and sand dunes to the North West. Two-thirds of the expropriated area is farmed, one-quarter is forest and scrub and the remainder consists of a variety of land uses such as abandoned farmland or marshes, the town of Ste. Scholastique, seven small villages and gravel pits.

Map 1 - Carte 1

MIRABEL

Location and Site Boundaries   -   Emplacement et limites du site

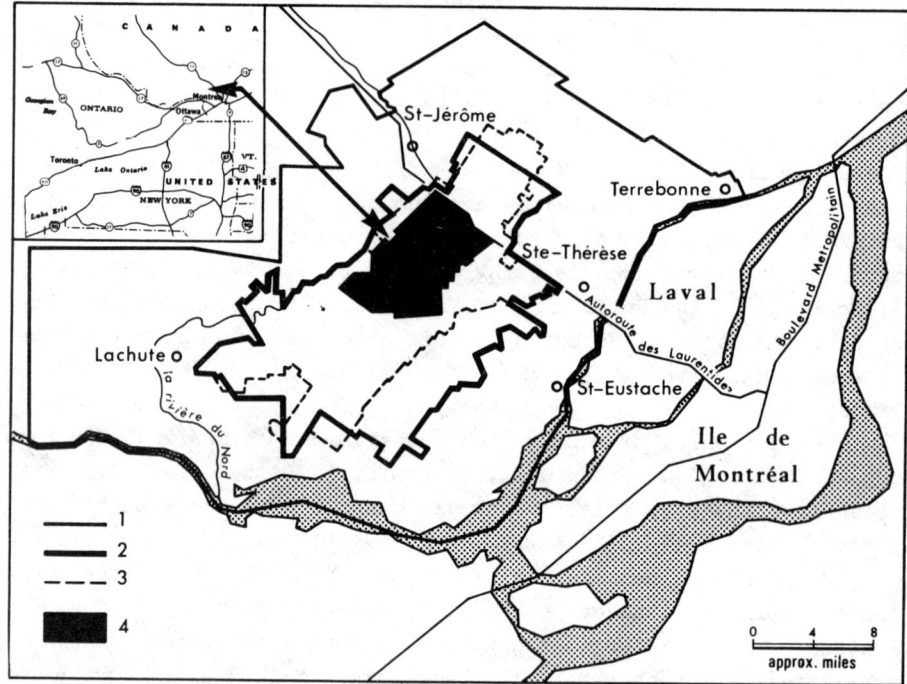

KEY - LEGENDE

1. Studied by SATRA - Du terrain étudié par SATRA
2. Of the new municipality of Sainte-Scholastique - De la nouvelle commune de Ste Scholastique
3. Expropriated - Du terrain exproprié
4. Of the Airport - De l'aéroport

Potential land use

Development potential was determined by labelling grid-square
maps of the area according to thirty-six variables such as drainage,
topography, vegetation, soil, susceptibility to erosion, habitats
and scope for recreation. Every variable had a map devoted to it
with every square graded in five classes for its suitability. Groups
of these maps were then put together and optimum land use patterns
produced (Map 2).

Sand and gravel pits

Sand extraction for airport construction was already destroying
dunes and animal habitats before the ecological studies began. Gravel
was also available closer to the airport on land that was biologically

Map 2 - Carte 2

MIRABEL

Integrated land use potential - Possibilités d'utilisation des sols intégrée

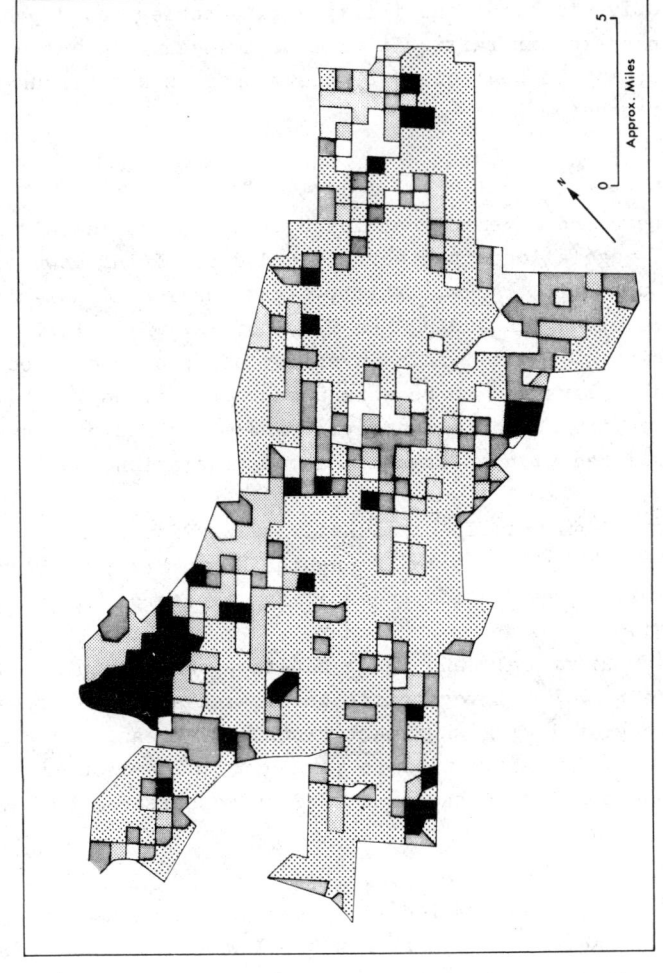

KEY - LEGENDE

Conservation and Education - Protection pour l'enseignement

Recreation - Loisirs

Commerce and Industry - Commerce et Industrie

Agriculture

Residential - Zones résidentielles

0   5

Approx. Miles

Source : Adapted from : Masan, A., Ecologie et Planification. - Adaptation de Masan, A., Ecologie et planification.
Centre de Recherches Ecologiques de Montréal, Oct. 1972.

poor and not in use for farming: extraction there would have been
environmentally and economically preferable.

Birds

Birds are a hazard at many airports but the 167 species recorded
at Mirabel are not expected to be a serious nuisance. The removal
of forest cover to make way for the airport will however create open
ground attractive to birds and thirty-eight species could present a
potential danger to aircraft. It will be necessary to watch these
species. They may be controlled by creating ground cover unattractive
to them or by other means.

Other animals

The numbers and movements of insects, birds and mammals living
in three soil-vegetation types were recorded by laying down belts of
sand to pick up their tracks. Thirty-eight species of non-bird verte-
brates were recorded, including red fox, coyote, white-tailed deer
and four species of snake. This inventory of species enabled food
chains and other linkages to be worked out. Relationships between
the human perception of animal activity and the effects of habitat
changes were linked with information about vegetation, soil and
climate.

The greatest amount of animal activity was found in the mixed
forests to the N.W. of the site, along the North River where the
greatest mixture of vegetation and soil types occurs, and in the
central forest.

Disruption of animals and their habitats can be minimised by
planting certain mixes of vegetation on cleared areas and by using
soil, sand and gravel from the least productive areas. Some impacts
will be short-lived, others will be permanent. The resulting changes
will cause some species to be threatened and others to thrive.

Water pollution

The North River was sampled at several sites along its course
and found to be badly polluted by municipal wastes but the effects
of the airport on the river and water quality in the area will be
negligible. Liquid waste from the airport is to be treated and solid
waste is to be removed from the area.

Noise

Studies were carried out at Dorval, the existing airport of
Montreal, to determine the noise that might be expected at Mirabel
so that land-use regulations could be designed to minimise nuisance
to people living and working nearby.

Sound was measured by sonar meters installed around Dorval and modelled after the TRACOR report on the reaction of urban communities to 10,000 flights over United States airports between 1967 and 1970(1).

The Dorval studies showed that noise was felt to be a nuisance most of all at night and in the early morning. Not only are background noise levels low at such times but many flights begin and end then as well. Among other things the study concluded:

a) that the best method of predieting discomfort from noise would be to combine the use of Composite Noise Ratings (CNR is explained in an appendix to this chapter) with psychological variables;

b) that 95 CNR appears to be a level above which discomfort increases sharply;

c) that noise should be given at least as much attention as air and water pollution;

d) that aircraft noise affects some people living up to 10 miles from Dorval;

e) and that aircraft on the ground can cause airport noise to reach 90 dB(A)(2) at the busiest times compared with the 70-75 dB(A) found in commercial areas of Montreal.

It was found that indoor noise levels were generally 20 dB(A) below outdoor ones and that:

a) above 40 dB(A) they interfered with home, medical and cultural activities;

b) above 45 dB(A) they interfered with activities in flats, hotels and schools;

c) and above 55 dB(A) they interfered with communication, business and indoor recreation.

Proposals were therefore made to identify the limits of areas where noise was expected to be a serious, moderate and a minor nuisance. These zones would correspond to exterior noise levels of 75 dB(A), 65 dB(A) and 60 dB(A) respectively. Sporadic noise can be tolerated up to no more than another 10 dB(A). The seriously affected places will be confined to farming, industry and transport. Some blocks of flats, offices, schools and recreation buildings will have to be located in the moderately affected zone but the nuisance is expected to be acceptable. Noise around Mirabel will be monitored.

---

1) Community Reaction to Airport Noise, Final Report, Vols. I & II, N.A.S.A., 1970, United States TRACOR Project.

2) To convert PNdB to dB(A): PNdB = dBA + 13.

PICKERING

Introduction

In December 1968 a decision was made not to promote the large-scale expansion of Malton, Toronto's existing international airport. At the same time a joint Federal/Provincial Committee was set up to prepare an aviation plan for Southern Ontario, and to find a site for a second airport for Toronto that would minimise the number of people affected by increases in air traffic.

Noise is a severe problem at Malton, and although opinion on the need for a new airport is divided, it has been estimated that 94,000 people would be affected by a full-scale expansion of the present airport and that 70,000 of them reside within the 100 Composite Noise Rating contour. Land at Malton is also valuable for housing.

A site for a new Toronto airport has been selected at Pickering-Markham, north east of the city, and 19,000 acres of land have been expropriated (Map 3). Sources drawn upon for this review of the site selection process are:

a) of the Ontario Department of Environment, Environmental Impact Study, February 1972;

b) press releases and reports of the Toronto Area Airports System Project Team of Transport Canada, 1972;

c) submissions from the Federation of Ontario Naturalists and other citizen groups.

Site selection

The limited amount of time available for research led the Ontario Government to identify "four areas of primary concern" to be observed in the site selection process:

a) the provision of ground transport,

b) the provision of physical municipal services within the area affected by the airport,

c) the planning and control of land use in areas surrounding all potential sites,

d) the planning and control of development in the Toronto region.

The provincial government also identified three criteria that would have to be met by a site before it could be considered suitable for a new airport:

a) it should permit safe and efficient flying and contribute to the profitability of aviation in Canada and Ontario;

Map 3 - Carte 3

TORONTO II AIRPORT - DEUXIEME AEROPORT DE TORONTO
General Location and Land Zones Affected by Airport Development
Situation générale et zones affectées par le développement de l'aéroport

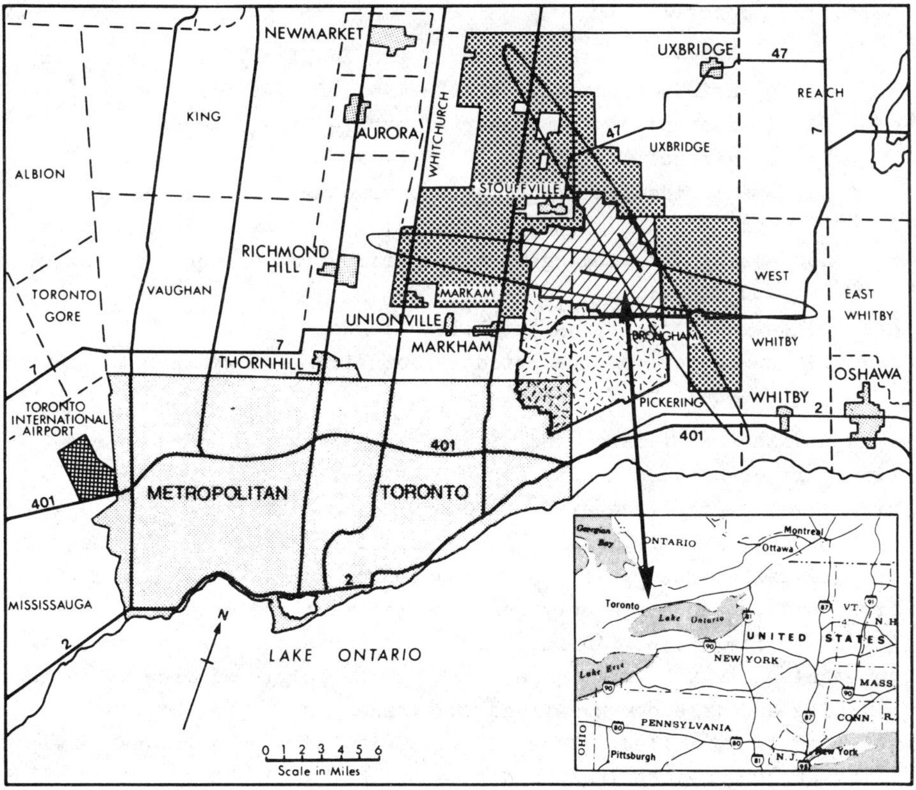

KEY - LEGENDE

  Land use freeze zone
Zone d'utilisation des sols «congelée»

  Airport site showing runways and noise cones
(approx. 95 CNR limits)
Site d'aéroport montrant les pistes et les courbes
d'égal bruit (limites, env. 95 CNR)

  Cedarwood

  Major urban centres
Grands centres urbains

223

b) it should help to achieve the greatest economic benefits
    from investment in the airport and its associated
    development;

c) it should be compatible with the development plan for the
    Toronto region.

Concern to limit the effects of airport development on ecology
led to the inclusion of the following considerations in the site-
selection process:

a) assessment of the number of people likely to be affected
    by noise, especially within the 100 CNR zone;

b) assessment of the number of people likely to be affected
    by air pollution;

c) identification of unique ecostructures or species that
    might be damaged or destroyed;

d) assessment of dangers of extermination of non-unique flora
    and fauna;

e) assessment of susceptibility to soil erosion;

f) assessment of the potential of birds and weather to reduce
    the safety of airport operations.

(The attitude of federal and provincial authorities that an eco-
structure or species needed to be unique to be worth preserving was
criticised by the Federation of Ontario Naturalists.)

Economic and regional planning considerations were dominant in
the initial stages of site selection. Ecological concerns, apart
from noise, were given only cursory treatment and were the subject
of little fieldwork. An initial list of 59 sites was whittled down
to eighteen, which were looked at from the points of view of regional
planning and telecommunications and then a short list of four was
selected for detailed site studies. This led to a site near Guelph
being chosen. Pickering was not on the original short list at all.

Early in 1971, work on an aviation plan for southern Ontario
established that two systems of airports - one based on Toronto and
another on Southwestern Ontario - would meet air travel needs better
than either a single new Toronto airport or an enlargement of Malton.
The Toronto II airport would require a maximum of four runways and
have a much reduced noise zone, which meant that sites other than
those considered previously could be reviewed. This led to the inclusion of Pickering and a site near the Niagara Escarpment in the
short list.

Factors considered in the final selection process included:

a) local government boundaries,

b) existing and potential land uses and population trends,

c) urban development prospects,

d) agricultural capability,

e) recreational capability,

f) each site in its fully developed state including transport
    links, land affected by flight noise and development out-
    side flight paths,

g) disturbance to existing populations and employment prospects
    and

h) the Toronto regional plan.

Questions of ecological impact were in theory covered under headings
b), d) and e) but in practice, played a very small part in determining the choice of site.

Ecological impacts: present government actions

As events have turned out the environmental impact assessment
is an "after-the-fact" affair aimed at influencing the design of
the airport, its access roads and service facilities and the development of the North Pickering community. A joint Federal-Provincial
Environmental Co-ordination Committee has accordingly been established,
and though it is not yet linked to another committee on airport
access a number of investigations are under way:

a) the monitoring of water quality,

b) a fisheries survey,

c) the management of stormwater and de-icer fluids,

d) the study of air pollution at Malton,

e) the study of wildlife on the airport site and in Pickering
    County.

Eleven firms have been selected by the Ontario Provincial
government to work on the design of a new community adjacent to the
airport in North Pickering Township.

A plan covering all social, ecological and urban aspects of this
development is expected in 1974. The development is part of a major
governmental thrust to encourage urban development to the east of
Toronto. Public participation will be encouraged throughout the
planning process.

Ecological issues

Climate. Pickering lies in a belt which has a snowfall of
sixty to eighty inches compared with forty to fifty at Malton. Such
an amount of snow is not a major problem but it will be sufficient
to close the airport for a few days in a year and should therefore
be considered as a factor in site selection. The site is not covered
by any fog records but its higher position than Malton will probably
result in fewer foggy days.

Air quality. United States studies have shown that less than
two per cent of national air pollution comes from commercial aircraft.

Comparable studies in Canada indicate an even lower figure and tests at Malton show that concentrations around airports do not exceed Ontario provincial standards.

Existing and potential land use. About 123,000 acres of rural land will be affected by airport development. The airport itself will cover 18,000 acres; Cederwood new town will involve 25,000 more and a further 80,000 acres will be within the 95 CNR limit and be subject to development restrictions (Map 3). About 8,290 persons would be displaced to make way for the airport or affected by noise.

The site is composed of Class I agricultural land, a classification embracing only 1.85 per cent of Ontario's farm land. The soil is deep, well-drained, holds moisture well, and in a virgin state is well supplied with nutrients. Under good management, such soils permit moderate to high production of a wide range of crops. The acreage involved is not great in the context of Ontario but its proximity to urban markets, its mild climate and fertility make it valuable for agriculture.

Farms are numerous on the site but many are in a state of ill-repair for the following reasons:

a) Pickering has become a place of retirement or escape for Toronto residents and

b) rumours of airport development have led to property speculation that has lifted land prices up to eight times above the level of farm land.

Recreation and retirement are thus land uses of increasing importance and explain why the site was designated for recreation, conservation and farming and open space in the Toronto Region Plan of 1971. These uses will be disturbed if not precluded by the development of an airport.

Conservation areas. Ten Conservation Areas, totalling 3,662 acres, lie within a ten-mile radius of the site. Although none of them will be displaced by the airport, four lie within the 100 CNR noise zone. Almost 250,000 people visited Bruce's Mills in 1970, 72,766 went to Greenwood and 22,594 to Claremont. Wildlife in these Conservation Areas would be disturbed by the noise, traffic and people associated with the airport and its associated urban developments. Aircraft noise would also reduce the value of the area for recreation. Furthermore two of the sites are downstream from the airport and would suffer loss of water-quality and silting if appropriate controls are not implemented.

Vegetation and wildlife. As there are only few large woods and no county forests on the site, development will not affect large or diverse forest stands. Furthermore clear cutting of trees throughout the entire site appears unnecessary for efficient and safe airport

226

operation. The absence of extensive tracts also limits the cover available for deer, grouse, partridge, and hare. Such species are accordingly limited and no rare or endangered species are present. Hunting in the past has been a significant recreational past-time in this site area, but recent municipal restrictions will have the effect of eliminating this activity.

Drainage and water quality. Three major creeks drain the site in a north-south direction and their efficiency is aided by man-made ditches. The presence of an airport and its associated paving could result in a slight depression of the water table but its magnitude is difficult to predict.

Silting and increased turbulence are likely in the lower reaches of the creeks as a result of the removal of protective vegetation in the course of airport construction. Silting is likely to continue as headwaters gain erosive power due to accelerated run-off and may reduce water quality. Removal of snow from the airport may modify the effects of the spring-melt but no study has yet covered this aspect of drainage.

Chemical pollution of waterbodies is a hazard from chemicals and oils, used during construction, and from chemicals used in the maintenance and operation of the airport and roads, Centralised chemical collection systems being tested at Dorval and Ottawa airports may help to solve these problems. Waste heat from the new Pickering power plant may be used for runway de-icing thus avoiding the need to use chemicals.

Bird hazards. Although Pickering does not lie on a main bird migration route and is not a major nesting or staging ground, certain hazards to aircraft are still present. Flocks of Blue and Lesser Snow Geese and Canada Geese cross the site area in Spring and Autumn at heights ranging from 2,000 feet to 10,000 feet in flocks of up to 10,000 birds. The site also lies on the migration route of the Eastern group of Whistling Swans which pass over the area at 12,000 feet in both Spring and Autumn. Ducks cross the area at heights up to 2,000 feet.

Radar can usually be employed to obtain warning of such bird flocks, though such hazards would apply to most other sites in the vicinity of Toronto. Broad-winged hawk migration on a couple of days in September can be forecast, as presently done at Malton, thereby reducing accident risk. Owl populations may become pests requiring culling.

Pickering County is a major flyway for Herring Gulls "commuting" between Lakes Ontario and Simcoe, and for the annual Ring Billed Gull migration. In contrast to other waterfowl, gulls do not necessarily flock, and their presence is hard to predict and difficult to detect by radar. As they travel at 2,000 to 7,000 feet depending on the

227

weather, they pose a hazard to aircraft. Gulls may create further problems by attempting to roost or feed in runway areas. The additional problems that would ensue if a new rubbish dump is allowed in Pickering County by the Ontario Municipal Board are the subject of a review by the federal Department of the Environment.

Noise. Eight villages with a total population of 1,778 people lie within the 100 CNR boundary and three of them lie within the airport site itself. Eight more villages, with a total population of 6,827 people, lie in the 95 to 100 CNR zone. Twenty-three schools (8,007 students), four Conservation areas (1,442 acres), a general hospital and a cerebral palsy hospital under construction all lie around the 95 CNR zone. The noise zones and development prohibitions needed to counteract noise nuisance are shown on Map 3.

Recommendations of the Ontario Department of Environment to minimise adverse environmental effects

Precautions should be taken to ensure that the construction and operation of an airport at Pickering does not impair the water quality or alter the rates of flow of streams in the area. It is therefore recommended that the following actions be considered:

a) the construction of two storm drainage systems serving the intensively-used parts of the site - the first to handle run-off from grassed areas, the second to handle and treat contaminated storm water from hangars and other paved areas;

b) the creation of settling ponds to capture silt and sand during construction and operation of the airport. The same ponds could be designed to retard rapid run-off;

c) the use of new techniques during the bridging of creeks to prevent silting and to ensure that river and valley banks remain stable thereafter;

d) investigation of way to minimise interference to water courses and their valleys;

e) natural vegetation should be removed from the site only to the extent necessary for the construction of facilities and the safe operation of aircraft and studies undertaken to understand the relationships between bird living habits, existing tree cover, aircraft safety and trees after the airport is built;

f) grass and other vegetation should only be stripped from sites immediately before construction in order to reduce erosion and silting. Reserves of fill and soil should be protected from erosion by wind or water by means of tarpaulins, sod or seeding of a cover crop;

g) Metropolitan Toronto's rubbish tips in Pickering Township
    and their attractiveness to gulls should be investigated
    to determine their compatability with the airport operation.

Land-use regulations should be applied to the surroundings of
the airport most affected by aircraft noise, to ensure that future
land uses are compatible with the anticipated noise levels in any
area. Land acquisition, soundproofing, runway layout and flight patterns should all be investigated before the airfield is built in order
to minimise the number of people affected by noise.

CONCLUSIONS

Great differences may be found in the two studies of environmental impacts described in this paper. The Mirabel studies were as
much concerned with developing new techniques as with forecasting environmental damage and were all carried out by the same research in-
stitution. The Pickering studies were more decision oriented, were
the work of both provincial and federal authorities and involved citizen groups. Site-selection procedures differed too. Pickering was
chosen following the consideration of other sites, whereas alternatives seem hardly to have been considered at Mirabel.

Environmental disruption is not expected to be severe at either
site yet the results of the studies are affecting the design, construction and operation of the airports and the use of the land around
them. Careful land-use zoning will be needed at both airports to
avoid the worst effects of noise. Avoidance of water pollution at
Pickering calls for modifications to the design and operation of the
airport.

The studies would have been more valuable had they preceded
construction. In the case of Mirabel, construction had been under
way for almost a year before the studies began.

Both site choices involved trading-off losses of farming and
recreation land against urban and aviation developments. Such trade-
offs involve judgement as well as analysis and such judgements might
be enhanced by involving the public more directly in them.

Experience of the Mirabel and Pickering studies suggests that
extensive research is rarely required in such exercises and that an
interdisciplinary team could speedily assess many of the expected
impacts. Full-scale research might then be devoted only to less-well
known and less-well-documented issues.

Appendix

CANADIAN MINISTRY OF TRANSPORT, TECHNICAL REPORT ON NOISE, 1970

The problem of aircraft noise extends beyond the physical boundaries of the airport, and involves the subjective responses of the surrounding community. Until a few years ago, noise associated with flying activity at airports created little more than a minor nuisance. However, rapid advances in aviation technology have caused airports to become major focal points of economic activity, attracting commercial, industrial and residential developments to locate as near as possible to their boundaries. This has had an inhibiting effect on airport expansion and resulted in the exposure of nearby residents to varying amounts of aircraft noise.

The growing percentage of jet aircraft in use has made matters worse by spreading higher levels of noise over wider areas than before. Residents who some years ago purchased homes outside what they thought to be the limits of noise nuisance have accordingly found themselves caught up in the very annoyance they took pains to avoid.

A scale of measurement that reflects public response to aircraft noise is required for airport planning. Annoyance factors such as frequency of occurrence, the measurement of sound energy, and particularly the time of day or night might form integral parts of such a scale.

The three main methods of measuring aircraft noise are: Perceived Noise in Decibels (PNdB), Composite Noise Rating (CNR) and Noise Exposure Forecast (NEF) - the last of which is not fully developed. The CNR method is most widely used and involves estimates of the land area exposed to varying degrees of aircraft noise for the various runways of an airport. The results are a guide to land use. They do not define at what level noise becomes intolerable or help to set standards. However CNR can be used to estimate response to existing noise conditions and to forecast the effect of changes in operations.

Once estimates for exposure to engine noise have been determined, contours representing various levels of exposure can be mapped. Such contours are based on the following factors:

a) the magnitude of the noise, measured in PNdB,

b) the number of occurrences,

c) the time of day or night,

d) and, for ground operations, the duration of the noise.

The next step is to assess public response to various noise levels for particular land uses. Interviews designed with this objective have indicated, for example, that construction of single-family dwellings should be avoided within the 100 to 115 CNR contours and prohibited within the next higher belt.

Tax exemption, tax abatement and other schemes have been adopted in a number of countries to encourage householders to soundproof their homes and to compensate them for the nuisance of aircraft noise. Such schemes have met with varying degrees of success. One of their weaknesses is that they are difficult to apply and administer uniformly where more than one local authority is involved. Another is their failure to offer protection for outdoor living.

Noise sensitivity is a personal thing. Many people consider a noise rating of 100 to 115 CNR unacceptable while others will accept it as a concomitant of progress. The purchasing of all dwellings within the 100 CNR and higher contours for each runway of an airport, and the relocation of them to other uses is the only way of ensuring that no one suffers.

In the case of proposed airports, steps must be taken to protect the airport investment by guarding against development on adjacent lands. Furthermore this protection should extend to cover long-range development plans containing various possibilities. Areas likely to be exposed to noise in the future may be derived from forecasts of aircraft movements, operating characteristics and route assignments. The introduction of data about preferences and noise exposure minimisation then allows traffic to be assigned to the runways and the delineation of CNR contours.

Neighbouring lands may be protected from development by the use of federal or provincial zoning powers or outright purchase. Zoning is the least expensive but also the least effective measure. Acquisition not only provides the best protection against incompatible land uses but can with good management be the least expensive in the long run. Revenues from noise-land management can offset the land purchase costs and possibly even yield net profits.

Noise-land protection measures have been taken at Mirabel and have been assumed in the Toronto II airport study for purposes of comparative cost evaluation.

Annex A

SOCIAL AND ECONOMIC IMPACT
OF AIRCRAFT NOISE

Results of Studies and Surveys

OECD Secretariat

Table of Contents

Part One

THE EVALUATION OF AIRCRAFT NOISE ANNOYANCE

Part Two

THE MONETARY EVALUATION OF DAMAGES
DUE TO AIRCRAFT NOISE

Part One

THE EVALUATION OF AIRCRAFT NOISE ANNOYANCE

1. INTRODUCTION

The considerable increase in international air traffic since 1960 and the generalised use of jet aircraft, in conjunction with the rapid urbanisation of airport neighbourhoods, have caused aircraft noise to become an international issue.

With the building of new airports and the enlargement of existing facilities difficult problems have arisen, as attested by the fact that certain countries have sited their airports well outside cities, restricted the use of older airports at night, imposed anti-noise flight procedures, etc. The seriousness of the noise problem is evidenced by the decisions taken in 1969 to include noise standards when certifying new aircraft in the United States; these acquired international scope when the International Civil Aviation Organisation (ICAO) adopted a recommendation concerning the noise certification of new types of subsonic aircraft[1].

Such decisions should hardly cause surprise when it is realised that in the United States, for example, the total area subjected to excessive aircraft noise (leading to numerous complaints) grew some seven times between 1960 and 1970[2]. Such noise, extending over greater periods of time as well as space, moreover threatens to exceed the threshold of human tolerance and to be harmful to the individual's health as well as his psychological and social balance.

While in theory the premise may be advanced that all human beings should be protected against noise, on the same footing as from hunger and disease, it must be realised that until now economic necessity and technological shortcomings have prevented noise annoyance from being taken into account when aircraft were being built or towns were being planned.

---

1) Aircraft Noise, Annex 16 to International Civil Aviation Convention, ICOA, August 1971.

2) "Transportation Noise and Noise from Equipment Powered by Internal Combustion Engines", Report NTID 300-13, U.S. Environmental Protection Agency, Washington, D.C., 1971, p.22.

Noise cannot be suppressed entirely. But as the complaints and protest movements against aircraft continue to grow, the authorities must acquire an objective knowledge of the impact noise has on man so that criteria can be defined on which to base appropriate protective measures at least economic and social cost.

To measure this impact is a difficult task, since while a number of direct physiological effects following prolonged, repeated exposure to intensive noise such as that found in certain industrial plants have been ascertained, so far none affecting residents in the vicinity of airports have been determined.

Noise annoyance in the vicinity of airports is rather of a psychosociological kind in that it interferes with such activities as speech, listening to the radio or television, reading etc., disturbs sleep, and creates a subjective feeling of annoyance.

As the cumulative effect of these annoyances may harm the well-being of the population (such as the repeated disturbance of sleep or frequent interference with work in the classroom), since an excessive amount of annoyance felt by a substantial fraction of the population may lead to complaints and organised protest and under certain conditions they may also cause the monetary value of exposed dwellings to depreciate(1), a fact to be determined is whether the effects bear any relationship to the level of noise itself. If such a relationship does indeed exist, it is on this that government decisions must be based.

So far research has consisted in:
- conducting surveys around airports to define the components of annoyance and calculate correlations between annoyance and noise;
- analysing the geographical location of complaints in order to deduce correlations with noise exposure;
- testing the direct effects of aircraft noise on sleep in the laboratory(2).

---

1) See Part Two of this report.

2) There has not yet been sufficient laboratory research on the effects of aircraft noise on sleep to draw reliable conclusions. Hence we shall not take them into consideration in the present report. Those interested in such research may consult two recent studies:
- "Effects of Noise Upon Sleep", By P.A. Morgan, Technical Report No. 40, Institute of Sound and Vibration Research, Southampton, 1970.
- "Les effets du bruit sur le sommeil", revue "Nuisances et Environnement" No. 13 et 14, Paris, 1972.

We shall begin by summarising the findings of the main surveys and by briefly commenting on the methods used. We shall then consider various implications of the criteria proposed, and finally list the advantages and shortcomings of the methods described.

2. DECISION CRITERIA BASED ON SURVEYS

Decisions for protecting the population around airports will depend on the annoyance criteria which are selected. But before settling on the criteria themselves, the question is how they can be calculated. At first sight, it might be thought that the leading components of noise perceived around airports should first be determined, then the main components of human response to aircraft noise, and finally that some connection between both these phenomena should be sought.

But in actual fact, although various objective data concerning the intensity and number of noises perceived at some particular site are certainly available, the best possible combination of such physical parameters cannot be determined unless there is a reliable yardstick for measuring the effects of noise. The evaluation of noise depends on evaluation of the associated annoyance rather than the other way round, since it is a matter of proposing noise criteria which best reflect human response.

In order to assess this annoyance it is necessary to conduct sociological surveys around existing airports.

The surveys will however be devoid of any real significance or practical value unless they lead to a precise definition of the parameters accounting for annoyance and to the latter's graduated quantification.

While a threshold of annoyance is likely to exist which cannot be exceeded without causing physiological disorders or escape responses, it is also likely that beyond this threshold a continuum will be noted, ranging from no reaction at all to many different kinds of response. But the degree of annoyance cannot be evaluated merely by asking people whether they feel any annoyance or not, since such a simple approach prevents various possible attitudes from being finely distinguished, while biased replies due to the semantic interpretation of questions may result if care is not first taken to ensure consistency. On this account, during the past fifteen years, sophisticated survey techniques have been developed providing for a fine, graduated analysis of response to noise:
  - by taking the replies to many open and closed questions into account;
  - by variously weighting the replies and ordering them according to seriousness of the response;

- by synthesising the replies into a single consistent "annoyance index".

The two most widely known techniques for obtaining fine measurements of aircraft noise annoyance are factor analysis and Guttman's scale analysis.

By means of factor analysis a large number of facts can be assembled and tested for the best combinations and weightings. An unfortunate drawback is that it is highly complicated to handle and a relatively abstract conceptualisation of annoyance is achieved. Among the surveys on aircraft noise whose findings have been published only one has made use of factor analysis: the one undertaken for NASA in the vicinity of several airports in the United States[1]. This survey showed especially the significance of personal factors in creating feelings of annoyance (a subject which will be discussed later).

Most of the other surveys of aircraft noise have used Guttman scale analysis.

Annoyance Scales

This method consists in constructing an annoyance scale and to assign a "score" to each informant according to the combined answers to a set of questions on a one-dimensional subject (in this case aircraft noise).

The Guttman technique ensures that the scale adopted will not be arbitrary and provides for the continuous measurement of attitudes towards noise. It has the advantage of testing the consistency of replies by an individual informant and of ordering them according to the degree of significance assigned by the entire population sample. Moreover, all informants can be correctly classified in terms of their annoyance scores, since by this method respondents with the same score are people who have replied in exactly the same way to the questions used for constructing the scale (interference with some given activity thus implies interference with all activities ranking lower on the scale)[2].

In short, an overall synthesis can thus be made of human reactions to aircraft noise.

Annoyance scales have been used in the United Kingdom for the purpose of two major surveys conducted around London (Heathrow)

---

1) "Community Reaction to Airport Noise", Tracor Staff, NASA CR-1761, Etats-Unis.

2) For a more detailed description of the method see "Aircraft Noise Annoyance Around London (Heathrow) Airport", by A.C. McKennell, Central Office of Information, London, 1963.

Airport in 1961 and 1967, in France during a 1965 survey around four airports, and in the Netherlands when a survey was made in 1964 of Amsterdam-Schiphol Airport(1).

The questionnaires developed by these countries either stem from studies undertaken in 1965 by Paul Borsky among residents near military airports, or from work by a Group of Experts on Aircraft Noise Abatement set up in 1961 by the OECD Committee for Scientific Research(2).

Although the questions adopted for constructing annoyance scales vary from survey to survey, some are universally used, particularly as regards noise-disturbed activities (conversation, radio/television reception and sleep)(3). In fact the annoyance scales developed in each country all measure the number of daily activities disturbed by aircraft noise.

Hence the criteria which can be proposed will not define some random sensation devoid of any precise significance; instead, the extent of activities daily disturbed by noise in a given community will be objectively determined.

Knowledge of a population's degree of annoyance will however be of no practical value unless the annoyance can be related to noise exposure of the population.

Noise Indices

The physical parameters available at some given point near an airport are:
- the sound levels produced by each aircraft at the point of measurement (loudness and duration of noise, spectral composition, etc.);
- the number and time distribution of sound peaks (during the day, at night and throughout the year).

---

1) Other surveys are under way in France, Switzerland and Israel, but their results have yet to be published.

2) See especially the questionnaire proposed in DAS/RS/63.144, OECD, Paris.

3) In the United Kingdom surveys, for example, the questions adopted for the annoyance scale were as follows: 1) Does the noise of aircraft bother you very much, moderately, a little or not at all? 2) Does aircraft noise wake you up (very often, fairly often, occasionally, not at all)? 3) Interfere with listening to radio or TV? 4) Make the house vibrate? 5) Interfere with conversation? 6) Bother you in any other way?
The replies to each question were dichotomised, enabling a six-point scale to be constructed: those who answered question 6 in the affirmative had usually also given positive replies to the previous 5 questions (following the very principle of scale analysis) and thus obtained a score of 6; those who replied negatively upon reaching question 5 scored 4, etc.

Such factors vary so considerably in terms of time and space that of course some simple expression must be found, since otherwise no correlation with annoyance would be possible and no criterion could be established.

The best combination of physical parameters will be that which enables the best possible correlation with annoyance to be achieved, while it must be relatively easy to calculate and applicable for different airports.

Based on survey findings (and the analysis of complaints), noise indices have been worked out in various countries by integrating into a single formula:

- the daily or yearly average of maximum noise levels produced by the various aircraft at a given point, such noise levels being expressed in dBA, PNdB or EPNdB units(1);
- a logarithmic function of the average daily or yearly number of such noise peaks, weighted as needed for the period when they occur (during the day, in the evening or at night);
- certain correction factors to allow for the percentage of runway utilisation, etc.

The underlying principle in combining average noise loudness with a logarithmic function of frequency of occurence in a single formula is based on a theory developed by Weber-Fechner in the 19th century: the sensation perceived by the ear varies as the logarithm of the stimulus. From this theory all noise-measurement units have been derived.

If the ear responds to the number of noise peaks in the same way as it reacts to their loudness, then the number of peaks should also be expressed in logarithmic form: this would imply that a loud noise rarely perceived produces the same effect as an average noise which is often perceived (principle of energy equivalence). In short, this would imply the existence of "trade-offs" between a change in the amount of loudness perceived and a change in the number of noises. If such a process could be really shown to take place the consequences for noise abatement and annoyance prediction would of course be significant.

---

1) PNdB (Perceived Noise decibel) and EPNdB (Effective Perceived Noise decibel) were especially developed to describe aircraft noise. A PNdB value exceeds by some 10 to 13 units - depending on whether the aircraft is taking off or landing and on the type of aircraft - a dBA value, which is read directly from the sonometer. As for EPNdB, adopted by ICAO for the acoustic certification of aircraft, this is a unit which in addition to loudness accounts for its pure-sound (highly annoying) sound components and duration. To calculate EPNdB is an extremely complex process (see ICAO, op. cit.).

It will now be seen that in most cases surveys have confirmed this theory, and that the findings only diverge as regards the weights which should be assigned to the number of noises perceived in relation to their loudness(1).

In order to simplify comparisons between the different surveys only the most commonly known and used indices (CNR and NEF in the United States; NNI in the United Kingdom and Switzerland) will be described(2). This is all the more legitimate as the various indices prove to be far more closely correlated with each other than with individual responses to annoyance, as will later be seen.

---

1) By countries, weights assigned to the logarithm of the number of sound peaks vary from 10 (United States, France, international recommendation of ICAO) up to 20 (Netherlands), intermediate values being 13 (Germany) and 15 (United Kingdom). In the United States and French formulas, this means that twice the number of sound peaks is equivalent to a noise increase of 3 dBA; in the United Kingdom formula of 4.5 dBA; and in the Dutch formula of 6 dBA. The greater the multiple of the logarithm for the number of peaks, the greater will be the weight attached to increases in air-traffic as contributing to annoyance.

2) The index formulas are as follows:

Composite Noise Rating (CNR) = $\overline{PNdB}$ + 10 log N - 12

where $\overline{PNdB}$ is the mean loudness of peak noises expressed in PNdB and N is the number of aircraft heard.

Noise Exposure Forecast (NEF) = $\overline{EPNdB}$ + 10 log N - 88
(a value expressed in NEF terms is roughly equivalent to a value expressed in CNR minus 70 to 75 units: e.g. 30 NEF = 100 to 105 CNR).

Noise and Number Index (NNI) = $\overline{PNdB}$ + 15 log N - 80

Table of equivalencies between NNI, NEF, and CNR indices

Number of aircraft heard per 24 hours	Average noise level in PNdB for CNR and NNI, and in EPNdB for NEF											
	90 PNdB EPNdB			100 PNdB EPNdB			110 PNdB EPNdB			120 PNdB EPNdB		
	NNI	CNR	NEF	NNI	CNR	NEF	NNI	CNR	NEF	NNI	CNR	NEF
10	25	88	17	35	98	27	45	108	37	55	118	47
50	36	95	24	46	105	34	56	115	44	66	125	54
100	40	98	27	50	108	37	60	118	47	70	128	57
200	45	101	30	55	111	40	65	121	50	75	131	60
500	51	105	34	61	115	44	71	125	54	81	135	64

3. SYNTHESIS OF SURVEY FINDINGS

The following synthesis mainly combines the findings of the United Kingdom (1961 and 1967), French (1965) and Dutch (1964) surveys, which all use Guttman scale analysis for measuring annoyance and correlating it with physical noise parameters.

As the following explanations cannot be greatly detailed only the main conclusions of the surveys will be commented upon(1).

In the matter of annoyance scores, the number of questions used in constructing the annoyance scale differed from country to country (5 questions for France, 6 for the United Kingdom and 7 for the Netherlands), so that for purposes of valid comparison the raw values of annoyance scores have had to be converted into relative values - or "degrees of relative annoyance", i.e. into percentages of maximum 5, 6 and 7 scores. Thus the maximum annoyance score obtained in France is regarded as equivalent to the maximum score obtained in the United Kingdom and in the Netherlands, while of course all intermediate scores have likewise been converted into "degrees of relative annoyance".

At first the annoyance scores were correlated with separate indices, since the precise purpose of the surveys conducted in each country was to calculate an index which would best represent annoyance. Calculations undertaken after the surveys were conducted, however, showed that all indices were strongly intercorrelated.

To make the consolidated findings intelligible a single index therefore had to be chosen. The one index used in common by the British, French and Dutch researchers was the NNI. This allowed international comparison of the findings to be made.

The combined findings of all three countries appear in Figure 1 herewith. These are the average annoyance scores classified by noise stratum (we have adopted the same 5-by-5 NNI classification as in the second United Kingdom survey so that all results might be referred

---

1) For a detailed description of the survey findings, see:

- United Kingdom surveys: "Noise, Final Report", Wilson Committee, HMSO, London, 1963 and "Second Survey of Aircraft Noise Annoyance Around London (Heathrow) Airport", Office of Population Censuses and Surveys, HMSO, London, 1971.

- French survey: "La gêne causée par le bruit autour des aéroports", CSTB, Paris, 1968 and "Enquête sur le bruit autour des aéroports", Report No. 16/67 of the Association d' Anthropologie Appliquée, Paris, 1967.

- Dutch survey: "Annoyance Due to Aircraft Noise", TNO Delft, 1964 (findings published in Revue Française d'Acoustique No. 10, 1970, under title: "La gêne due au bruit des avions").

to the latter, the most extensive investigation so far conducted in Europe on aircraft noise)(1).

It will be noted that the average annoyance scores are closely linked to values for the NNI and that differences between countries are extremely small (the difference within each noise class does not exceed ± 5 per cent).

Although all the enquiries show a very clear-cut correlation between aircraft noise indices and average annoyance scores by noise class or location of the survey correlation (correlation coefficients above .90 in France, the Netherlands and the United Kingdom) they show relatively low correlation between the noise indices and individual annoyance scores (correlation coefficients under .50). Noise does not therefore alone account for annoyance reactions. Various personal factors, and doubtlessly also those related to the kind of life one leads (children or none, all-day round or occasional presence at home, windows habitually opened or closed) as well as certain acoustical factors (apartment exposure, window size, etc.) play a role in the creation of the feeling of annoyance. Recent research(2) has shown that fear of aircrashes, greater or lesser sensitivity to noise in general, and attitude towards the usefulness of aviation and airports alter annoyance reactions. "Appropriate educational compaigns" would therefore somewhat reduce subjective annoyance. Whether they would also reduce objective annoyance i.e. disturbance of daily activities, is far less certain. The elimination of fear and hostility with respect to an airport can only modify reactions up to a certain threshold, i.e. where sleep or conversation are objectively disrupted, irrespective of the individual's attitude towards aviation. It must also be borne in mind that the public as a whole is increasingly seeking quality of life and fewer daily annoyances. It is therefore highly probable that compaigns to promote the easier acceptance of aircraft noise would be offset by

---

1) Sources of combined data in the figure:
   - page 207, "Noise, Final Report", op.cit. (London findings);
   - page 192, "Second Survey of Aircraft Noise around London (Heathrow) Airport", op. cit. (London findings);
   - pages 32 and 142 of Report No. AAA - 16/67 of Association d'Anthropologie Appliquée: "Enquête sur le bruit autour des aéroports", op. cit. (Paris findings);
   - page 92, No. 10-1970 of Revue Française d'Acoustique, op. cit. (Netherlands findings).

2) In particular, see "Community Reaction to Airport Noise, Final Report", TRACOR No. T.70-AU-7454-U, Austin (Texas), United States, 1970. The enquiry by TRACOR covered seven United States airports and showed that the correlation between individual annoyance scores and the values of the NNI index increased from .37 to .79 when these personal variables where included in the calculation of annoyance.

campaigns for environmental improvement led by associations for the protection of residents in the vicinity of airports.

Knowledge of some personal variables therefore seems to be of limited value for decision makers. However, the following important conclusion emerged from all the surveys:

- even at high noise levels, a small number of people suffer little or no annoyance,
- even at low noise levels, a small number of people are always annoyed.

The existence of "imperturbable" just as "eternally dissatisfied" subjects is a relatively stable factor in all problems and for decision-making purposes must therefore be taken into account.

It is obvious, however, that some dissatisfied group in any population will create more problems for the public authorities than a group of people who are always satisfied with their environment. Complaints made in the vicinity of airports are indeed likely to come primarily from a dissatisfied group whose general discontent will be cristallised around the noise question. If these complaints increase in number they will finally set in motion a true wave of public protest which could then be joined by those people who are truly annoyed but who don't necessarily belong to the "eternally dissatisfied" group.

Figure 1

MEAN ANNOYANCE BY CLASS OF NOISE

GENE MOYENNE PAR CLASSE SONORE

(Results from 3 european countries - Résultats de 3 pays européens)

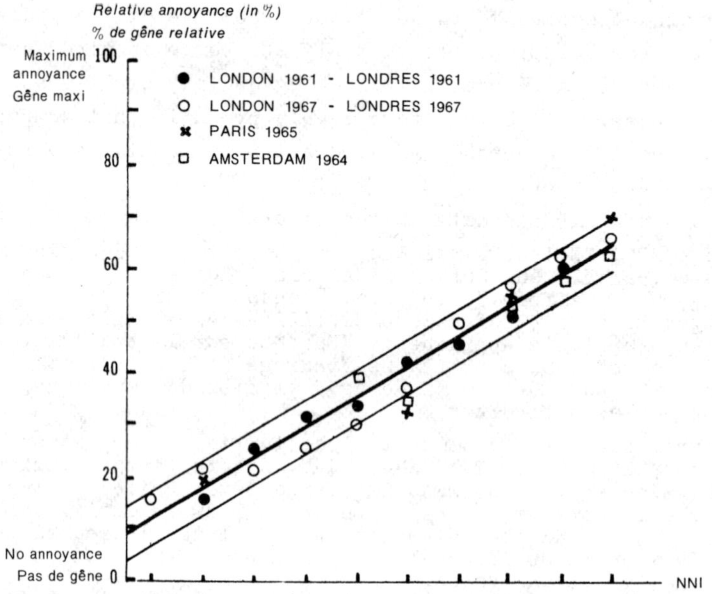
Relative annoyance (in %)
% de gêne relative
Maximum annoyance
Gêne maxi
No annoyance
Pas de gêne
100
80
60
40
20
0
LONDON 1961 - LONDRES 1961
LONDON 1967 - LONDRES 1967
PARIS 1965
AMSTERDAM 1964
NNI
<15
15-19
20-24
25-29
30-34
35-39
40-44
45-49
50-54
≥55

4. ANALYSIS OF THE COMPLAINTS

The location of complaints in the vicinity of airports could therefore in itself be an indication of the extent of annoyance to which the population is subjected. Indeed, the noise indices developed in the United States (CNR and NEF) are based on complaints, whereas European indices are based on annoyance as expressed in the surveys. The American indices are thus, as it were, based on the extroverted form of annoyance (manifest reaction) and the European indices on its introverted form (latent reaction). In the United States complaints are regarded as the ultimate form of annoyance(1), which suggests that their number and pattern of development provide pragmatic evidence of the scope of the problem and determine what action should be undertaken.

A synthesis of United States case studies relating to complaints is given in Figure 2 below(2).

The recent survey conducted by TRACOR has actually resulted in the formulation of an equation for predicting the number of highly annoyed persons in relation to the number of complaints per thousand households:

Number of highly annoyed households per 1000 exposed = 195.5 + 2.07 (complaints per 1000 households exposed)(3)

TRACOR however notes that the ratio "highly/annoyed/complainants" diminishes as complaints increase; consequently an increase in complaints does not entail a proportional rise in the number of people annoyed.

It is therefore by no means certain that complaints are a good indicator of annoyance in all countries(4), especially as the

----

1) The process by which annoyance develops may be illustrated as follows:

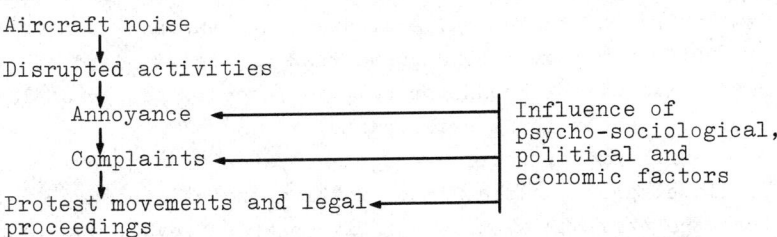

2) Figure taken from Report No. NTID-300-7 of the U.S. Environmental Protection Agency: "Effects of Noise on People", Washington, D.C., 1971, page 110. (The approximate scale in NNI has been added.)

3) "Community Reaction to Airport Noise, Final Report", TRACOR, op. cit., page 83.

4) Nonetheless complaints do precipitate an awareness of the problem and it quite often happens that surveys are organised only after complaints have been repeatedly made.

Figure 2

TYPES OF COMPLAINT IN RELATION TO NOISE

TYPE DE PLAINTES EN FONCTION DU BRUIT

(Results obtained in the United States - Résultats portant sur les Etats-Unis)

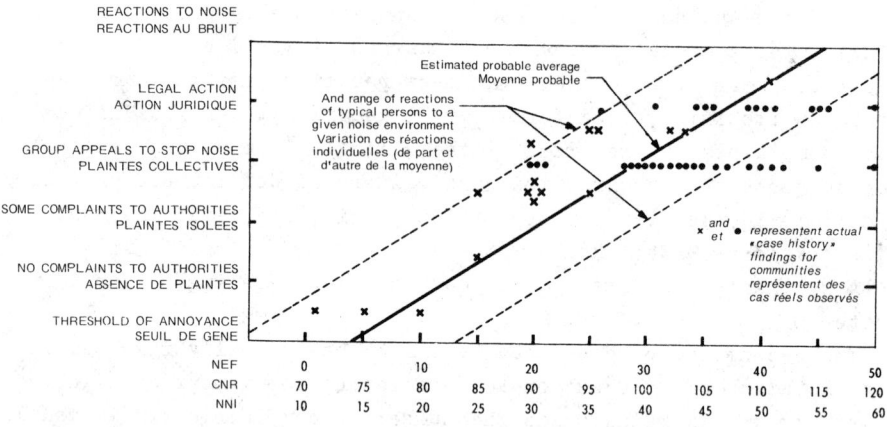

INCREASING NOISE EXPOSURE - EXPOSITION AU BRUIT

formulation of a complaint depends on many exogenous factors of a practical (to whom should the complaint be addressed?); political (to what extent does one believe the complaint will be taken into consideration?) and economic nature (according to the United Kingdom and United States surveys, complaints depend on levels of education, family income and the value of dwellings exposed to noise(1). From this it may moreover be deduced that as the standard of living rises, complaints will increase or be formulated by people at lower noise exposure levels than in the past.)

Furthermore, while average annoyance in a given area can be predicted on the basis of the level of noise exposure in that area (see the previous synthesis of European surveys), complaints can only be predicted by considering all the sociological, political and economic variables characterising the population exposed to noise.

In view of all the foregoing reasons, it seems advisable to take account of annoyance rather than simply to count complaints.

---

1) "Aircraft Noise Annoyance Around London (Heathrow) Airport", by A.C. McKennell, op. cit., p.p. 7.1 to 7.4 and "Community Reaction to Airport Noise, Final Report" by TRACOR, op.cit., p. 84.

5. PRACTICAL USE OF SURVEY FINDINGS FOR DECISION MAKING

We have already seen that a certain segment of the population is hardly ever annoyed even at very high noise levels, whereas even at very low noise levels a small section of the population will feel annoyed.

To circumvent this problem of individual variations of attitude with regard to noise, it would thus be enough to consider the percentage of people annoyed according to locality (instead of considering the average score, which conceals individual variations). On what criterion would decisions then have to be based - when 30 per cent of people are annoyed or 90 per cent? The need to satisfy 95 per cent of the population rather than 50 per cent cannot be established scientifically (not to mention that the satisfaction of 95 per cent of the inhabitants of a community numbering 500 people is radically different from trying to satisfy 50 per cent of the people in a town with a population of 20,000).

Although this problem cannot be resolved, it is still possible to use the ratio established between the percentage of people annoyed and the noise level for predicting the results of any decisions which may be taken, "people annoyed" being defined by their individual annoyance scores.

As an outcome of the first United Kingdom survey, the investigators estimated those people to be highly annoyed whose annoyance score equalled a minimum of 4 (on a 6 point scale the relative score comes to 65 per cent because above this score aircraft annoyance prevailed over all other causes of dissatisfaction with living conditions(1).

The reasons alleged by investigators in determining annoyance thresholds are of course more complete and numerous than those here summarised (for details, reference may be made to the researchers' reports). But the survey findings agree at least on two major points: an annoyance threshold is exceeded when the annoyance score indicates frequent disturbance of speech communication (conversation and radio or TV reception), this annoyance threshold proves to be much the same for all the surveys when expressed in relative terms. Unquestionably, whenever the spoken word - man's principal means of contact with the outside world - can no longer be perceived on account of noise, annoyance reaches a limit of tolerability which if exceeded interferes with the normal pattern of daily living.

Figure 3 combines the findings of the European surveys by taking the above annoyance criteria into account.

---

1) In France, anyone who scored 3 or more (on a 5 point scale) is considered highly annoyed. In the Netherlands, anyone who scored 4 or more (on a 7 point scale) is also considered highly annoyed.

As these results expressed in NNI have been found to correspond closely with those obtained in the United States by K.D. Kryter using the CNR and NEF indices, the NNI, CNR and NEF indices may be regarded as virtually interchangeable, subject to the margin of error which must necessarily be expected in any such evaluation(1).

Figure 3

PERCENTAGE OF ANNOYED PERSONS IN RELATION TO NOISE
PROPORTION DES GENES EN FONCTION DU BRUIT

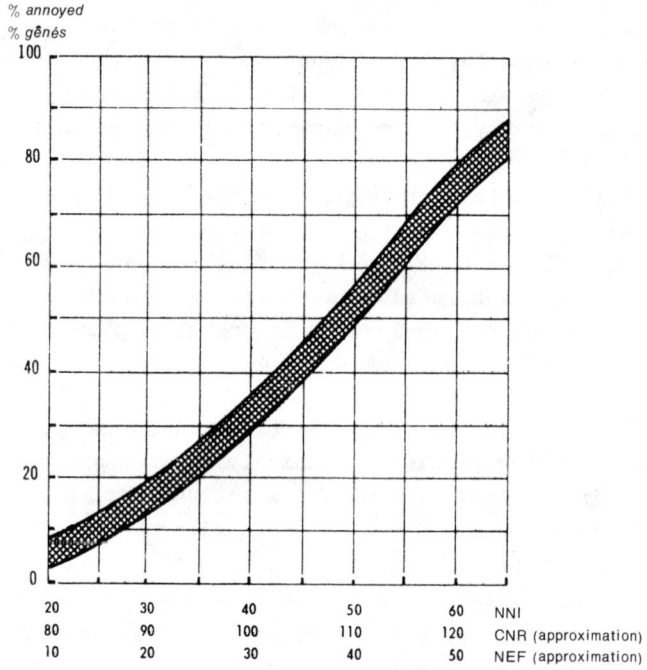

This method provides a valid tool for predicting the probability of annoyance: if, for example, in areas currently subjected to 60 NNI, the noise of each aircraft were to be reduced by 10 dBA or the air traffic were to be cut by three-quarters, the proportion of people annoyed would fall from 75 to 50 per cent. It would thus be enough to know the level of noise exposure for each area (in terms of NNI or CNR) to ascertain and predict how many people will be objectively annoyed (according to the meaning attributed to "annoyance" during the surveys, which implies the disruption of a number of activities).

1) Kryter's estimate (which corresponds to the lower part of the curve on our figure) is quoted from "The Effects of Noise on Man", by K.D. Kryter, Academic Press, New York, 1970 (figure 238 a).

The percentage of annoyed people in each area can be predicted in simple terms by using one of the following two formulas(1):

$$\text{percentage of annoyed people} \simeq \begin{cases} 2(\text{noise level in NNI} - 25) \text{ or} \\ 2(\text{noise level in CNR} - 85) \text{ or} \\ 2(\text{noise level in NEF} - 15) \end{cases}$$

To sum up, the surveys so far conducted have made it possible to determine noise indices which are closely correlated with average reactions of annoyance in a population to establish limits of noise acceptability based on the number and scope of activities disrupted by noise, and to estimate the proportion of persons annoyed (i.e. whose annoyance goes beyond the threshold of tolerance) among a population in terms of the latter's exposure to noise.

These conclusions drawn from the surveys provide virtual decision-making criteria. Such a criterion as the "percentage of annoyed persons in terms of level of noise exposure" may prove to be a most useful decision-making tool, since it provides an evaluation of annoyance in probablistic terms, i.e. by allowing for likely individual variations (which would not be taken into account if average annoyance were merely ascertained in each area).

This criterion thus makes it possible to calculate the number of people annoyed in some area in absolute terms: the percentage of people annoyed - which can be predicted whenever the noise to which the area is (or will be) exposed is known - need thus only be set against the population density for the area. Actual "maps of annoyance" might hence be plotted around airports, and used for reaching certain decisions concerning landing and take-off paths, noise abatement procedures, the preferential use of certain runways, etc. so as to subject the smallest possible number of people to noise.

To minimise the number of people annoyed could also be a factor in decision-making when extending or constructing an airport. For example, the lay-out of runways could be so planned that aircraft would fly over the least populated areas.

Hitherto, only equivalent noise contours - 50 NNI, 60 NNI, etc. - have been plotted around airports and the areas so circumscribed are sometimes subject to zoning measures which vary according to locality.

---

1) We shall here consider the indices to be interchangeable because, as already pointed out, they show much greater intercorrelation than correlation with the annoyance experienced by residents around airports. In view of probable errors of estimation (at least ± 5 per cent in relation to the values obtained from the preceding figure), the multiple of the logarithm for sound peaks (15 in the case of NNI and 10 for CNR and NEF) has but a secondary effect The proposed formulas may be applied when the noise level is at least equivalent to 30 NNI (or 90 CNR or 20 NEF).

These contours show, for example, that in the area between the 50 NNI and 60 NNI curves some 50 to 75 per cent of the population are annoyed (figures derived from figure 3 above).

But as earlier indicated, from a policy-making standpoint 75 per cent of a population of 500 is not equivalent to 50 per cent of another amounting to 10,000. This is not to imply that protective measures need only be taken with regard to densely built-up areas while sparsely populated villages can be neglected. All we mean is that if the choice is between overflying a population of 10,000 or a population of 500 adoption of the second alternative would enable compensation or soundproofing to be offered at far cheaper cost, since such solutions would then apply to a minority only. Furthermore, when noise is not uniformly distributed around an airport but concentrated instead along well-defined corridors, the people living in them can move to a quieter area. In cases where annoyance is evenly distributed, too many people may wish to move and quieter areas prove too remote.

The question set forth here - is it better to subject fewer people to more noise or more people to less noise? - has already been discussed at length elsewhere(1). The problem is an important one, since the policy adopted by airport authorities may depend on how it is answered: to concentrate or disperse take-off paths (landing paths are much more rigidly circumscribed since the aircraft descends along a 3 per cent slope and must line up with the runway more than 10 kms before touching down).

The arguments for and against either of the two solutions are political rather than scientific (except when the technical limitations of the two solutions are examined). No attempt will be made to settle the question in the present report, since the subject properly belongs to a cost/effectiveness study dealing with various methods of aircraft noise abatement. It is however well to point out that the conclusions of social surveys may prove useful for some types of decision: possible restriction of night flights or limits on night-time noise, flight paths minimising the number of people exposed to noise, soundproofing of houses located in excessively noisy areas, etc.(2).

_____

1) In particular, see "Aircraft Noise: Flight Routing Near Airports", The Noise Advisory Council, HMSO, London, 1971.

2) Many measures based on social surveys have already been adopted in various countries, such as grants for sound-proofing dwellings exposed to more than 55 NNI around London (Heathrow) Airport, or the concentration of flights along a few paths known as "Minimum Noise Routes"; classifying noise areas around airports (in France, Germany, the Netherlands and the United States) has also been the result of social surveys in most cases.

6. SHORTCOMINGS OF THE SOCIAL SURVEYS AND OF NOISE INDICES

However, the proposals here formulated should be considered cautiously, as the social surveys and noise indices are guilty of a number of shortcomings which cannot be ignored.

It was pointed out for instance that as reactions to noise vary so greatly from one person to the next predictions can only be considered as relating to an entire population.

Is this a major shortcoming of social surveys? True, the effectiveness of some noise-abatement measure for a community's benefit may well be questioned if overall annoyance diminishes while a few individuals remain dissatisfied with the steps taken. Actually this problem would assume major importance if noise were the only issue revealing comparable individual variations. But there are many fields where major variations in behaviour occur. It may even be asked whether there is any single field unaffected by such variations and where all decisions result in unanimous approval.

Since variations in individual behaviour are universal and by no means peculiar to noise, there is no reason why they should create any specific problem for decision makers.

The real drawback of the social surveys is that they provide a good correlation between annoyance and noise only for the daytime. In regard to night-time noise it is not yet possible to define an objective threshold of disturbance. It would appear that in-depth studies concerning the effects of aircraft noise on sleep are urgently needed. These studies should include the measurement of secondary effects of the disturbance of sleep: fatigue, consumption of sleeping pills, job alertness and performance, etc. No overall study of this kind has yet been undertaken, yet one is needed if any standards of night-time noise which the majority of the population can accept are to be proposed.

The noise indices also have undoubted drawbacks. To begin with a common index would be desirable so that noise abatement measures taken at international level could be based on coherent conclusions. At present the conversion of one index into another is complicated by the fact that the weighting for numbers of aircraft heard as well as units adopted to measure noise vary from one country to another, whereas these units are so closely intercorrelated that the use of dBA, recorded directly on a sonometer, proves fully adequate.

Furthermore, noise indices give rise to problems of application. The contours of noise equivalence plotted around airports should be calculated generously rather than over-accurately, since the paths followed by the various types of aircraft are shown to be far from

precise and levels of noise transmitted to the ground depend on
various meteorological and other factors. Great care seems to be
called for in this connection, since otherwise the plotting of some
index values may fail to match the annoyance which is actually felt.
Because of the drawbacks inherent in the use of calculated noise contours, some airports propose more comprehensive noise monitoring
systems (for example London-Heathrow). All these problems are important and should not be overlooked on the premise that they have not
yet been sufficiently investigated.

The social surveys have however already contributed a great
deal. They have made it possible to determine noise tolerance limits
based on simple criteria (the disturbance of essential daily activities) and also to calculate noise indices which, notwithstanding
certain shortcomings, are simple handy tools for predicting which
areas around airports will be exposed to noise causing some given
degree of annoyance.

The findings of the social surveys must now be supplemented by
an evaluation of financial damage caused by aircraft noise.

Part Two

THE MONETARY EVALUATION OF DAMAGES DUE TO AIRCRAFT NOISE

Huib Jansen and Hans Opschoor
Amsterdam Free University

1. INTRODUCTION

In the first part of this document it has been shown that aircraft noise disturbs certain activities, thus leading to annoyance,
complaints and sometimes even community action, and that many other
factors, including psycho-sociological and political ones, may influence the frequencies of these effects.

From an economic viewpoint, one may say that, generally, annoyance is expected to result in a lower level of satisfaction for
those activities where noise intervenes and where intervention is
judged to be significant. Attempts have been made to transform
lower levels of satisfaction into monetary values.

In itself, annoyance is one result of noise exposure; there
may also be other consequences of exposure to noise;

- a loss of productive efficiency resulting in lower production;
  e.g. noise may disturb employees during their working-hours;
  sleep disturbance (whether noticed or not) may have the same
  results (see Part One);
- a change in behaviour whereby an increased amount of resources
  will be spent with the purpose of reducing the exposure to
  noise (the undertaking of extra weekend trips to the country,
  etc.) or its effects (the purchase of tranquilizers).

The "amount of noise" (expressed in indices such as NNI, CNR,
etc. (see Part One) may be taken to be seen, by the individual, as
one of the characteristics or fixed properties of a given geographical location. His evaluation of the effects of noise (or some of
these effects, depending on the amount of information the individual
has, and his perception of those effects) will enter into his evaluation of that location as say, a dwelling area. What happens to the
value of the area as such will, of course, depend on what happens to
the totality of the evaluations for that area of all agents in the
economy, whereby allocation of the land to other purposes may play
an important role.

In the following, some models that aim at associating a monetary
value to aircraft noise, using house price depreciation, will be
discussed and some of the evidence that is used in those models will
be reviewed. It may be useful to keep some of the remarks made in
this introduction in mind:
- of the great many effects that noise may have, only effects
  on people are regarded;
- these are only regarded insofar as they enter people's valuations, and may thus be subject to criticism due to the fact
  that people may not always be believed to be adequately informed, aware and/or concerned in order to be the ultimate
  evaluator of all effects associated with noise.

The monetary evaluation of noise nuisance has been studied in the
context of a search for some of the costs associated with locating a
major airport in an area. The most elaborate study of this kind has
been performed in the United Kingdom, where the so-called Roskill
Commission was asked to determine the "best" location for the Third
London Airport (TLA)(1). The impact of this study, including the
part dealing with noise, has gone well beyond the frontiers of the
United Kingdom. In reaction to the work done by this Commission,
improvements have been proposed with regard to the collection of

---

1) The Roskill Commission, "Final Report", HMSO, London, 1970.

some of the vital data in the model (by METRA-Consulting Ltd.)(1),
but also a completely different approach has been suggested, also
based on houseprice depreciation data (by Wise and Pearce of
Southampton University)(2). These models and some of their results
and properties will be analysed here, in the order given above. Some
preliminary results of similar research in the Netherlands will also
be included. Finally, an appraisal of this way of attaching "economic" values to noise nuisance, as we see it, will be given.

2. THE MODELS USED TO EVALUATE THE IMPACT OF A THIRD LONDON AIRPORT (UNITED KINGDOM)

A. The Roskill Model

The Roskill model of evaluating the noise nuisance is mainly
based upon an investigation regarding the decision a household has to
take when confronted with a noise situation. Such a household has
to decide whether to move or to stay within the area exposed to noise.
Thus, movers because of the noise are to be distinguished from the
other residents. The latter category can be divided into two: those
that will stay, and those who would have moved out of the area any-
way (the so-called "natural movers"). Natural movers (a given fraction of the population) may suffer a loss on the price for which they
can sell their house compared with the no-noise situation; this
value is called D. Also, they will suffer the cost of enduring the
noise N, during the time they remain in the area. N is taken to
equal the sum of money which would just compensate them for the
nuisance suffered and make them as well off as without the noise.

Those who remain are taken to suffer the annual equivalent of
N, each year. Those who move because of the noise suffer D, but
also their removal expenses R, which they would not have suffered,
had there been noise, and an amount called S, representing the difference between the householder's subjective value of his house and the
market value (this value is equal to the sum of money which the householder would consider just sufficient to compensate him for the loss

---

1) S.P.C. Plowden, METRA, "The Cost of Noise", unpublished,
   London, 1970.

2) D.W. Pearce, "The Economic Evaluation of Noise-Generating and
   Noise-Abatement Projects", in: "Problems of Environmental
   Economics", OECD, Paris 1971.

of the property, representing the surplus due to relations built up with the area and people living in it, etc.(1).

Non-natural movers will move, when for them N>S + D + R, since in that case, moving would entail a loss of satisfaction smaller than the loss they would suffer by staying. They will suffer a cost equal to S + D + R. Note that some of the terms represent actual financial losses (D, R) and that others are monetary equivalents to welfare or utility changes (N, S).

Those that move into the area exposed are taken to be at least compensated for the nuisance by the depreciation of the house value. The model allows each family to make this decision year after year; D and N are taken to grow at 5 per cent p.a.; S and R are taken to grow at 3 per cent p.a.(2). It is therefore possible that some households decide to stay for a number of years but close to the time-horizon (the year 2000) wish to move out.

D has been estimated by a survey among house-agents: R has been estimated by asking professional experts. S has been estimated through a survey among households (see also below, para. C). It is calculated as follows: for each level of noise (NNI) the distribution of individual annoyance scores was known from the Wilson Report (op. cit. p. 207), and with the medians of these distributions the depreciation of house-values was then associated. This association was taken to hold also in other noise-zones. Thus, for each noise-zone and for each price-level, a distribution of the capitalised noise endurance

---

1) Glossary of terms and symbols:

d = percentage of depreciation of house price of a house suffering from noise compared with a similar house in a quiet area.

D = percentage of depreciation of house price of a house within a certain noise contour around an airport, compared with a similar house far away from any airport. D may thus reflect more "influences" than d, which only reflects noise.

N = the monetary equivalent of enduring noise associated with an airport, estimated as a sum of money which would compensate someone for having to suffer a given noise, compared with a situation where no such noise was present.

P = price of house.

R = removal expenses, including costs associated with the transactions of buying and selling a house, as well as financing the house.

S = difference between someone's subjective value of a house (as part of a certain environment) and the market value of that house.

s = some factor relating the surplus-value of a house (the house itself as well as its environment) to the market price of a house.

2) The 3 per cent growth rate reflects the growth of real income expected for the United Kingdom. "Quiet" was taken to be a luxury good, therefore a larger rate was taken for D and N.

costs N was calculated(1). These values were subsequently converted
into annual values.

B. The METRA Approach

The calculations performed by METRA differ from the ones done
by Roskill on several points, although the basic principles are very
similar. This model also starts from decisions taken at household
level, although a distinction is made between movers because of the
noise and other residents only. Thus, the natural movers are neglected. The movers because of the noise are, again, taken to suffer
S + D + R. This may result in over-estimating the costs to the
"natural movers", if the Roskill approach would be the correct one.

Some other differences with the Roskill approach are:

a) METRA distinguishes between owners/occupiers and tenants
plus houseowners, whereas Roskill does not. This may be an improvement from a theoretical point of view, but on the other hand, the
calculations that have to be performed in the case of tenants may
lose much of their relevance in cases where the housing market is a
regulated or structurally unbalanced one, such as, e.g. in a country
like the Netherlands. The METRA evidence shows that house owners/
occupiers suffer the greatest loss; ignoring this point may therefore lead to an over-estimate, when their costs are also taken to
represent those of tenants.

In what follows, we shall confine ourselves to the case of
owner/occupiers, for practical reasons.

b) N was not calculated from D, as by the Roskill team. Rather,
its distribution was estimated through a social survey that was also
used to assess S. Households were asked to imagine they were moving
and to imagine what sort of a house they would then wish to buy, as
well as the price they were willing to pay for it. Next, some eight
negative aspects were attached to that house, including three that
were to represent different NNI-levels, and the respondents were
asked how much cheaper the house would have to be before they would
again consider taking it. Thus, N values were established as compensations that people would require.

c) The surplus on the house was estimated by asking people for
what lower value of a similar house some 5 miles or more away they
would consider moving to that other area. The difference was taken
to represent the cost of disruption, of making new friends and building up a new life in the new area.

---

1) For a more detailed description, see Appendix D of M.E. Paul,
    "Can Aircraft Noise Nuisance be Measured in Money?", Oxford
    Economic Papers, 1971.

Roskill, however, confronted the respondents with a hypothetical situation in which the land on which their house was situated was required as part of some development plan. Respondents were then asked how much the owners would ask for their house from the developer; the difference between this value and the market value was taken as an estimate for S. Roskill's S includes R; METRA's does not. This brings in an element of unexactness, since householders may be unaware of the magnitude of R.

Also, Roskill's way of phrasing the question puts respondents in a situation where they would <u>have</u> to move, whereas this aspect is absent from the phrasing used by METRA.

It seems to us that from a theoretical point of view METRA's way of assessing both S and N is to be preferred; some important practical difficulties that have appeared will be discussed in the next paragraph.

3. SOME COMMENTS ON THE ROSKILL AND METRA APPROACH

A. <u>The Decision Criterion</u> $N \gtrless S + D + R$

Households are taken to move when $N > S + D + R$. It seems however, that these items do not include all possible consequences, or do not only deal with the noise of an airport. The airport may have other (valued at E) effects on residential conditions than just noise (e.g. air pollution), so that E is in fact taken into account when a decision whether to move or not is taken. Actually, METRA implicitly assumes: $E = 0$ and Roskill supposes that some of these effects are accounted for in N, through D. Furthermore, the criterion implicitly assumes that losses of wealth that do not actually realise themselves in money terms within the planning period play no role; however, D is a loss of wealth, also to those who stay and insofar as this loss might lead to a loss of satisfaction to the present owner or that of his heirs, this should be taken into account The latter argument implies that the model actually used underestimates the number of those who move as well as the total noise costs. The consequences of the first argument depend on the sign of E, i.e. on whether the net effects of the airport other than noise are a benefit to those living around it, or a disbenefit.

B. <u>Mobility</u>

The models assume that all households that might wish to move are in a position to actually do so. However, a closer look at the terms appearing in the criterion reveals that D and R are actual financial losses (both appearing on the same side of the inequality sign), but that N and S are hypothetical equivalents of utility losses. Moving then will _always_ lead to a reduction of material welfare to any family, and this financial restraint may lead to the decision that the family will stay, disregarding the fact that moving might, after all, lead to a situation of greater utility. This situation arises when even _financial_ losses are not in fact compensated. The consequence of this argument is that again the models tend to _under_-estimate noise costs(1).

A second mobility restraining factor that may be relevant is the ease (both in terms of labour market conditions as well as the "psychological" ease of changing) with which one may take on another job in another area. If this change is difficult, people will tend to stay to a greater extent than the models predict, thus again leading to _under_-estimate noise costs, unless this sort of immobility is included in the values given for S(2). This, however, seems hardly likely since the phrasing of the questions to determine S by both Roskill and METRA do not make it clear at all that one might have to move over a considerable distance.

C. Noise Sensitivity, Surplus and Distance

S is taken to depend on the web of relationships that a household has built up with the area it lives in and the other people living in it. Moving away therefore may entail a loss of S, as a function of the _distance_ over which one moves. Equally, N will decrease as one moves farther away from the airport and the "gap" in house value will be depending on distance, as noise exposure varies with it. Thus moving over only a _small_ distance might prove to lead to a situation of greater utility than staying or moving out of the noise area altogether. This argument shows a case where the models used lead to an _overstatement_ of the noise costs since the only alternatives granted to a household are either to stay or to move out of the noise area.

D. Categorisation of Households Involved, and their
    Ascribed Costs

Those who stay would bear N. However, this is not their full cost. As people that are more noise sensitive leave the area, the relative attractiveness of the area to those who stay must decrease,

---

1) See e.g. M.E. Paul, op. cit. p. 308, and D.W. Pearce, op. cit. p. 110/111. Some other arguments yet to be presented here are also taken from these sources.

2) D.W. Pearce, op. cit. p. 110.

thus leading to a decrease of S, which has not been accounted for in the Roskill or METRA model.

Those who move into the area are assumed to be fully compensated for the noise by the fact that they get their house cheaper. This assumption is a very debatable one: it is not at all certain that in-movers are aware of the noise or its effects. In fact, house agents may even have an incentive to leave potential buyers without full information. Therefore one must not be surprised to find that for many in-movers D was not enough to compensate their N. In that case a category of noise costs has been ignored.

The "Second Social Survey around London (Heathrow Airport)"(1) indicates that the average annoyance in a given noise zone has not gone down to any great extent, compared with the annoyance registered six years earlier.

One might argue that those who are fully aware of the noise and its consequences might possibly be able to purchase a house for less than what they would be willing to pay, and gain the difference between the two sums of money. This argument is valid and it is a second instance where the Roskill and METRA models lead to an over-estimate of noise costs. This category of people is, we believe, small compared with those who will find that for them $N > D$.

In several respects, potentially relevant households have been ignored. To begin with, as far as noise contours are concerned, people suffering from noise<35 NNI have been ignored. It has been argued that this is incorrect; in the first part of this report an equation has been given that relates the percentage of people seriously disturbed to NNI: per cent annoyed $\simeq 2$ (NNI-25)(2). Although this percentage decreases rapidly with decreasing NNI, the number of people living in a low-NNI area may be quite large. Thus, a serious under-estimation of noise costs may be the result.

Also, the models ignore people who might have wished to live in the area but are stopped due to the noise. Finally, the building of a new airport may disturb social or ecological patterns in an area to the extent that people elsewhere feel they are now well off. Also this category of people and the loss they suffer is ignored, so again one may speak of an under-estimation of noise costs.

---

1) op. cit., pp. 7 and 8.

2) This compares very favourably with a result reached by J.B. Ollerhead for the United Kingdom alone; see "Estimating Community Annoyance due to Airport Noise", 1972, Loughborough University of Technology, TT 7203; for the Netherlands, a similar equation can be derived.

E. Some Comments on the Data Used

D is influenced (among other things by the situation on the housing market. If demand for houses in the area is great relative to supply (the usual case around airports close to large cities), D might be lower than would be the case when supply and demand were, quantitatively speaking, closer to one another.

Also D will depend on the average space of time people are willing to offer their house for sale: the larger this period is, the more chance one has of finding a buyer that is not very much disturbed by the noise(1). Therefore, in a situation with a low supply and patient sellers, it is possible that for some houses $D \leqslant 0$! Finally, mobility may influence the supply and therefore D. A related cost aspect that has not been taken into account is the cost associated with the extra time during which houses remain unsold. Again, this leads to an underestimate of noise costs.

In view of what has been said about D, it is hard to accept the attempts to derive N from D. In fact, Roskill derived distributions of values for N, depending on house price levels and noise levels. As there are reasons to believe that mobility is lower in the lower income classes, D for cheaper houses might be relatively low. Deriving N from D thus leads to values of N illegitimately influenced by differences in income(2). A more fundamental criticism, however, is that it is difficult to see why noise endurance costs would be a function of the structure of the housing market and the relative levels of supply and demand on that market. Measured D-values do reflect such factors, and hence they do enter the estimates of N as used by Roskill.

The METRA model uses an estimate of N derived from a social survey which took place in an area that was not (to be) disturbed by aircraft noise. Verbal indications of noise exposure levels were used to allow respondents to give different money values to different noise situations. The fact that people are not familiar with noise and its effects may lessen the "value" of their responses. Also, the indication chosen to represent different noise levels may well have been interpreted in a variety of ways by different respondents, especially since they have no experience with living around an airport. Extremely high percentages of respondents gave no money value, or stated that no sum of money would compensate them for

1) This argument was put forward by A. Lassiere, "The Economic
    Effects of the Disamentiy due to Urban Road Noise in Residential
    Areas", unpublished, London, 1970.
2) These points were mentioned by Paul, op. cit., and Pearce, op.
    cit., who especially stressed the "equity" issue involved.

enduring noise of given levels: 53 per cent at 50-60 NNI, 47 per cent at 45-50 NNI and 33 per cent at $\leqslant$45 NNI. This decreases the value of models that are based on information acquired through surveys of this kind.

Surplus has been estimated differently by Roskill and METRA, as was indicated above. The Roskill questionnaire put people in a situation where they would <u>have</u> to move, and asked them to state what sum of money they would then ask from a developer. (They were not offered a new house.) This sum may, however, be influenced more by people's experience with the behaviour of developers, or their beliefs about that behaviour than by the factors underlying S. Also, one wonders if people would associate all their loss of surplus with a move of at least 5 miles from their present location.

METRA's questionnaire evades these difficulties, but again at a price: in Roskill's sample, 8 per cent indicated that no sum of money would be high enough to compensate them for having to leave the area, whereas in METRA's sample this percentage rose to 43! Finally, METRA's questionnaire suggested that a new house had actually been found; compared with Roskill's S this implies that an element of uncertainty has been taken away, which decreases the estimate people give.

F. Treatment of "Infinities"

Both for N and for S some people will indicate an economic infinite value (or non response). In applying so-called neo-classical economic welfare criteria, one either has to take these replies seriously, which leads to the conclusion that no airport should be built, or one ignores them. The latter procedure was adopted both by Roskill and by METRA. Roskill takes the highest possible value of N to be £4,000; responses for S are cut off at 200 per cent of the value of the house respondents live in. METRA assumes that those giving a value of N exceeding the price of their present house will move. Of course, no cut-off procedure can be defended on logical grounds, it leads at least to an understatement of the actual noise costs and at most to the conclusion that methods such as the ones discussed here cannot be used at all.

4. THE WISE/PEARCE MODEL

Rather than start from a - debatable, as has been seen above-categorisation and cost imputation, Wise and Pearce analyse the value of noise based on house price differentials in the setting of demand function for houses (more exact: a marginal utility function) in a given area. Once noise is introduced, the demand for these houses will fall, leading to a lower equilibrium price. One can show that the loss of willingness to pay (a measure for the decrease in satisfaction) includes not only this difference in price, but also a measure of surplus lost.

They assume that in the future, amenity goods such as quiet will become increasingly scarce, both in relative and in absolute terms. If gross national product will grow at a given rate the value society attaches to quiet will grow faster. Discounting future losses at a given rate yields some measure of the value that people in an area attach to the quiet of that area.

Anybody who feels interested in living in the area under consideration is taken into account, including those who would have entered in the absence of noise, but who are now deterred.

For reasons of equity the model is used, employing average house prices and depreciation percentages of the highest price class as data(1).

The surplus factor has been estimated using the Roskill results. The reason for taking depreciation values of the highest price class is that mobility-restraining factors are assumed to be less severe in that class than in any other. Clearly, the authors try to evade the objections raised in para. 3.A through 3.D above; they have not solved the problems with regard to estimating the data involved or with regard to the cut-off procedure.

Disadvantages of this model include:

a) the sensitivity to the values of the depreciation percentage and the surplus factor used, whereas all the estimation problems discussed above have not been solved; this is the more important as we have seen that there are so many important other factors that intervene on actual housing markets that percentage depreciation may well be found to be low in areas with very high noise sensitivity: there is no one-to-one relationship between the two, and hence the model fails, especially in the context of imperfect housing markets. The

---

1) This brings in an element of arbitrariness: if one distinguishes other house price classes, other depreciation percentages will result. This may mean that distinguishing a class of houses with higher prices than, e.g. £12,000, all houses would have allowed a greater depreciation due to noise, according to this method.

depreciation used here reflects the impact of noise <u>alone</u>: D as
defined above measures some mix of all influences generated by an
airport. Generally, land values around airports tend to increase due
to additional demand for other uses of the area, which may well lead
to a <u>market</u> price difference lower than the value put on noise:
Pearce's model will then underestimate total noise costs.

b) The model is specified in a way which makes it rather sensitive to the values used for the different rates. In the United
Kingdom the discounting rate of future losses is taken to be 8-10 per
cent. Some will favour lower values, going down to, say 4 (these are
"real" rates corrected for inflation). But the lower this rate, the
greater the chance that the time horizon becomes an increasingly
important determinant.

5. SOME GENERAL REMARKS

Looking at the models discussed above, the following remarks
can be made. All wish to give a complete evaluation of the noise
which is generated by an airport as a negative external effect, as
it reaches residential areas as such. Possible negative effects on
the value of the area as a recreational resort, or as an industrial
area, etc. are thus ignored except to the extent that the latter
effects influence the valuation of an area as a residential one.

Actually, some of the models may evaluate both more and less
than the noise effects. House values may be influenced by other
positive and negative factors associated with the airport. This will
influence the outcome in the case of the Roskill model and the Wise/
Pearce model. In general, however, we feel that especially the
Roskill and METRA approach tends to <u>under</u>-value the effects of noise,
that of Pearce/Wise may in principle take away some of the deficiencies, but this is acquired at the price of a rather influential sensitivity to variations in essential parameters, which are difficult
to estimate. Also, vital variables such as house price depreciation
and consumer surplus are used and these are open to some of the most
essential criticisms of the Roskill and METRA approaches.

In the British case a 10 per cent discount rate has been applied
to determine a capital value of the costs, including noise. Some
economists will agree that this is a rather high rate to use. Real
rates of 4 per cent to 6 per cent can be found in the literature;

these are taken to reflect "time preference" rather than "productivity of investment", two concepts having an equal numerical value in an economically "perfect world" only. The effect of using a high rate rather than a low one is to decrease the influence that costs in future periods have on the capital value.

So far, the criticisms have not been of a very fundamental kind, except perhaps the points raised in connection with immobilities and infinities. We shall now turn to a more profound point: some of the implicit value judgments.

Ultimately all three approaches aim at establishing the monetary equivalent of the (consequences of) noise on the people exposed as they value it. However, this procedure is debatable.

In the first place, some money equivalent of noise or its effects is aimed at. This implies, essentially, that for every situation which may arise as a consequence of a new airport, it is assumed that there exists at least one other situation which will yield at least the same "amount" of utility, and which can be reached through operations on economic markets. People are basically asked what (least cost) set of other goods and services will compensate them for things like enduring noise for a number of years and/or leaving the area they are living in. It is but an assumption, however, that such situations of equal utility or satisfaction to be reached through the market exist.

Also, the assumptions implied regarding the household's forecasting and discounting capacity are tremendous, as well as those regarding the ability to find marginal rates of substitution over time.

On top of this, households are sometimes (when the survey approach is used) required to produce an answer to questions pertaining to external effects of this sort within a few seconds. Assuming that economists themselves correspond most closely to the economist's conception of a "homo economicus", and assuming that we are in that respect not too much different from the average economist, we can say that even if one allows a person a few hours to sort out the implications of these questions, it still might be difficult to put faith in the answers produced. As an example: what sort of answer might one expect on questions regarding the noise endurance costs? Most likely, if they are sensitive to noise they will mention some arbitrary sum of money that they consider large. Others may give their estimate of the cost of moving out of the noisy area as the only way of keeping their levels of satisfaction from decreasing. Some, too, may give their estimate of N (if it exists).

Another way of getting the wanted monetary information is by deriving it from market behaviour, as some sort of sedimentation of preferences, in what economists call "revealed preference", such as

the derivation of N from D, by Roskill. This raised tricky questions
as to the degree of purity and perfectness of the markets involved.

Next, the value that <u>people</u> put on something is the relevant
value only, if:

  i) individuals are the best judges of the effects of noise on
       them;

  ii) individuals have been weighted properly in the process of
        getting overall figures.

Proposition (i) raises questions with regard to the degree of
knowledge and awareness that people have about noise, the way it
affects them, and the development of both over time.

Considering that even medical experts are not certain what influences noise may have on health, and that elementary information
such as threshold values for e.g. sleep interference is still not
entirely available (see above in the first part), one may well doubt
the validity of this first proportion - the cons quence being, of
course, that the valuations based upon it lose much of their
relevance.

The second proposition - the "equity problem" - is one of the
well-known ones in the set of problems that economics seem to be un-
able to deal with in any satisfactory way. Still, the issue is
vital in problems of evaluation, such as the one we have at hand.
It has been shown(1) that in the case of the Third London Airport,
applying different weighting factors (including e.g. the "one dollar
one vote" system explicitly used by Roskill) will alter the relative
preferences between alternative sites. The Pearce/Wise approach
tries to avoid using the market weighting system by making no distinction between houses in different price classes. Calculations
are based on the median house price (the mean might have been better)
and (to take the most favourable situation with respect to mobility)
the depreciation rate of houses in the highest price class was used.

Our general impression, then, is that attempts to evaluate the
effects of the noise due to (new) airports, such as those discussed
above, have not been very successful. Use has been made of assumptions that clearly are violated in the actual circumstances that
have to be dealt with, the way the various entities have been quantified can often be debated, some "political" elements associated
with all normative economic statements arise. Whether or not socio-
psychologists will eventually be able to measure annoyance properly,
and to "explain" variations in it, whether or not other health effects
will be better known and quantified, we tend to believe that deciding
to use non-monetary measurements of noise effects in policy-oriented

1) See e.g. "Evidence to the Commission on the Third London Airport"
     J. Wise, C. Chapman, D.W. Pearce. Roskill Commission Proceedings
     5021/3/5/6/7; and "Vestigingsplaatskeuze voor Grote Luchthavens"
     D.W.Pearce and J.B. Opschoor, Econo. Stat. Berichten, vol. 57,
     No. 2853.

calculations rather than transformations of these in "economic" terms seems much better.

A final point (of rather general nature) concerns the distributional effects of an airport, in connection with the compensation principle.

Noise costs have been calculated as hypothetical sums of money. They will not actually be (fully) covered by monetary or any other kind of compensation. Unless a "social welfare function" would be known, this means that nothing can be said about the effective welfare change to the community associated with any alternative.

What is required is that no one should experience a welfare loss and that some should experience a welfare gain (one may speak of a movement toward a Pareto-optimum). However, when compensation is not given, some will in fact realise a welfare loss. We feel that either compensations should be paid, or the "ethical" or "political" nature of such decision problems should have to be realised more fully

6. SOME QUANTITATIVE INFORMATION

We have seen that house price differentials play an important role in the assessment of the "cost of noise" due to a new airport. In this paragraph, we shall review some of the results of attempts to arrive at the necessary data.

Although depreciation of house values may be easily understood to be a possible effect of exposing an area to noise, this does not mean that it is easy to show these differences when actual market transaction data are considered. In several cases, mainly in situations of air pollution, where similar effects may be expected, this has appeared to be very difficult. For this, several arguments can be put forward which will not be discussed here. We shall concentrate mainly on survey results derived from samples of house agents.

Table 1 contains depreciation percentages as a function of noise and price level, as reported by the Roskill Commission. Surveys were held among house agents in the areas mentioned.

In another British study (concerning the costs and benefits of retrofitting aircraft), the relation shown in Table 2 (based on estate agents' estimates in the Heathrow area) was introduced.

In the METRA report mentioned above, one can find the result of a regression analysis based on a survey of estate agents around (outside) London:

$$X_1 = 1.73 + .00107 \ V$$
$$X_2 = 0.0295 + .00070 \ V$$

Table 1

AVERAGE PERCENTAGE DEPRECIATION OF HOUSE PROPERTY VALUES
(re houses outside 35 NNI)

		Noise exposure		
A. Heathrow Area		35-45 NNI	45-55 NNI	>55 NNI
price range (£)				
0 -4,000		0	2.9	5.0
4,000-8,000		2.6	6.3	10.5
>8,000		3.3	13.3	22.5
B. Gatwick Area				
0 -4,000		4.5	10.3	
4,000-8,000		9.4	16.5	
>8,000		16.4	29.0	

Table 2

Noise exposure	percentage depreciation
<35 NNI	0
35-40 NNI	3.5
40-45 NNI	7.5
45-50 NNI	10.0
>50 NNI	15.0

where X_1 = percentage depreciation of houses assumed to be in the
45-50 NNI zone (compared with <35 NNI value)

X_2 = percentage depreciation of houses assumed to be in the
35-45 NNI zone

V = value of the house (£) when in <35 NNI zone.

These data have been assembled in Figure 1.

It appears that important differences between depreciation data
exist, even if price and noise exposure are controlled as far as
possible. Several notes may be added:

- Gatwick houses suffer from a rapid growth in air traffic forecasts; it is at a greater distance from London, and it is more
rural, thus having a lower background level. One can perhaps
imagine other significant variables to differ at the two
locations, thus leading to differences in house price
depreciation.

- Price differentials have been established by consulting a
sample of house agents. These agents will not all give the
same answers. Exactly how much they vary can be shown for the
Gatwick data; the outcome may surprise some and they certainly
cast further doubts on the figures discussed:

Table 3

RANGE OF DEPRECIATION PERCENTAGE ESTIMATED (35-45 NNI)

House price range	<4,000	4,000-8,000	>8,000
highest estimate	10	15	25
average estimate	5	9	16
lower estimate	0	3	5

Two observations relevant to these figures seem to be:

i) It is not at all clear whether house agents' estimates relate to noise only, or include other effects of having an airport as well, such as the increased attraction of the area for commercial and industrial uses, air pollution, etc.

ii) It has been found that the NNI contours used around existing airports (based among other things on prescribed take-off and landing procedures) do not all correspond with actual contours (based on radar measurements of actual take-offs and landings). This may lead to a situation where some house agents will associate different qualitative descriptions of noises to different NNI values, a confusion which may well lead to greater variation around the mean depreciation percentage.

In the Schiphol Airport area (the Netherlands) all house agents working and residing in the ≥35 NNI area have been interviewed personally. House agents were shown a map of the area around Schiphol, with several noise contours in it. They were then shown a map without these contours, containing a marked spot representing a house of a given value (four levels were studied). This house was then hypothetically exposed to four different noise levels (levels were explained to vary due to changes in take-off procedures, landing strip configurations, etc.), which was demonstrated by moving a transparency holding the actual noise contours, across the map. This procedure was devised to control all variables possibly effecting house values: ceteris paribus, one would therefore expect to be able to isolate the effects of noise on house prices for different levels of noise and of house prices.

However, the experiences during the interviews indicate that it is not certain that all responses have to do with equal interpretations of the (identical) stimulus: some house agents completely ignored the existence of house price differentials but were willing to state percentages that would be applicable when the housing market would be in equilibrium. Others mentioned very high actual figures.

A direct comparison of the Dutch data (which are preliminary only) with the United Kingdom figures is difficult due to the fact that different monetary units (for different years) have been used, as well as different units for noise exposure. However, it seems that the Dutch results indicate a smaller influence of the house price level and that, on the whole, they tend to indicate a greater marginal effect of noise on depreciation percentages. The Dutch percentages tend to remain within the range indicated in figure 1.

The range of the depreciation percentages for any given noise level and price level is disappointing, as was the case with the United Kingdom data.

As has been stated, house price depreciation figures give only a partial approach to the total damage due to noise; more elaborate models such as those discussed above have tried to take other elements into account as well.

In order to give some ideas as to the order of magnitude one might expect for total noise costs, the results of METRA's calculations will reproduced here (table 4):

Table 4

Noise level	Type of social cost	% of households for which each type is smallest	Average minimum cost (£ 1968)
50 NNI	endurance costs moving costs modified moving costs	37 35 28	951 2,599 4,396
	TOTAL	100	2,506
45-50 NNI	endurance costs moving costs modified moving costs	42 33 25	689 2.184 4,128
	TOTAL	100	2,028
35-45 NNI	endurance costs moving costs modified moving costs	55 23 22	571 1,791 3,615
	TOTAL	100	1,508

The term "modified moving costs" merits some explanation. Many people (18 per cent) stated that no sum of money would induce them to move out of the area they lived in, thus in fact placing an infinite surplus value upon this property and its surroundings. For these people (and also for those mentioning a compensation of more than 50 per cent of their house value) a cut-off figure of 50 per cent of their house value has been used, yielding the so-called "modified moving costs" in those cases where moving was the outcome.

Another interesting point to compare Dutch and British results is the non-response (or rather: non-monetary response) to the questions with regard to surplus and noise endurance costs. Table 5 summarises these percentages.

In general, one may note that the non response in the Dutch case is larger than in the case of the British surveys. This is not due to the way the questions have been phrased.

Regarding the Roskill approach to estimating S, which results in a much more promising non-response percentage, it may be revealing to

Figure 1

HOUSE PRICE DEPRECIATION PERCENTAGES AS A FUNCTION OF NOISE EXPOSURE
DEPRECIATION DU PRIX DES MAISONS (EN %) EN FONCTION DU BRUIT

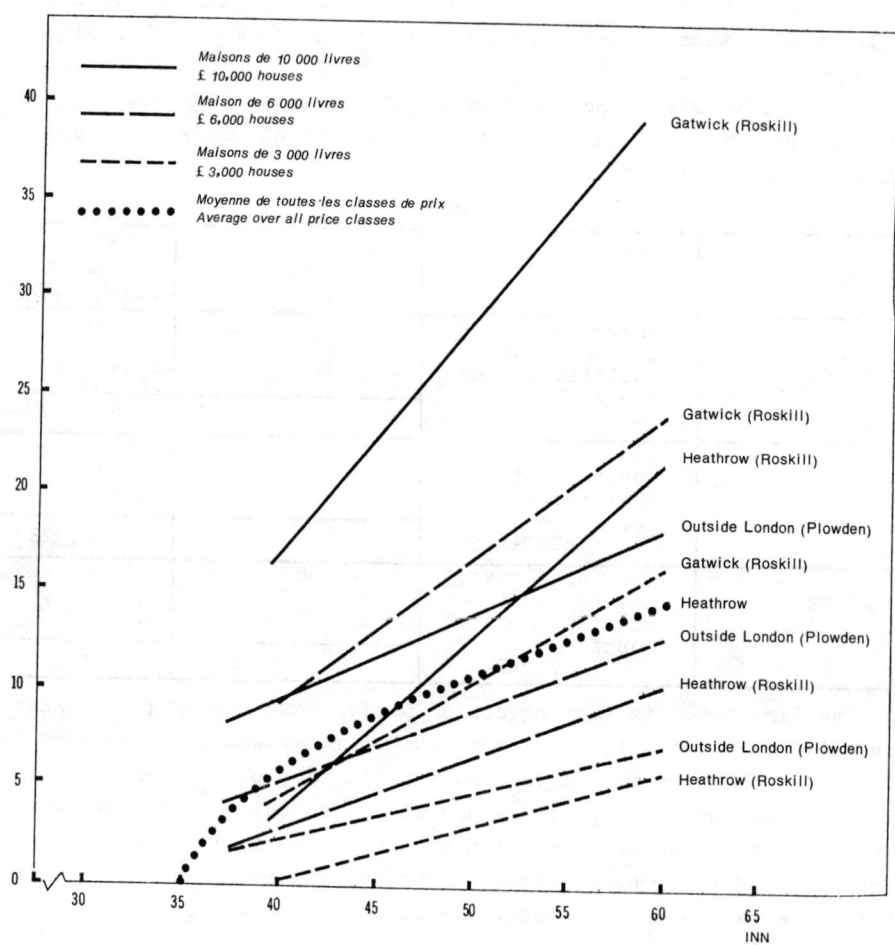

Average % depreciation
of house value
*Dépréciation moyenne de la
valeur des maisons (en %)*

Maisons de 10 000 livres
£ 10,000 houses

Maison de 6 000 livres
£ 6,000 houses

Maisons de 3 000 livres
£ 3,000 houses

Moyenne de toutes les classes de prix
Average over all price classes

Gatwick (Roskill)

Gatwick (Roskill)

Heathrow (Roskill)

Outside London (Plowden)

Gatwick (Roskill)

Heathrow

Outside London (Plowden)

Heathrow (Roskill)

Outside London (Plowden)

Heathrow (Roskill)

INN

Table 5

NON (MONETARY) RESPONSE ON QUESTIONS REGARDING S AND N

	Roskill survey	Plowden survey	Dutch survey
Surplus (Roskill)	8%	-	9.2%
Surplus (Plowden)	-	43%	55.8%

Noise endurance cost survey by Plowden;
  non response for noise   >50 NNI: 60%
                          45-50 NNI: 55%
                            >45 NNI: 38%

Noise endurance cost - Dutch survey;
  non response for noise   >50 NNI: 77.8%
                          41-50 NNI: 71.3%
                         32.5-41 NNI: 60.7%
                          <32.5 NNI: 46.7%

add that a large number of persons who, confronted with the Plowden
question in fact said that no sum of money would compensate them for
leaving the area, now stated that they would require a zero surplus
or even a negative one, according to the Roskill logic.

7. CONCLUSION

Models that aim at producing monetary evaluations of the damage
due to aircraft noise have been applied in the United Kingdom and are
at present being applied in other countries.

To a greater or smaller extent they are all based on information
regarding house prices; other relevant variables are often connected
with differences in valuations for houses with different sets of
characteristics.

It seems that the logical basis of these models is weak on
several points and that in other cases the correspondance with what
one might expect to hold in "real life" is rather vague.

Data collection has taken place using both estimates derived from
market information and social surveys. In general, the survey approach has led to a situation that is essentially inconsistent with
the basis of cost-benefit theory: one had to disregard high percentages of people that could not (or were not willing to) attach
money values to the alternatives presented to them or that indicated
that no sum of money would compensate them for prepared alternation.

The effect of noise on house prices has been illustrated with
some numerical results. It appears that the values given are heavily
dependent on the area where the airport is situated - which is to be
expected - but also that taking different samples of house agents
yields highly differing estimates. In the Dutch case a 100 per cent
sample of, say the 35 NNI area around Schiphol was taken which confirmed that even if one tries to create a complete "ceteris paribus"
situation, greatly varying answers still will be produced.

One may wonder why all this trouble has to be taken. Evidently, if one is able to estimate the money value of noise nuisance, decision problems such as where to locate an airport (or even: should we build another airport) could be solved more easily since the result would be a figure which could be added to, say, the cost of building the airport, in order to compare the sum with the benefits of the airport.

In view of the arguments presented above our conclusion is that this is not yet possible and may well prove to be impossible at all.

Approaches such as outlined in the first part of this document are at present more significant than the ones discussed in the second part.

At least for several years ahead one has to accept that noise nuisance will remain one of the economically speaking "intangible" items on the balance sheet of advantages and disadvantages of an airport site.

ECONOMIC AND URBANISATION IMPACTS OF INTERNATIONAL AIRPORTS

OECD Secretariat

Development, operation and maintenance of a major international airport requires not just a substantial capital outlay and continuing investment to keep facilities up to date, but the allocation of a parcel of land far larger than would be necessary to support almost any other single land use function. In densely populated urban areas, this investment of land represents a significant opportunity cost which deserves careful examination. From the viewpoint of the host community, the costs and benefits derived from airport investment can be measured in terms of the airport's role as a mover of people and goods into and out of the region, in terms of its role as a generator of regional economic activity, and in terms of its influence on urbanisation processes in the surrounding sub-region. This paper will focus on several issues relating to the airport's role as land user and commercial enterprise, arguing that in a variety of ways, airports leave their imprint on the form, structure, and pattern of growth of the urban areas they serve.

I. PERSPECTIVE ON AIRPORTS AND URBAN DEVELOPMENT
SUMMARY OF THE ARGUMENT

Airports can be distinguished from other land uses in the following ways:
1. They tend to be very large land users;
2. Their work forces are large as are the number of individuals and families dependent on them;
3. They are indispensable parts of the transportation network - movers of increasing numbers of people and goods (as were the railroads a century ago);
4. They generate innumerable social disamenities and physical environmental impacts which affect not just their "neighbours" but those far from the site itself; and
5. They must be served by extensive roadway systems, for airport traffic flows are often higher than those converging on any other single activity centre outside the central business district.

Given these characteristics, this paper argues that airports and an airport's location have a definite relationship to the growth process in urban agglomerations. Airports are not, after all, foot-loose in the classic sense. There are constraints on their location alternatives, for they cannot be far removed (in time or distance) from their market areas.

Since airport development invariably requires major investment in infrastructure and public utilities the surrounding area becomes a natural focus for urban development. Except in cases where strict controls are applied, one can expect that in the long run, airport sub-regions will become dense, urbanised zones. That is to say, a symbiotic relationship exists between airports and urban development - growth is a natural byproduct of the airport location process. Although causal relationships may be difficult to demonstrate, it is apparent that airports provide several essential ingredients that encourage urban growth - jobs; extensive roadway systems; a generally undeveloped setting where reasonably priced land is available; and public utilities which can easily be tapped by other land users. This paper concludes:

1. that airports may have a rather profound influence on the pattern of development in the sub-region around the site; although

2. the significance of the economic impacts may be more localised, varying from one airport to another - the degree of impact being relative to the scale of other economic activities in the area.

II.   SCOPE OF THE PAPER

Airport planners have not always considered regional impacts as basic elements in the planning process. Two or three decades ago, when a major airport was built, more often than not aeronautical considerations were the sole focus of attention. At that time three issues seemed to dominate location decisions: where could a site be found that was close to the city, that would be relatively inexpensive to acquire, that was flat and topologically appropriate to meet the necessary technical standards. Many of these airports were converted wartime military installations, located on what was then the outer fringe of the urban agglomeration, where there were few buildings to obstruct landing approaches, and few residential developments to disturb.

The emergence of an important civilian aviation sector after World War II coincided with the rapid acceleration of urbanisation and suburbanisation in cities throughout the world(1). What were once "airports in the country" are now "airports in the city", often surrounded by development which stretches far beyond the facility itself. The coincidence of rapid urban growth, rapid technological advances in the aviation industry, and increased demand for air transport, set the stage for the airport dilemma of the 1970s. Just as airports began looking for room to expand, they fell out of favour where they were most in demand: in highly urbanised, metropolitan areas. To understand why this has happened it is necessary to examine the impacts of the airports on their hinterlands. The questions range from environmental and ecological issues to more subtle and complex economic and social ones.

This paper is not concerned with the impacts of airport location on the natural environment. Rather, it focuses on a broad cross-section of economic and urbanisation impacts that are basic to understanding the airport as a part of the regional and sub-regional system.

To document the scale of these effects, it is essential to develop some frame of reference describing the relevant variables. There are, of course, innumerable combinations of characteristics that one could study under the heading "urbanisation and economic impacts of airports". This paper represents only one such configuration, discussing impacts in relation to land use, the demands of competing land users for space, and the effect of airports on the locational decisions of other land users.

III. SOME THEORETICAL CAVEATS

Regarding the data available for this study, several caveats are in order:

1. Impacts uniquely due to the presence of an airport are often difficult to identify. Major studies of airport impacts on land use are just now appearing and few have found a strong cause/effect relationship between airports, per se, and the evolution of land use outside the site. Rather, one finds support for the thesis suggested above - that the relationship is symbiotic, airports nurture and accelerate urbanisation trends in the surrounding area.

2. In a metropolitan context the effects of any particular activity or land use are often hard to single out. An airport's impact is relative. It varies with the scale of

---

1) Warren Deem and John S. Reed, Airport Land Needs (New York: Arthur D. Little, 1966) p. 5.

273

other economic activities in the region. In some cases it may be of region wide significance, in other cases it may be be just one of many enterprises distinguished neither by the size of its contribution to the economy nor by its effects on urban growth patterns.

3. One of the major theoretical issues concerns the identification of the area of impact. While it is obvious that the impact of an airport declines as one moves away from the site, there are few studies that document the magnitude of impacts even in close proximity. This points to a larger question that will be of special concern in this paper: what are the intensities of economic and urbanisation impacts and are they predominantly local, sub-regional or regional?

IV. CHARACTERISTICS OF IMPACTS

With these caveats in mind, section IV will define a set of characteristics that might be used to describe an airport's urbanisation and economic impacts. It should be noted that these variables have several dimensions: impacts can be direct or indirect, and they can be of regional or sub-regional significance. Annex I, at the end of this paper, attempts to set each characteristic into context in terms of these four dimensions.

A. Direct Impacts

At least four types of direct airport impacts can be identified:

1. Employment - on site employment, services immediately related to airport and aircraft operations. Perhaps the most important region-wide impact, as airports are typically one of the largest single employers in an area, often paying higher than average wages.

2. Payrolls in relation to employee expenditure patterns.

3. Airport purchases of local goods and services.

4. Land use restrictions within the immediate sub-region resulting from safety and noise regulations.

a) Airport Employment and Payrolls

With the growth in air traffic, airports have become employment centres in their own right. Los Angeles International, for instance, which employed 37,000 in 1970(1) is the second largest employer in

―――――――――

1) Waldo and Edwards, Inc., The Economic Impact of Los Angeles International Airport on its Market Area (Los Angeles, November, 1971), p. 2.

the county. O'Hare is the sixth largest employer in the Chicago area(1). Similarly, at Heathrow, employment doubled between 1956 and 1967(2), and in 1966 it was estimated that 14 per cent of the jobs in West Middlesex (the Western fringe of Greater London) were located at the airport.

There have also been a number of studies analysing the through-put of airport employee payrolls to regional expenditure patterns. Los Angeles reported a $1.4 billion gross payroll impact generated by the airport, taking into account successive rounds of expenditures. This included $211.5 million in Los Angeles County, $126.1 million in Los Angeles City, and $93.3 million in the immediate airport area(3). A report of the Miami Airport Authority based on 1961 data counted 25,000 airport employees with gross personal incomes amounting to $141.6 million, generating regional retail sales of approximately $90.0 million. On site employment at Chicago's O'Hare was 22,000 in 1970. Airport employees were paid an average wage of $13,000, making them among the highest paid workers in the metropolitan area. They collected nearly $300 million in salaries equalling nearly 1 per cent(4) of the estimated total disposible income for all employed persons in the Chicago SMSA.

An airport's direct employment impacts, then, can be significant in themselves. The scale of operation is such that airports often have a marked influence on the distribution and structure of the sub-regions job market(5). But the work force on the airport site is only one side of the employment impact picture. Measurement of the other category - "indirect" and "secondary" employment - discussed in a later section is far more difficult.

b) Land Use Restrictions

Public safety and noise regulations related to airport operations have a direct impact on the kinds of land uses permitted in

1) William E. Downs Jr., "O'Hare International Airport: What It Means to Chicago," Papers of the Air Transportation Conference (Washington D.C., 31st May-2nd June, 1972), p. 29.

2) Peter S. Smith, "A Study of the Economic and Social Effects of a Major Airport, with Special Reference to Heathrow Airport", (London: University of London, Unpublished M.Phil. Thesis at Kings College, December 1967), Chapter 5.

3) Waldo and Edwards, Op. cit., p. 8.

4) Landrum and Brown, Inc., "Economic Contributions of O'Hare Airport to the Community" (Chicago, 1971), pp. 6, 9.

5) Richard de Neufville and Takashi Yajima, "Economic Impact of Airport Development,"Proceedings of the Twelth Annual Meeting of the Transportation Research Forum (Oxford, Indiana: Richard Cross Co., 1971), p. 123.

the area immediately around the site. Most countries have established safety zones and noise zones (e.g. no buildings within a certain distance of the runways, and controls on land use within high annoyance areas) in order to protect areas over flight paths. In some cases, like Frankfurt, the airport is at the centre of a greenbelt area - perpetually free from development. In other cases, with the introduction of jet aircraft, to comply with land use restrictions some airports have been forced to acquire developed land (e.g. Los Angeles), or even close a facility to jet air traffic (e.g. Chicago's Midway and Stockholm's Bromma). Stockholm Arlanda shows one way airports can affect land use: when the airport was planned, predicted noise annoyance contours were used as the basis for zoning throughout the surrounding region[1]. In general, however, as the urbanised zone has engulfed what used to be the metropolitan periphery, development pressures around many airports, in spite of noise and safety regulations, have become intense. Hence Heathrow and the Boroughs immediately surrounding the airport eye the Greenbelt both looking for "space" but both recognising the dangers of attempting to open the zone to development.

c) Airport Purchases of Local Goods and Services

Like any other business enterprise, airports must rely on local suppliers for certain goods and services which can not readily be produced on site. The benefits accruing to the community can be quite significant if the scale of operation is large.

Calculating successive rounds of impacts resulting from an airport's demand for services is a difficult task. Nonetheless, an important indicator of economic impact is the flow of revenue from the airport to local suppliers. For example, in 1970, Los Angeles International reported $258.2 million in local purchases of goods and materials (in the five counties nearest the airport), mostly by airlines[2]. Similarly, a study of the New York airports reported that local purchases by air carriers alone amounted to $234.4 million in 1959[3].

To gauge the importance of these purchasing patterns it is necessary, of course, to compare airport purchasing power with that of other large businesses in the region. Unfortunately, comparative

1) Karl Ahlberg, "Airports and Town Planning." Paper delivered at the Fifth International Symposium of the Institut de Transport Aérien (Paris, November,1972), p. 3.

2) Waldo and Edwards, Inc., Op. cit., p. 43.

3) Port of New York Authority, "Importance of Aviation to the Economy of the Region," A Report on Airport Requirements and Sites in the Metropolitan New Jersey - New York Region (May 1961), p. 6.

data of this kind is rarely available. Even so, it appears that
large airports create not just employment impacts (as discussed
above and in the sections to follow), but significant revenue flows
to enterprises around the site.

B. Indirect Impacts

While the direct impacts of an airport on the economy and urban
system are easier to identify and quantify, the indirect effects are,
perhaps, of more interest from the viewpoint of land use and land
user demand. Indirect impacts may be categorised as follows:

1. Secondary and service employment - not on the airport site -
    associated with the airport employment base ("multiplier
    effect");

2. Influence of the airport on off-site land uses (industry
    offices, hotels, etc.);

3. Impact of the airport on housing markets, land values, and
    population movements; and

4. Relationship of the airport to the supporting transportation
    and public utilities network and infrastructure.

a) Employment Multiplier

Economists, urban geographers, and land use planners have long
been interested in the concept of the "multiplier effect". With
reference to airports, the multiplier has two components:

1. Indirect employment. Ancilliary activities that are crea-
    ted to serve the airports, the airlines or passengers. In
    this category fall hotels, car hire agencies, catering
    firms, etc.

2. Secondary Employment. Service sector activities such as
    laundries and grocery stores, whose existence is derived
    from the needs of those directly employed by, or indirectly
    dependent on the airport.

In other words, the multiplier accounts for indirect and service
sector activity that would not have otherwise occured. The question
is not whether induced activity results from the location of an airport (for it certainly does) but how much. Since techniques of
estimating the airport multiplier differ, the size of the multiplier
is subject to spirited debate among planners. But the multiplier is
crucial to discussions of airport impacts as the level of employment
induced may run well over 50,000 jobs for a large airport. The concept of the airport multiplier has been described as follows:

"The location of a major airport in any area will mean the rapid
introduction of a large number of new basic jobs, and a consequent

increase in population due to the influx of workers and dependent families. This initial increase in basic workers and their families will create a demand for services in the form of retailing and other non-basis activities, and thus an increase in the number of service jobs in the sub-region. Employees who fill service jobs, together with their dependent families, will bring about a further increase in population."(1)

Some claim that to accurately estimate the airport multiplier, a model describing the regional employment market with and without the airport must be developed(2). Nonetheless, on a cruder level several studies do attempt to trace the multiplier effect of large airports.

A recent study of Chicago's O'Hare estimates that the airport generates 30,000 additional jobs in the metropolitan area. That is, 30,000 people working outside the airport are "directly dependent" on air transportation (or on the servicing employees of the air transport sector) for their livelihood(3).

A study of the New York Airports (1960) found 51,000 employed in direct airport activities, 70,000 indirectly, but dependent on the air transport sector. This indirect employment was broken down as follows:

		Number Employed
1.	Purchase of materials locally by the air transportation and related services industries	10,530
2.	Passenger activities including:	
	a) taxi cab and ground transportation	1,150
	b) company personnel arranging transportation	2,860
	c) convention or visitor generated business	20,235
3.	Business activity generated by spending wages and purchasing goods and services	35,280

The study also notes that this "still may not account for all the substantial inter-industry consequences of the employment".(4) In 1965, an updated study reported 61,000 employed at New York airports, another 101,000 indirectly(5), reflecting the rapid growth of the industry.

---

1) E.L. Cripps and D.H.S. Foote, "The Urbanisation Effects of a Third London Airport," Environment and Planning, 2, No. 2, (1970), pp. 153-154.

2) Ibid., p. 154.

3) Landrum and Brown, Inc., Op. cit., p. 11.

4) Port of New York Authority, Op. cit., p. 8.

5) Ibid., p. 8.

A regional impact study of the Miami, Florida International Airport found 25,000 directly employed at the airport and 43,500 jobs induced by airport operations, with some 28,000 households directly dependent on the airport for the bulk of their family's income(1).

Studies of Heathrow found approximately 50,000 jobs created by the airport in addition to the 30,000 on site(2).

Studies of L.A. International estimate an airport work force of 37,000, with 64,500 others employed in indirect and secondary jobs(3). (See Table 1.) Furthermore, it was estimated that each direct and indirect airport related job generated 1.5 additional service sector jobs(4).

Although there are differences of opinion as to the size of the airport multiplier, there is no question that it will be substantial for a large airport. These differences of opinion can be important as they have a direct bearing on the process of planning for regional growth associated with the development of a new airport. Continued study and further clarification of the relationship between direct, indirect, and secondary employment impacts is essential, otherwise gross over-estimations of under-estimations of an airport's potential employment impact may result.

Table 1

ECONOMIC IMPACT OF LOS ANGELES INTERNATIONAL AIRPORT

	1970	in 1975	in 1980
1. Employment Attributable to:			
Direct - Airport Activities	37,076	51,581	63,703
Indirect - Hotel/Motel(1)	1,739	2,305	2,839
- Travel Agents	400	535	665
Construction - Airport	1,446	1,340	1,340
- Hotel/Motel(1)	14	116	116
Sub-total	40,675	55,777	68,663
Secondary (Induced employment in housing, food, clothing, entertainment and services)	61,013	83,666	102,995
Total	101,688	139,443	171,658

1) Immediate LAX Area only

Source: Waldo and Edwards, Inc., The Economic Impact of Los Angeles International Airport on its Market Area (A Study Prepared for the Los Angeles Department of Airports and The Air Transport Association of America, Nov., 1971), p. 76

1) Quoted in Peter Smith, Op. cit., Chapter 1.
2) K.R. Sealy, "The Environmental Effects of Large Airports", in N.W. Essex and E. Herts Preservation Association, ed., Studies of the Site for the Third London Airport (December 1965), p. 47.
3) Waldo and Edwards, Inc., Op. cit., p. 7.
4) Ibid., p. 63.

In general:

1. The multiplier effect seems to be sub-regional. The notion of a "zone of intensity" is a useful concept here, as it appears that the airports impact on regional employment decreases with distance from the site itself(1).

2. On a sub-regional level, airport employees tend to receive higher than average wages(2) suggesting that airports provide attractive employment opportunities and that they are likely to have a significant impact on the structure of the sub-regional market(3). This may place other businesses at a severe disadvantage (in competing for workforce) and, in some cases result in decisions to relocate further away from the airport zone. So, while airport sub-regions are attractive for some kinds of activities, others may find such locations relatively unfavourable and undesirable.

b) Related Land Uses

Airport sub-regions are often thought to be favourable locations for industry and tertiary services. A careful survey of the literature, however, suggests that airports themselves may have little effect on industrial location decisions(4). A study of 124 manufacturing firms in the Heathrow area found almost complete indifference to the airport as a factor in locational decisions (nb. many of the firms surveyed were in the area even before the airport became a major air transport facility)(5). On the other hand, the same study concluded that offices and firms dealing in tertiary services placed considerably greater importance on the airport as a factor in their locational decisions. There are several reasons for this.

1. Firms with overseas offices and markets find sites near airports convenient for travel by both staff and clients.

2. Airport locations tend to have a certain "prestige" that some firms find attractive.

3. Airports tend to be located at the nexus of well developed road transportation networks, which, in themselves, attract certain industries and tertiary services, including(6)

1) Peter Smith, Op.cit., Chapter 1.

2) A.G. Hoare, "Heathrow Airport: A Spatial Study of its Economic Impact." Paper presented at the Annual Meeting of the British Association for the Advancement of Science, 1971, p. 12.

3) Richard de Neufville and Takashi Yajima, Op.cit., p. 128.

4) R.C. Fordham, "Airport Planning in the Context of the Third London Airport," Economic Journal, (June 1970).

5) A.G. Hoare, Op.cit., p. 8.

6) K.R. Sealy, Op.cit., p. 49.

a) transport-oriented industries with national or international markets, including manufacturers of electronics components, television and radio and transportation equipment;

b) regional market industries serving the metropolitan area;

c) research and new product industries;

d) hotels, offices, catering firms, carhire outlets, and warehouses, often serving the airport or airline passengers.

For the purposes of this study the last category is especially important, for there is evidence that as an airport grows, these related services grow along with it. As Figures 1 and 2 indicate, hotels in particular have benefited from the trend in air travel. For example, at Los Angeles International there are now 18 major hotels with 3,700 rooms (up from 450 rooms in 1960). Another 3,100 rooms will be added by the end of 1973(1). Similarly, with government assistance, Heathrow is now experiencing a rapid increase in hotel accommodations. Even for the short four year period 1968-72 the trend is clear.

Table 2

GROWTH OF HOTEL ACCOMMODATIONS AT OR
NEAR MAJOR AIRPORTS 1968-72

Airport	Number of rooms	
	1968	1972
Atlanta	920	1,414
Seattle	900	2,108
San Francisco	760	3,480
Toronto	500	1,590
New Orleans	400	1,117
Houston	210	1,346
Detroit	200	1,037

Source: ITA Bulletin No. 32, 25th September, 1972, "What is the True Economic Impact of an Airport," p. 692.

These hotels serve a varied clientele ranging from stop-over travellers and airline crews, to tourists, conventioneers and business-men holding meetings at airports as a matter of convenience. This trend was hardly anticipated when these airports were planned but they are now becoming important economic activities in themselves.

In the past few years, office building complexes have grown in airport areas. Between 1961 and 1969 the area immediately surrounding Los Angeles International captured almost 10 per cent of the total new office space in the County(2). In the last 5 years, 12 complexes with

1) Waldo and Edwards, Inc., Op.cit., p. 49.

2) Ibid., p. 67.

Figure 1

HOTELS LOCATED IN THE IMMEDIATE AREA OF LOS ANGELES INTERNATIONAL
HOTELS SITUES A PROXIMITE DE L'AEROPORT INTERNATIONAL DE LOS ANGELES

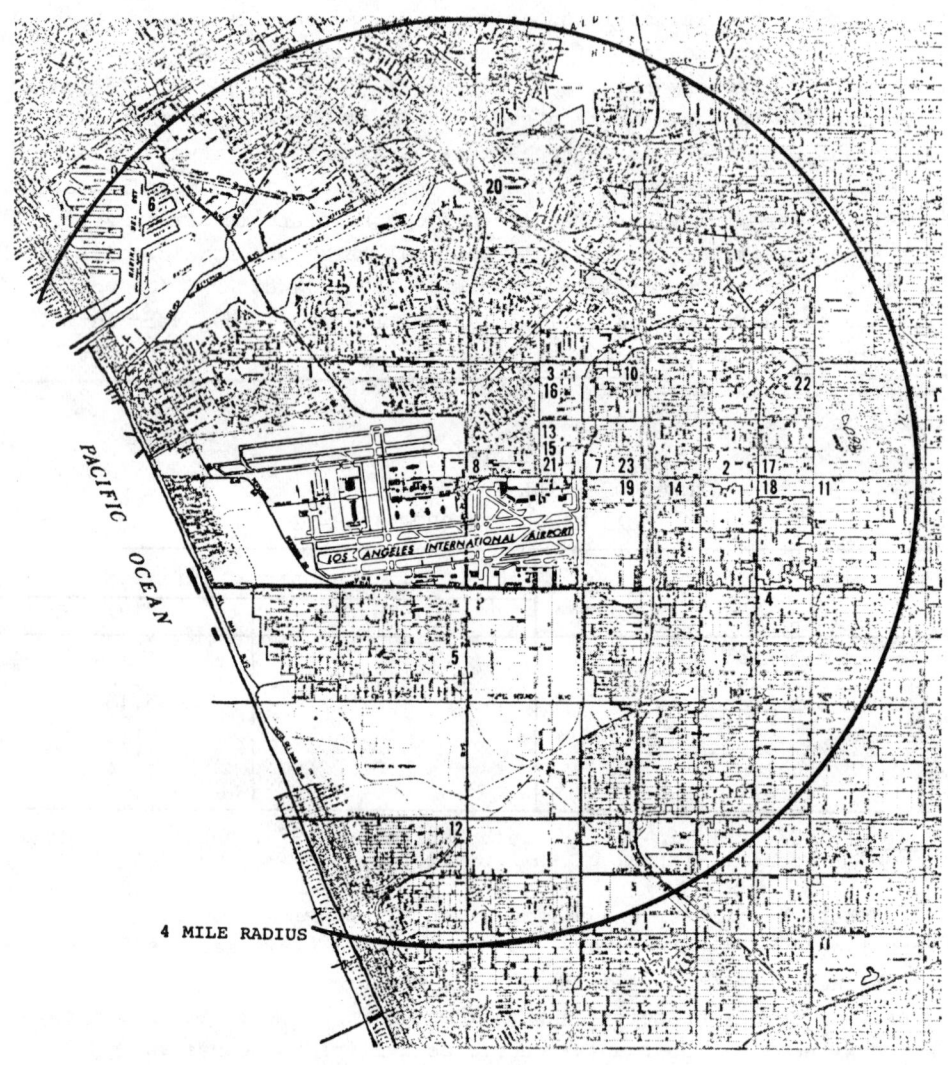

Numbers indicate locations of hotels and motels.
Les chiffres indiquent la situation des hôtels et des motels.

Source : Waldo and Edwards, Inc., *Op. cit.,* p. 51.

Figure 2

LARGE HOTELS (MORE THAN 200 ROOMS) IN THE GREATER LONDON AREA
GRANDS HOTELS (PLUS DE 200 CHAMBRES) SITUES DANS LA ZONE «GREATER LONDON»

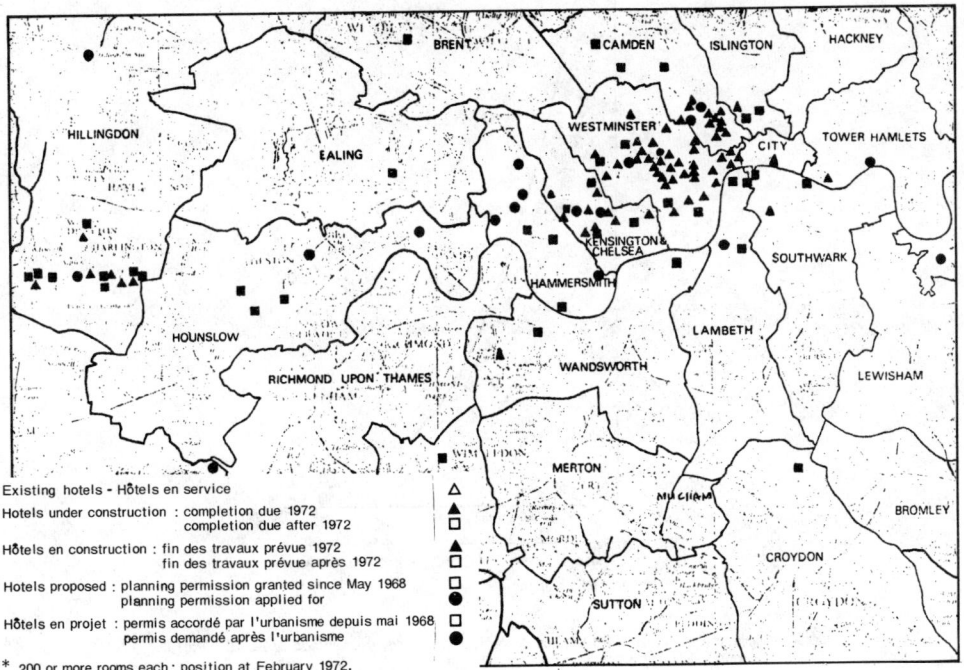

Existing hotels - Hôtels en service

Hotels under construction : completion due 1972
completion due after 1972

Hôtels en construction : fin des travaux prévue 1972
fin des travaux prévue après 1972

Hotels proposed : planning permission granted since May 1968
planning permission applied for

Hôtels en projet : permis accordé par l'urbanisme depuis mai 1968
permis demandé après l'urbanisme

* 200 or more rooms each ; position at February 1972.
200 chambres ou plus chacun ; situation en février 1972.

The Airport is located on the left of this figure, in the Borough of Hillingdon - Note number now under construction.
L'aéroport est situé à gauche de ce diagramme, dans le Borough de Hillington - A noter, nombre d'hôtels en construction.

Source : Greater London Council, *London Facts and Figures* (London, GLC, 1972), p. 19.

over 100,000 square feet of office space have been built within 5 miles of the O'Hare airport site(1). Here, too, it is difficult to say whether prestige of the location, access to transportation networks, or the airport itself is responsible for these developments. Suffice to say, the strength of the relationship is apparent.

Finally, as one might expect, airport-related services - bonded warehousing, car rental agencies, catering firms, etc. have moved into the airport sub-region. Warehousing is, perhaps, the best example of this trend. Although still of relatively minor significance, air

1) Landrum and Brown, Inc., Op.cit., p. 35.

Figure 3

GRAPH OF JOURNEY TO WORK - HEATHROW AIRPORT EMPLOYEES
GRAPHIQUE DE DEPLACEMENTS MOTIF TRAVAIL
PERSONNEL DE L'AEROPORT DE HEATHROW

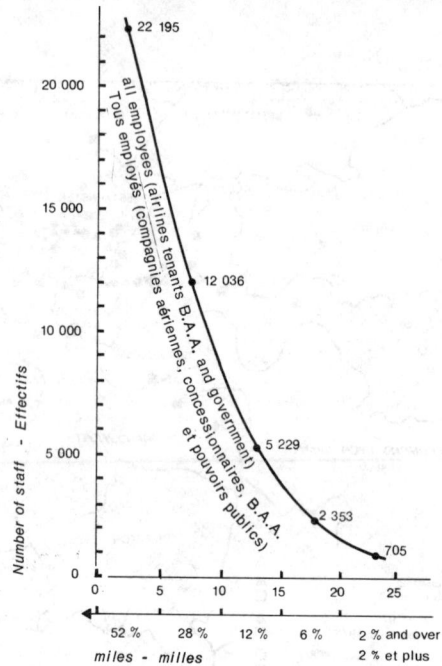

Source : Commission on the Third London Airport, *Papers and Proceedings,* Vol. VIII, Part I
(London : HMSO, 1970), p. 1/ 14.

Figure 4

INCREASES IN LAND VALUES AROUND US AIRPORTS
AUGMENTATIONS DES PRIX DE TERRAINS
A PROXIMITE DES AEROPORTS DES E.U.

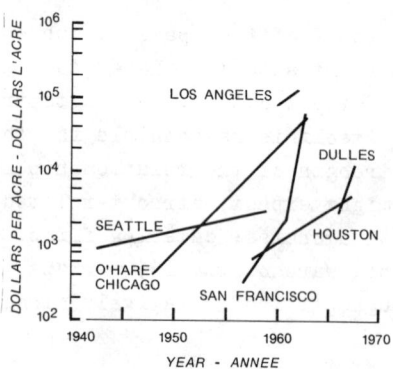

Source : US Department of Transportation and National Aeronautics and
Space Administration, *Civil Aviation Research and Development
Policy Study* (Washington : GPO, March 1971), p. 5-12.

cargo shipping is growing at a rapid annual rate of 10-20 per cent in
major hub airports like JFK, O'Hare, Orly, Heathrow and Frankfurt(1).
Necessarily a concomitant trend can be found in the growth of storage
and transfer facilities near these airports. This category of airport related services, as vital to the operation of an airport as
aeroplanes and maintenance bases, has become a major land use category in its own right.

C. Housing Markets and Land Values

   Research in this area suggests several trends.
   1. Although the desirability of land near airports for residen-
       tial development does not seem to be significantly affected
       by the disamenities of near airport locations, there is evi-
       dence that the rate of depreciation of housing values is
       greater in high noise annoyance (above 35 NNI) zones around
       airports than in comparable areas elsewhere.
   2. Located as they are, often in high demand areas, it is hard
       to distinguish demand for housing associated with direct and
       indirect airport employment from general residential deve-
       lopment(2). Nevertheless, there are a number of studies of
       airport employee residential patterns. One study indicates
       that the vast majority of employees at Heathrow live within
       five miles of the airport (see Figure 3). In 1966, a study
       at Gatwick Airport found that 64 per cent of the employees
       live within five miles of the site (mostly in the towns of
       Crawley and Horley) and only 23 per cent live more than ten
       miles away(3). Of Orly's 25,000 employees it is estimated
       34 per cent live within 5 kilometres of the airport(4)
       placing considerable pressure on the local housing market.
       It is likely that preference for relatively short journeys
       to work favours concentration of airport employees close to
       airport sites elsewhere as well.
   Data on the effect of airports on land values must be drawn
largely from the North American experience. Indications there are
that airports have had no negative effect on land values per se.

_____

1) International Civil Aviation Organisation, Air Freight: Europe-
    Mediterranean Region (Montreal, 1970), Chapter 2.
2) Peter Smith, Op.cit., Chapter 5.
3) Surrey County Council, London Gatwick Airport, An Environmental
    Study (Surrey: 1970).
4) J.V. Block, "Surface Access to Paris Airports," in Air Transport
    Access to Urban Areas (O.E.C.D. ed.), June 1971, p. 122.

Figure 4 shows the trend around several large United States airports. When land was assembled for Chicago's O'Hare, the average price was $400 per acre (early 1940s). In 1967 the average price was $100,000 per acre(1). This has, in effect, excluded any possibility of airport site expansion. Land values around Los Angeles International were estimated at $120,000 per acre in 1966, and a study of the Salt Lake City Airport reported that land values were increasing at a rate of 8 per cent per year(2). Since 1965 land prices around Washington's Dulles have increased by five or six times, even though the airport is located in a rural area, zoned to minimize development. While this data does not imply a strictly causal relationship, one can conclude that disamenities aside, land around airports is sufficiently desirable to force competing land users to bid prices up substantially.

Recent research in the Toronto area, however, suggests that land values tend to falter during periods of "perceived" technological change (e.g. after the introduction of the jet aircraft), but that over time they recover and continue to increase at their previous rate. This same study hypothesises that during these periods of change, some residents may leave, only to be replaced by others who are relatively indifferent to the new condition. Furthermore, as disamenities are more widely perceived, some land is shifted to other uses, thereby altering the character of land use in the long run(3).

In general, it must be recognised that most of the urban development that has taken place around airports has no relationship to the airport itself and is a part of the larger metropolitanisation phenomena that has fundamentally altered the structure of the land market in these areas. Furthermore, to accurately assess the impact of airports on land values, it would be necessary to study a situation where the amenities and disamenities of such locations are not obscured by the general demand for housing and "space" in the sub-region.

a) <u>Public Utilities and the Supporting Transportation Infrastructure</u>

One element of the planning process which necessarily received extensive consideration as airport plans were developed, was the access and transportation infrastructure.

Traffic generated by the airport - by employees, passengers, service vehicles, and the like - as well as unrelated road utilisation, has placed a heavy burden on access routes leading to many

1) William E. Downs Jr., <u>Op.cit.</u>, p. 270.
2) Warren Deem and John S. Reed, <u>Op.cit.</u>, p. 18.
3) R.W. Crowley, "<u>The Effects of an Airport on Land Values</u>". (Ministry of State for Urban Affairs, Canada, February 1972), p. 19.

international airports. Ironically, when these roadways were planned, they were though to be monuments to modern design: sufficient to meet demand for at least several decades. Consider, however, the expressway between O'Hare Airport and Chicago's Loop completed in 1961. By 1963 usage exceeded estimates for 1980. Hence, while it may seem woefully inadequate now, infrastructure must be viewed as one of the more fundamental impacts of an airport on its region and sub-region. While some research has concluded that infrastructure plays only a small role in the regional development process[1], several things should be noted.

1. Since many airports were built on the urban periphery, improvement of highway access was essential.

2. There routes often passed through relatively undeveloped areas, improving access and, thereby, heightening the potential for development.

3. Other utilities - particularly sewerage, water, gas telephone - installed to meet airport needs, could easily be tapped for other uses, reducing capital outlays that would otherwise be necessary if these services were not already available.

At a time of rapid urbanisation, it was reasonable to expect that this infrastructure would accelerate the development process in that sector of the region.

V. AIRPORTS AND DEVELOPMENT CORRIDORS

It appears that airport location has had some major, unanticipated effects on the urban growth process. As noted earlier, for technical reasons many airports were sited on inexpensive, flat land near the urban periphery. There can be little doubt that improvement of the infrastructure servicing the airport ripened the development potential of these "corridors." As cities began pushing out into the less populated hinterlands (especially during the 1950s and 1960s) the infrastructure designed to serve the airport provided a ready link to the relatively undeveloped areas beyond. The ensuing development, which may have had little to do with the presence of the airport itself was, nonetheless, stimulated or accelerated by the airports need for extensive road transport systems. Thus, inadvertently, airports may have played a role in opening new corridors for development just when many large cities were witnessing major population redistributions.

---

1) Richard de Neufville and Takashi Yajima, Op.cit., p. 124.

VI. IMPLICATIONS:
POLICY FOR EXISTING INTERNATIONAL AIRPORTS

Hemmed in by surrounding development, or sterilised by zoning, many of the last generations's airports have "no where to grow"(1). Until recently these airports have been able to meet most of their expansion requirements on site. Now, however, the situation is different. Urban encroachment on the one hand, incompatability of land uses in the airport sub-region on the other, sets the stage for misunderstandings: airports seeking to expand, local authorities seeking to contain. These conflicts are often exacerbated by the fact that airports can fall under several political jurisdictions: governed by one authority, but necessarily dependent on the co-operation of other government authorities at the local and regional level.

Efforts to attract compatible land uses to airport areas (i.e. non-residential uses thought to be appropriate in areas adjacent to airports)(2) is helpful, but often unrealistic for it may be too late to think in terms of "compatible" land uses when the urbanised area has already engulfed and swept beyond the airport(3). Needless to say, opportunities to control sub-regional development should not be missed (some planning authorities admit that they themselves have too readily granted zoning variances that have in turn contributed to the current problem)(4). Controversies around existing airports will continue through the decade. Fortunately, ecocomic and urbanisation issues have now become an integral part of the airport planning process. This suggests that those planning the next "generation" of airports will be better prepared to deal with impact questions before difficulties arise, if, in fact, large airports continue to be built in relative proximity to their market areas,

VII. CRUCIAL QUESTIONS:
THE FUTURE OF EXISTING AIRPORTS IN HIGHLY URBANISED AREAS

This paper raises several issues that are of special importance from the standpoint of future land utilisation around major

---

1) "The Airport Crisis: No Place to Land," Business Week, (30th September, 1972), p. 43.

2) CONSAD Research Corporation, "A Community/Airport Economic Development Model." Prepared for the Department of Transportation, Federal Aviation Administration (May 1972), p. 3.

3) Warren Deem and John S. Reed, Op.cit., p. 13.

4) San Bernardino County (California) Planning Department, Airport Impact (San Bernardino: Planning Department, 1970), p. 22.

international airports. These issues are based on several assumptions.

1. That most existing airport facilities will remain operative for the foreseeable future.
2. That airport site expansion opportunities are increasingly limited by urban encroachment and political controversy.
3. That new airport sites, reasonably close to their service areas, are increasingly difficult to find.
4. That the absolute demand for air traffic services will continue to climb.

Given these assumptions, several important questions arise.

A. Will continued growth of the air transport network be curbed in intensely developed areas if airports cannot meet site requirements to support increased service levels? What is the relationship between site capacity and restrictions on further expansion of services?
B. How might land use impacts in the airport region, and competition for space with other land users, influence the adoption or rejection of future technologies? What effect will space constraints have on the speed with which technological innovations are introduced? Will these developments occur faster if major airports experience difficulty expanding or locating new, larger sites?
C. In what ways might future service levels, and airport capacity to meet demand, be affected by environmental, economic and urbanisation impacts?

These questions are particularly important given that unlike many services - which are footloose and can move to outlying areas for the sake of convenience or economy - airports are tied by large capital investments and by the fact that they must be relatively near their markets. In this respect, one must ask: what is the future for large land users like airports, which are inextricably imbedded in the urban areas they serve? How can they meet demand for air transport services without major expansion programmes or without transfer to new sites? Finally, in what ways can interagency cooperation at the local and regional level help to ameliorate tensions between airports and their neighbours, given that in highly urbanised areas, both must continue to co-exist for many years to come.

VIII.   URBANISATION AND ECONOMIC IMPACTS:
LESSONS TO BE LEARNED

With planning already underway in many countries, professionals have turned their attention to the problem of building yet another generation of international airports. Interest in urbanisation and economic impacts, it seems, is based on the assumption that new airports can serve as central components of regional development strategies. This paper has simply tried to describe the impact process at the local, sub-regional and regional levels, drawing whenever possible, from studies of the first jet-age airports.

Decisions on airport location are properly left to the political process. This paper serves only as a guide of sorts suggesting (1) that the costs and benefits to the regions in which the last generation of airports were located were largely unanticipated; and (2) that the impacts of airports being planned now, designed to serve into the next century, can not also be left to chance.

While it may be easy to argue that one or another of the variables discussed in this paper has greater or lesser importance than suggested, the point is that airport planners must recognise that the airports of the 1940s, the 1950s, and the 1960s are now integral parts of the urban system. Inevitably much the same thing will happen with airports that will be built in the future. At best we can try to understand the nature of the development process that took place in the areas around international airports so that planning for new airports does not continue in a technological vacuum - blind to its effect on the urban growth process and, therefore, likely to raise political controversies not unlike those which plague the air service sector today.

Annex 1

Airport Impacts: Selected Characteristics

	Regional	Subregional
Direct Impacts		
Employment	*	*
Payrolls		*
Airports Purchases of Goods and Services	o	*
Land Use Restrictions		*
Indirect Impacts		
Employment	o	*
Related Land Uses		*
Housing Markets and Land Values		*
Infrastructure and Public Utilities	o	*

* Primary significance.

° Secondary significance (if applicable).